Selling
the Indian

Selling
the Indian

*Commercializing & Appropriating
American Indian Cultures*

EDITED BY
Carter Jones Meyer
Diana Royer

The University of Arizona Press
Tucson

The University of Arizona Press

© 2001 The Arizona Board of Regents

First printing

All rights reserved

⊗ This book is printed on acid-free, archival-quality paper.

Manufactured in the United States of America

06   05   04   03   02   01   6   5   4   3   2   1

Library of Congress Cataloging-in-Publication Data

Selling the Indian: commercializing and appropriating American Indian
cultures / edited by Carter Jones Meyer and Diana Royer.

p. cm.

Includes bibliographical references and index.

ISBN 0-8165-2147-6 (cloth : acid-free paper)

ISBN 0-8165-2148-4 (paper : acid-free paper)

1. Indians of North America—Public opinion. 2. Indians in popular
culture—United States. 3. Indians in literature. 4. Stereotype
(Psychology)—United States. 4. Public opinion—United States. 5. United
States—Civilization—Indian influences. 6. United States—Cultural policy.
I. Meyer, Carter Jones, 1957– II. Royer, Diana, 1959–.

E98.P99S45 2001

305.897′073—dc21   00-0013100

British Library Cataloguing-in-Publication Data

A catalogue record for this book is available from the British Library.

For Bruce and Carl

Contents

Acknowledgments

WE WOULD LIKE TO THANK numerous people who have contributed to this collection. Our appreciation is extended first to our contributors, all of whom were a pleasure to work with. The energy they put into their scholarship and their diligent responses to deadlines have been praise-worthy.

We also thank our colleagues at Miami University and Ramapo College of New Jersey. In particular, Pete Martin, Jack Rhodes, Dianne Sadoff, Lee Sanders, and Carol Hovanec have provided encouragement and support of our research. Special thanks must be extended to George Scheper, who gave us the initial inspiration for this book. Among our friends and family, Terry Stretch, Leslie Vernon, and Meade Jones deserve our deepest appreciation for their ongoing interest in our work.

Finally, we wish to thank the staff of the University of Arizona Press. Patti Hartmann's guidance was integral to the success of the anthology, as was the fine work of our copyeditor, Lisa DiDonato. All of these people believed in the project and contributed in essential ways to its completion.

Introduction

ONE OF THE MOST CRITICAL ISSUES facing American Indians is the persistence of a highly corrosive process known in academic circles as cultural imperialism.[1] Non-Indians, enamored of the perceived strengths of native cultures, have appropriated and distorted elements of these cultures for their own purposes, more often than not ignoring the impact of the process on the Indians themselves. "They came for our land, for what grew or could be grown on it, for the resources in it, and for our clean air and pure water," writes Margo Thunderbird, reflecting on the process. "They stole these things from us, and in the taking they also stole our free ways and the best of our leaders. . . . And now, after all that," she acidly concludes, "they've come for the very last of our possessions; now they want our pride, our history, our spiritual traditions. They want to rewrite and remake these things, to claim them for themselves. The lies and thefts just never end."[2] A number of prominent Indian scholars have echoed her sentiments, including Vine Deloria Jr., Ward Churchill, and Pam Colorado.[3] Anthropologist Wendy Rose, lamenting the impact of cultural imperialism on Indians' ability to know their own traditions and spiritual beliefs, argues that the process is really "the extension across intellectual terrain of the more physically oriented nineteenth-century premise of 'Manifest Destiny'."[4] The net effect will be the displacing and then the replacing of Indians within their own cultural contexts. In short, they will no longer own their own identity in the same way that Indians no longer own most of the land that was theirs when whites began to settle in the New World. For many Indian scholars and activists, it is a form of cultural genocide. That this process should elicit so strong an indictment demands that we look more closely at its manifestations in the twentieth century, particularly in the hope that past injustices may be resolved as we move into the next century.

The essays that appear in this volume challenge the reader to look anew at some of the more significant ways in which American Indian cultures were commercialized and appropriated in the twentieth century. By commercialization, we mean very broadly the exploitation or appropriation of native cultures by non-Indians either for monetary profit or for some other form of personal and/or cultural gain. Although other scholars, notably Geary Hobson, Ward Churchill, and Wendy Rose, have focused on the commercial tendencies of white shamanism—the practice by non-Indian poets and writers of appropriating an Indian identity or higher Indian "powers" to convey certain mystical truths to their followers—there have been few explorations of the many other important commercial ventures in the twentieth century.[5] This book reaches across space and time to explore some of these ventures and to uncover the extraordinary complexity that marks each of them. We have organized them within two arenas where Indians have figured prominently and where their identity has been forged most completely by and for non-Indians. Part I, "Staging the Indian," analyzes some of the ways in which Indians have been displayed to the public, beginning with the 1904 Louisiana Purchase Exposition and extending to contemporary stagings at a well-known tourist attraction and in the popular media. Part I concludes with a study of how one American Indian challenges stereotypical displays for his audiences on the performance circuit. Part II, "Marketing the Indian," explores not only the origins and motivations of non-Indian reformers involved in Indian arts and crafts, but also the role played by Indians themselves and the impact of their involvement on their own cultures and identities. Taken together, these essays suggest that the rubric of cultural imperialism is made more complex when we consider such critical issues as economic need in combination with the need for cultural integrity and self-determination. They also tell us much about the impact of commercialism on identity formation, not only among Indians but among non-Indians as well.

That there are important connections between commercialism, appropriation, and the formation of modern American identity cannot be denied. From one perspective, Americans have always defined themselves in opposition to others. Opposing Britain, opposing Mexico, opposing American Indians, opposing the Soviet Union, opposing Iraq—the list can become quite lengthy with a few moments' thought. Employing stereotypes to characterize those we set ourselves in opposition to is the simplest way to deal with them, because reduction of a human to a symbol—especially a negative one—makes fighting them, whether physically, ideologically, or both, easier. Thus, our various stereotypes and images of American Indians have changed over the centuries as our need to define ourselves in relation to them has changed. In their typological view of the New World, the Puritans cast American Indians as servants of the Devil. Convert or exterminate was the attitude of these New England colonists, and because extermination did not carry the extra work of assimilation, it was more often opted for when Satan's hand servants were encountered. In a less fierce but nonetheless destructive stereotype, Thomas Jefferson picked up ideas from Jean-Jacques Rousseau and portrayed the American

Indians as a race of noble savages doomed to extinction. This concept neatly served nineteenth-century expansionists who emphasized the Indians as relics of a time past whose very presence on the land hindered a divinely ordained progress of white civilization. John Louis O'Sullivan told the nation it was our Manifest Destiny to overtake the lands American Indians let lie fallow; basically, American Indians were "wasting" natural resources by not using them.

Casino gambling on reservations has given rise to a new stereotype of American Indians: as wealthy. Jim Northrup shows the fallacy of such thinking by explaining that "only a small percentage" of Indians profit from gambling and that "each Reservation decides how to spend its gambling profits. Some people get a lot of money and some don't. I think it is creating a class-based society." Northrup adds, "I don't think gambling contributes to racial harmony either. Since the casino always wins, there are more losers walking out than winners. I can just about picture the losers saying, 'Those God damned Indians got all my money again.' Since the experience is negative, I don't see how they can think positively about us."[6]

In contrast, as Americans have come to realize, at least intellectually, that natural resources are not endless, the stereotype of American Indians as the original environmentalists, respecting and living in harmony with nature, has surged. A related stereotype, developed by the New Age movement and promulgated by white shamans, has imagined Indians as spiritually in tune with all of life. Many Americans, instead of placing themselves in opposition to Indians, want to be associated with what they perceive to be a positive aspect of Indianness. So despite ongoing mistrust, misunderstanding, and discrimination toward American Indians, many people seem eager to claim Indian heritage. Philip J. Deloria addresses this topic in his book, *Playing Indian,* by probing "the connection between 'the Indian' and American identity" and seeing playing Indian as "a persistent tradition in American culture," one in which Americans "reinter[pret] the intuitive dilemmas surrounding Indianness to meet the circumstances of their times."[7] Statistics support these observations about the recent surge of identification with Indians: The number of American Indians recorded by the U.S. Census Bureau doubled between 1980 and 1990 (all one has to do is claim such heritage to be counted).[8] Non-Indians participate in Indian ceremonies, wear American Indian religious symbols on clothing and jewelry, and purchase smudge bundles and dream catchers for use in their homes. A commercialism that operates on the view of American Indians as spiritual reduces a wide variety of cultures and individuals to a flat image.

And it is an image of the consumer's own making: In purchasing sacred items or paying to participate in a sweat-lodge ceremony, we are adopting rituals that we had in part projected upon American Indian cultures through our beliefs about what those cultures embody or represent. Also, as Deloria reminds us, "At the very same moment that it was suggesting Indians' essential place in the national psyche, playing Indian evoked actual Indian people and suggested a history of conquest, resistance, and eventual dependency."[9] In this kind of commercialism and appropriation, non-Indians who reinvent American Indian traditions for their own use are committing cultural imperialism.

In chapter 1, Nancy Parezo and John Troutman discuss how, in 1904, a contingent of Cocopa Indians left their homelands in northern Mexico and southern Arizona and traveled across the country to participate in the 1904 Louisiana Purchase Exposition in St. Louis. The group of families was showcased within a living exhibit of American Indians hired to wear "traditional" clothing, demonstrate their daily routines, and sell their arts and crafts to an eager crowd of rubbernecking tourists. "The 'Shy' Cocopa Go to the Fair" reveals how the Cocopa culture as presented in the exhibit became a commodity of exotica for the millions of tourists who visited the native village, yet the essay also shows that the Cocopa by no means lost control over their own experience at the fair. At a time when economic and subsistence opportunities were shifting and dwindling at home, the Cocopa negotiated their own terms for traveling to the fair and used the opportunity of their own exhibition to place themselves in a better position economically through the selling of their wares within an increasingly receptive market of native crafts. Parezo and Troutman demonstrate how the Cocopa, living in a compound within the largest world's fair ever held, tried to make the best of a situation full of gaping crowds, racist rhetoric, and nationalistic propaganda.

A contemporary situation of American Indian display is assessed by Katie N. Johnson and Tamara Underiner in "Command Performances: Staging Native Americans at Tillicum Village." Tillicum Village is a four-hour spectacle of Northwest American Indian traditions performed in a state park a short ferry ride from downtown Seattle. Described as part "ancient culture," part dinner theatre, the authors say the event raises questions that are not easily answered: Is Tillicum Village a recent example of a long and lamentable history of natives appearing as cultural artifacts on the (white) stage? Or is there, perhaps, more to Tillicum Village than meets the tourist gaze? Johnson and Underiner situate this tourist attraction between the politically charged history of such performances and the increasingly global nature of tourism, where perceiving groups as Others can occur along axes of privilege as well as ethnicity. Combining performance and cultural analysis with informal interviews, they consider the varying degrees to which cultural appropriation and commodification are both hidden and revealed by the event's rhetoric of authenticity. Finally, they consider the participation of American Indians themselves as conscious, politically significant subjects in the coproduction of Tillicum Village's many (mixed) meanings.

S. Elizabeth Bird extends the discussion of spectacle and display by analyzing how Indian men and women have become sexualized in relation to the white gaze—an important component of colonial domination. "Savage Desires: The Gendered Construction of the American Indian in Popular Media" traces this gendered way of seeing American Indians from captivity narratives through anthropological discourse to contemporary representations in popular media such as television, movies, and romance novels, all of which appropriate these images to ensure commercial success. Many Americans will never encounter a real, living Indian, and media fill a knowledge vacuum with outmoded and limited stereotypes. As Bird discloses, the 1990's lovely Princess, Wise Elder, or Stud may be more benign images than the earlier Squaw or Crazed Savage, but they are equally unreal and dehumanizing.

Pauline Tuttle's " 'Beyond Feathers and Beads': Interlocking Narratives in the Music and Dance of Tokeya Inajin (Kevin Locke)" provides good insights into one American Indian's response to the commercialization of his culture. Thus far, scholarship on American Indian music and dance has been slow to move beyond the descriptive mode and to bring us closer to an understanding of the complementarity of the life-work of the ethnographer and that of the performer, or their roles in reinscribing notions of how the sharing of song, dance, story, and performance space give form to cultural knowledge, social progress, and individual agency. Tuttle builds her theoretical approach on studies of the performing arts in Africa, and her work is rooted in modes of consultation and collaboration that aim to give voice to the performer at the heart of this chapter, Kevin Locke. Locke, a preeminent figure in the revitalization of both the Hoop Dance and traditional courting flute repertoire, strives to extend the contextual and conceptual parameters of performance beyond the rigidity and stasis of what we have come to think of as "tradition." Locke performs an almost exclusively traditional repertoire and is dedicated to the preservation and development of ancestral heritage. However, when donning the traditional regalia of his Hunkpapa Lakota ancestry, Locke is quick to take his audience beyond a simple collection of feathers and beads in motion—beautiful, but void of meaning if not coupled with a deeper understanding of both their cultural and spiritual significance and their historical and contemporary representation in popular culture. Tuttle's study of the integration of Lakota and Bahá'í teachings in Locke's performance fills a void in an ethnomusicological discourse that has all but ignored both the "sacred space" and "intersubjective time" that is integral to much American Indian dance, music, and ceremony and that is marked by the confluence of past, present, and future, of this world and the world of the spirit.

In Part II's " 'The Idea of Help': White Women Reformers and the Commercialization of Native American Women's Arts," Erik Trump discusses Indian reform organizations that advocated Indian arts as a means of developing economic self-sufficiency for Indians and promoting philanthropic enthusiasm among whites. Trump argues that these organizations differed from commercial marketers in their attention to the gendered nature of the production and consumption of Indian arts. He describes the negative images of Indian women that late-nineteenth-century Indian reform organizations initially used to guide their activities, and he shows how after 1900 numerous voices, many of them feminist, began to revise those negative images. Trump analyzes how one reform organization, the Indian Industries League of Boston (1893–1922), adopted the new image of Indian female artistry and used it to spur the consumption of Indian arts by reform-minded white women. His examination of the rhetoric of the league's public appeals demonstrates that these organizations challenged the injustices of an economically exploitative commercial market by creating a complex image of Indian women's labor that featured women's struggles.

A different view of the marketing of American Indian arts is given by Carter Jones Meyer in "Saving the Pueblos: Commercialism and Indian Reform in the 1920s." While the federal government was intensifying its efforts to detribalize American Indians and incorporate them into the larger American culture, a small but influential group of Anglo intellectuals began a massive campaign to save native cultures and turn back the policy of assimilation that threatened them. Although much is known about the political thrust of the campaign, led by John Collier, little attention has been given to its cultural component, molded and shaped by writer Mary Austin and archaeologist Edgar L. Hewett. Meyer explains how through their respective organizations, the Indian Arts Fund and the School of

American Research, each based in Santa Fe, Austin and Hewett worked to resurrect the ancient arts and crafts of the Pueblo Indians, seeing in this work a means by which to educate the American public about the value of Indians *as Indians*. Only in this way, they surmised, could the assimilation policy be overturned and Indian self-determination established. Their work did help increase Americans' general knowledge of the Indians, and their defense of Indian self-determination provided an important foundation for postwar Indian activists. Nevertheless, Meyer reveals that excessive infighting and competition, in combination with persistent paternalism, undercut much of their work on behalf of the Indians and brought confusion to the more immediate reform campaign. Austin and Hewett should be regarded as transitional figures in the early phase of a larger cultural reorientation in twentieth-century America, a reorientation predicated on the shift from an Anglocentric to a multicultural ideal.

Sarah H. Hill provides another stepping stone in this progression toward valuing the artisans, not just their products, in "Marketing Traditions: Cherokee Basketry and Tourist Economies." Hill's examination of Clark Field's 1940's collection of Cherokee baskets allows us to view multiple processes at work in the lives of weavers. Whereas the containers point to market trends and the interests of collectors and scholars, they also inform us about women's work, environment, and values. As a source of recorded prices, they document the economy of Cherokee weavers in the era of the arts and crafts revival, the work of Indian reform groups, and the interventions of the federal government. Although all initiatives undertaken in the first half of the twentieth century promised economic relief to Eastern and Western Cherokees, the experiences of basket weavers reveal how slowly economic change came even in the face of persistent efforts to shape their markets. Hill looks at current enterprise as well to show that as the twenty-first century begins, basketry is a more viable industry among Eastern Cherokees, where a crafts cooperative has helped insure a year-round market and higher prices.

In "Crafts, Tourism, and Traditional Life in Chiapas, Mexico: A Tale Related by a Pillowcase," Chris Goertzen looks at weaving in a contemporary Indian culture. Goertzen works outward from the genesis, appearance, and sale of a single handmade souvenir to explore the conditions under which crafts made for outsiders can meet the psychological and practical needs of the tourist and, under the best circumstances, not abuse the letter or spirit of tradition living in modern craftspeople. He shows how the negotiated identity of the craft object relates to the embattled complex of identities of the modern Maya. Sales of crafts make these Indians more visible to foreigners and to a historically hostile state government—this factor has made a previously despised (and defensively maintained) ethnicity economically indispensable to the state. Craft sales have a modest but real impact in easing dislocations caused by religious conflict in the highlands and are helping shift gender relationships in Maya families. By lessening pressure to ease the strain of burgeoning populations through the usual means—massive outmigration—these sales help families and communities stay intact.

The essays presented in this anthology reveal that the commercialization and appropriation of American Indian cultures were naggingly persistent practices of American society and culture in the twentieth century. According to many prominent Indian scholars, these trends are part and parcel of cultural imperialism, and their continuation may eventually cause the destruction of native cultures and identity. Yet, as many of the authors suggest, there are important issues that make for a more complex interaction between Indians and non-Indians in the commercial sector, among them economic need and its relation to cultural integrity, self-determination, and the formation of native as well as non-Indian identity. In spite of cultural imperialism, it seems, many Indians still manage to negotiate autonomous voices and identities. We offer these essays as a new step toward understanding this complex process and hope that the dialogue begun here will continue.

Notes

1. The terms non-Indians use to refer to American Indians are in themselves part of the marketing of cultures. "Indian," "Native American," "American Indian," "Amerindian"—these shaping labels have all been created by outsiders over the centuries. Whereas individual tribal names seem to be the preferable signifier, at times—such as when writing this introduction—one finds the need for an encompassing term, in the way "European" serves to designate the various peoples of those nations. Bordewich settles on the term Indian, because it "has the virtue of clarity" and is "by far the most commonly used term among natives themselves" in the titles of organizations developed by Indians, such as the American Indian Movement and the National Congress of American Indians, and in the names of most existing tribes (19). Therefore, throughout our introduction we choose to use American Indian, while allowing each essayist in the volume to use the term he or she has chosen for particular reasons.

2. Quoted in Churchill, 99.

3. Churchill refers to each of these scholars in his essay.

4. Ibid., 300.

5. In addition to Churchill and Rose, see Hobson.

6. Hobson, 215, 216, 224.

7. Ibid., 8, 7.

8. Bordewich, 66. Bordewich explores this issue of claiming American Indian heritage; see especially 65–68.

9. Ibid., 186.

Works Cited

Bordewich, Fergus M. *Killing the White Man's Indian*. New York: Doubleday, 1996.

Churchill, Ward. *Fantasies of the Master Race*. San Francisco: City Lights Books, 1998.

Deloria, Philip J. *Playing Indian*. New Haven, Conn.: Yale University Press, 1998.

Hobson, Geary, ed. *The Remembered Earth: An Anthology of Contemporary Native American Literature*. Albuquerque: University of New Mexico Press, 1981.

Northrup, Jim. *The Rez Road Follies: Canoes, Casinos, Computers, and Birch Bark Baskets*. New York: Kodansha International, 1997.

Rose, Wendy. "The Great Pretenders: Further Reflections on White Shamanism." Pp. 296–307 in *Native American Voices: A Reader*, ed. Susan Lobo and Steve Talbot. New York: Addison Wesley Longman, 1998.

PART I
Staging the Indian

1

The "Shy" Cocopa Go to the Fair

NANCY J. PAREZO AND JOHN W. TROUTMAN

The Anthropology exhibit has the interest of strangeness, for it is an
exhibit of races of men whose lives and whose crafts have no counterpart in our lives and crafts. The hairy Ainu, the Aborigines of Japan,
whose race descent is not yet known; the large Patagonians; the shy
Cocopa Indians, of Mexico and Lower California, who have never
before left their homes; and the American Indians, of many tribes, from
the warlike Sioux to the gentle Pueblo peoples, living here as they do in
haunts away from civilization, tell by their customs, their dress, their use
of colors, their expressions, and their figures, and not least by their
vocations, what many long chapters of human evolution have been.
—WILLIAM J. MCGEE[1]

SCHOLARS HAVE RECENTLY POSITED that museums are active institutions that
continually fabricate identities.[2] Museums have also served as meeting
grounds between cultures. The same can be said of the anthropology exhibits at world's fairs in the late nineteenth and early twentieth centuries. These exhibits presented viewers with paradigms and canons through
which a broad audience of the "civilized" world could meet, interpret, and
ultimately commodify the "noncivilized" world. Through the interpretive
lens crafted by those in charge of the exhibits and their own touristic gaze,
middle-class Anglo-Americans encountered native peoples and purchased
their art and other souvenirs of exotica before returning home. Due to such
an interpretive framework, intercultural meetings held for these tourists, as
W. J. McGee, the head of the anthropology exhibits at the 1904 Louisiana
Purchase Exposition in St. Louis, said, "the interest of strangeness."

But what really occurred at these exhibits? How did the tourists' gaze
of strangeness and the tenements of fin-de-siècle anthropology embodied
in the exhibits affect the experience of the native peoples at the fairs? These
living exhibits of American Indians and various Others were popular at

many world's fairs. We are exploring an anthropology exhibit at one particular fair, the exhibit that W. J. McGee took charge of in 1904 at St. Louis. Although representatives from many native communities participated, we will detail the experience of the Cocopa Indians from the conception of the exhibit and all of its ideological underpinnings to the return trip of the Cocopa to their villages in the Lower Colorado River Valley.

By the turn of the twentieth century, world's fairs were established, universal meccas for the display and dissemination of knowledge about the peoples of the world and their material and technological accomplishments. The fairs also served as tools for the imperialist countries who staged them to justify and essentially celebrate the subjugation and dispossession of indigenous peoples worldwide. The 1904 Louisiana Purchase Exposition, held in St. Louis to commemorate the Louisiana Purchase, covered more than 1200 acres; twice as large as Chicago's, it was the largest fair ever attempted. The St. Louis fair was open from May to December and attracted more than 19 million visitors. Exposition President David Francis called it "the world's first assemblage of the world's peoples."[3] It contained ample evidence of the world's native populations and their arts in many venues. The Idaho state exhibit had Native American–made baskets, textiles, and pottery, and the Alaska territorial exhibit featured two plank houses and a group of Haida totem poles, as well as a resident Nootka family who performed, made baskets, hats, mats, and carvings and lived in a special house. The Arizona territorial building contained agricultural products, a model of the Tonto Basin reservoir and cliff dwellings, and a full-scale Mexican adobe house.[4] The Bureau of American Ethnology (BAE) of the Smithsonian Institution erected an exhibit prepared by Jesse Walter Fewkes and Matilda Coxe Stevenson that compared aesthetic principles and designs in Hopi and Zuni pottery, while in other parts of the government pavilion motion pictures of Pueblo Indians energetically dancing at the Grand Canyon were shown to encourage tourism in the new national parks. Anthropologist Alfred Jenks arranged an ethnological display for the War Department: a village of more than 1,200 Filipino natives— Igorot, Negrito, Bagobo, Bantoc, Tinguien, Moro, and Visayan—as representatives from the lands on which the United States had recently engaged in war. Private firms and individuals, sometimes in conjunction with national governments, produced displays focusing on indigenous populations and their industries and arts; the German–East African exhibits in the Palace of Agriculture contained African tools, while Maori paintings were seen in the New Zealand exhibit in the Forestry, Fish and Game Palace.

The midway (known as the "Pike") also had numbers of native peoples from around the world. They were found along the Pike at "Jerusalem" and "Fair Japan," billed as Burmese "devil dancers" and the "Mysterious Asian-Indian," and seen within the "Streets of Cairo," "Tyrolean Alps," "Streets of Seville," "Irish Village," "Chinese Village," "Bazaars of Stamboul," and the "Moorish Palace."[5] Even historic events featured native peoples: native South Africans, accompanied by a display of African artifacts, reenacted the Boer War. There was a four-story cliff dwelling that visitors could enter for 25¢ to experience "precontact" Puebloan life and see "the strange rites and dances" of the Hopi and Zuni Indians, according to entrepreneur W. Maurice Tobin.[6] Actually, visitors watched San Juan and San Ildefonso men in Plains and Pueblo attire impersonate Hopi dancers in pseudo-Snake, Kachina, and Flute Dances or perform their own Eagle Dance; San Juan women produced and sold pottery in the plaza modeled on Zuni Pueblo. In "A Trip to the North Pole" and at Crane's Esquimaux Village tourists could see Inuit families who were attending their third world's fair, including the much photographed Nancy Columbia, who had been born at Chicago in 1893. They could also witness native sports, marriage ceremonies, seal hunting, or even a fight between Inuit hunters and polar bears. And more than 200 Sioux and other northern Plains men and women performed in Cummin's Wild West Show and Indian Congress.[7] McGee estimated that more than 3,000 non-Caucasians demonstrated, lived, sold art, and performed in St. Louis.

The main anthropology exhibits were the creation of the Louisiana Purchase Exposition (LPE) Corporation, a for-profit company that organized the entire exposition. The corporation saw the fair as a unique opportunity to educate the general public in an informal setting, combining entertainment and enlightenment, while making a profit.[8] Called the "University of the Future" by William F. Slocum, president of Colorado College, the fair allowed millions of Americans to learn about the technology, colonization, and development that had become enshrined in Western ideologies of progress. Four hundred international congresses and conventions brought internationally known scholars, such as sociologist Max Weber, to expand people's minds, while the second Olympiad of the modern era celebrated the human body and "the national culture of strenuous living." The novelty of eating an ice cream cone, gasping at a monumental display of oranges, hearing John Philip Sousa's band, riding on a Ferris wheel, seeing thousands of "exotic" people, and actually meeting members of "several of the most striking tribes known to science" was enticing.[9]

But the exposition was designed to be more—it was an attempt to summarize or compile all existing knowledge as people entered the new century and tried to find purpose in a rapidly changing society.[10] The fair, wrote Slocum in *Harper's Weekly,* would give a visitor "new standards, new means of comparison, new insights into the condition of life in the world he is living in." The emerging discipline of anthropology would provide *the* central educational paradigm; according to Frederick J. V. Skiff, Director of Exhibits, "a universal exposition is a vast museum of anthropology and ethnology, of man and his works." The central theme of the fair was "process rather than products," and evolutionary anthropology was concerned with understanding the process of universal cultural and racial development rather than understanding people as members of individual communities or societies with unique cultural histories.[11] Anthropology would also help support the economic elite's messages regarding race and social progress and would intellectually and "scientifically" validate U.S. overseas economic expansion, for the anthropological paradigm used was based extensively on the principles of what came to be labeled social Darwinism.[12] In this way new knowledge and almost incomprehensible diversity would be made lucid and controlled politically, economically, intellectually, and symbolically.

The anthropology exhibits were conceptualized and organized by William J. McGee. The centerpiece was an outdoor village of native peoples. In the village, hundreds of Native American people lived and worked in full-scale, "traditional" (i.e., uncivilized) dwellings and villages arranged to create a sense of uniqueness, "strangeness," and inherent inferiority as prototypic representatives of races considered less technologically, intellectually, and artistically evolved than enlightened civilization, represented in its high form by Euro-Americans. "In order to illustrate the development in the arts," McGee told a newspaper reporter, he was designing the exhibits to "display family groups living in the Stone Age, others just at the beginning of metal working, others engaged in primitive pottery-making and basket-weaving, and so on through." Because McGee was head of the fair's Anthropology Department and thus presented native peoples to St. Louis (and in the process both reaffirmed notions of racial superiority and challenged some popular stereotypes), he was crowned by the *St. Louis Post-Dispatch* as "The Overlord of the Savage World."[13]

This title was fitting for the field of anthropology itself. By 1904, anthropology had secured the status and recognition among all other professions as the authority on non-Western peoples and their arts. McGee presented a very powerful image of native peoples and their dissimilarities to Anglo-American society as well as a vision of a hopeful future for them, that is, the possibility for native peoples' "progress." This was done through an orchestrated sequence of before-and-after encounters: Tourists met native peoples in settings that demonstrated the assimilation process from both before and after they had been "civilized." Although they were framed and conceptualized in a manner that was often strange or completely foreign to them, native peoples formed their own opinions of the fairgoers they met and controlled and manipulated their own experience at the fair as best they could. They retained control over the manufacture and marketing of their individual works of art, and tried, sometimes successfully, sometimes not, to limit and bound the taking of photographs and the arenas in which touristic encounters took place.[14] With the exception of boarding school children, native peoples came of their own free will to work at the fair. The fair offered families a chance to travel and earn money from the sale of their art and performance of other types of cultural capital (music, storytelling, secularized rituals and dance) at a time when many of their previous economic pursuits were no longer possible.

These encounters were not completely symmetrical, of course. In this chapter we look at the experiences of the Cocopa Indians who traveled to St. Louis as a case study in how native families were treated, based on archival collections in the Library of Congress and the Missouri Historical Society. We review how McGee conceptualized and marketed them as shy, strange peoples who represented a racial type and a cultural stage, people who were worthy of being known and interacted with, that is, worthy and deserving of the touristic gaze. We have no primary data from interviews with the Cocopa participants, who are all deceased, nor written documents penned by them. However, we can provide some tentative indications of how the Cocopa reacted to living and demonstrating on the fairgrounds, being under the almost constant gaze of visitors, and their first trip outside their homeland along the Lower Colorado River Valley—to a strange place where they met strange people who wanted to pigeon-hole and ultimately commodify them by taking home their images and art as memories of their encounters.

The Anthropology Display in St. Louis

Even though observing "progress" and understanding humanity's evolutionary development were two of the exposition's central themes, the anthropology exhibits were, in one sense, an afterthought for the fair corporation. They were conceptualized early in the planning process as a comprehensive presentation of the world's "primitive" and "barbarous" peoples, based on a plan commissioned from Smithsonian Institution anthropologists William J. McGee and William H. Holmes.[15] The LPE Executive Committee only finalized the plans in mid-1903, however, when they began to fear they would not attract sufficient visitors to make a profit. Nevertheless, by the summer of 1903 the LPE Corporation enthusiastically supported the creation of an Anthropology Department, and the anthropology exhibits quickly became one of the fair's central features.

To organize this "Congress of Races," the executive committee appointed one of the most prominent anthropologists of the day: geologist, ethnographer, and theoretical evolutionist William J. McGee, as chief of the Department of Anthropology.[16] McGee accepted the position in August 1903 after resigning as director of the BAE under allegations of financial misconduct.[17] McGee quickly tried to initialize his grandiose plans to comprehensively "diffuse and incidentally to increase knowledge of Man and his Works," in essence bringing to fruition the scheme he had wanted the Smithsonian Institution to enact at the 1901 Pan-American Exposition in Buffalo, New York, and which the LPE Corporation had approved in principle.[18]

McGee wanted his department and the exhibits involved to create for fairgoers a narrative of human "progress." The centerpiece was a living exhibit of people from seventy-five groups, residing on 40 acres of land in their "traditional" habitations that were distributed around a lagoon. These native peoples would demonstrate their industries, games, and ceremonies; produce aesthetic products; and speak their native languages. McGee also planned indoor and outdoor exhibits to systematically trace the paths of human progress. He divided the indoor exhibit into five sections: archaeology, history, anthropometry, psychometry, and ethnology.

The archaeology section contained displays of cultural artifacts from around the world, arranged "in synthetic series illustrating the stages of human development shown also in the ethnologic section."[19] As befitting an industrial fair that celebrated technological innovations and new knowledge, visitors saw artifacts in exhibit cases that demonstrated "how the cave-man wrought with stone hammers and knives" as well as "the prehistoric means of fire-production" and presented "the relics of Egyptian and Central American civilizations, now discoverable only in ruins."[20] The section of history, in contrast, displayed the artifacts of the Euro-Americans who aided in the "transformation of the Louisiana Purchase Territory from a wilderness ranged only by wild beasts and savage men into a family of great commonwealths."

The sections of anthropometry and psychometry, located in the basement of the anthropology building, were established for "comparing the physical and mental characteristics of all the world's peoples. The measurements comprise not only external physical characteristics such as stature and weight, but rates of respiration and pulsation, acuteness of the senses, times of sense reactions, capacity for coordinating impressions, and other faculties of the human creature, so that the race-types and culture-grades assembled on the grounds may be brought within the range of comparative study."[21] Dr. Frank G. Bruner and Dr. R. S. Woodward, psychology professors from Columbia University, researched the hearing, sight, color blindness, and memory of native peoples, while St. Louis physician Dr. Phil Hoffman studied feet and the effects of wearing shoes. The Cocopa, like other native peoples, were the subject of intensive anthropometric and psychometric research. Six Cocopa were measured for height, head size, eye color, and the shape of the cornea and were tested for visual acuity, color blindness, intelligence, manual dexterity, handedness, and motor skills.

COMPARE TO CURRENT DNA SAMPLING

In addition, anthropologist Frederick Starr of the University of Chicago, who had brought the Ainu contingent from Japan, ran an ethnographic field school in the exhibit. The Cocopa were the subject of ethnographic interviews and observations by Starr's students.[22] Thus, the anthropology department would contribute to scientific research as well as general education.

McGee anticipated that after viewing the interior displays visitors would examine the dynamic outdoor exhibits. Instead of dedicating the ethnology section to displaying only the material culture and artistic products of native peoples and relying on dioramas or mannequins, McGee decided to center the space around live displays of indigenous peoples who represented "human progress from the dark prime to the highest enlightenment, from savagery to civic organization."[23] These ethnographic displays were composed of an assemblage of more than 300 American Indians living in family groups, punctuated with celebrities like Geronimo and Quanah Parker, as well as Ainu, Patagonians, and Pygmies who lived and worked in housing they built.[24] The ethnology section was thus the cornerstone of the department. According to McGee, it was "devoted to types of both race and culture (or development). . . . Generally, the primitive folk will occupy

NEGRIN ~ EXHIBIT

MATSUA'S WIFE

habitations erected by themselves from materials brought for the purpose, and will live and work in their accustomed ways; so that on the Exposition grounds may be seen every stage in industrial progress with the development in the arts, languages, social customs, and beliefs characteristic of each stage of human advancement."[25]

Another important feature of this celebration of "progress," illustrating "the best way of bearing the white man's burden," was the government-sponsored model Indian school, the final section of the anthropology exhibit.[26] Samuel M. McCowan, the head of the Chilocco Indian Training School in Oklahoma, built the school next to the native village, significantly placing it at the top of a small rise.[27] Here visitors could observe the "civilizing" effects of Christianity, nationalism, and the Protestant work ethic among Oneida, Sioux, Pima, and Arapaho children, thereby witnessing "the normal course of human progress—which is from ignorance toward knowledge, and from helplessness toward competence."[28] According to McCowan, the school would "illustrate the most advanced methods of raising our surviving aborigines to the plane of citizenship. . . . [T]he interest of the modern training [at the school] will be constantly enhanced by the contrast between aboriginal handicraft and that of the trained pupils, both displayed in the same building."[29] "Blanket Indians" (i.e., older men and women from the reservations who wore Pendleton blankets over their attire and were considered traditional) demonstrated their art manufacturing processes and sold their products to the public on one side of the hall. These artisans included Pueblo women grinding corn; Geronimo making souvenir bows and arrows; Pueblo potters; Pomo, Jicarilla Apache, and Pima basket makers; and Sioux and Cheyenne bead and buckskin workers.[30] In open rooms on the other side of the hall, children from several government schools attended classes and demonstrated their prowess at manual labor: washing clothes, cooking and dining-room serving, embroidering, sewing, furniture making, printing, farming, raising livestock, and blacksmithing. There was also a band of forty students that gave two concerts daily. The past and the future, "the aboriginal and the cultural, the old and the new" were collated.[31]

According to McGee, the juxtaposition of the Indian village and the Indian school told "two living stories. It presents the race narratives of odd peoples who mark time while the world advances, and how savages [are] made, by American methods, into civilized workers." An "old-fashioned" frontier sutlery, under the direction of trader J. W. Benham of Phoenix, was built next to the Indian school to serve as a trading post and leisure-time meeting place for the native demonstrators.[32] McGee and McCowan wanted the Indian village to resemble a "typical" reservation; this necessitated a trading post where the American Indian residents were able to "purchase everything they need, from evaporated apples to pens and ink, and where visitors may buy Indian work, from Navajo blankets and Pueblo pottery to wonderful basketry, the best examples of which are works of art." Here visitors could watch these economic transactions as the Indian artists traded their "products for supplies just as they did in the early days." According to one newspaper article, the native people had no reason to leave the fairgrounds because all of their needs could be satisfied through the goods offered them for trade: "beads, baskets, and leather articles will be taken in exchange for food, blankets and anything else wanted. The post will be so well equipped that the Indian may produce everything he needs without leaving the exposition grounds."[33] Benham, in turn, sold the art as well as Southwestern pottery, basketry, and rugs from his own collections to tourists. The tourists and native peoples witnessed and engaged in the market economy through a fabricated trading post where articles made by the native peoples were commodified, exchanged, and sold. The value of the articles lay essentially in whose hands had produced them—American Indian arts and crafts, marketed as such, became an industry largely responsible for the increasing commodification and popularity of American Indians themselves and their communities as tourist attractions.

In many ways, the native village constituted a semicaptive research laboratory, reinforcing anthropology's claim that its professional knowledge was based on scientific research. The village displays were supplemented by both serious and entertaining public programs (lectures, congresses, band concerts by the students, athletic contests, and special events) designed to prove McGee's theory of racial and cultural development. To promote the second Olympiad of the modern era, McGee even held a "savage Olympics" called "Anthropology Days," held August 12 and 13 and again in September, in which native people competed in contests of spear throwing, shot put, racing, broad jump, throwing a baseball, weight lifting, pole climbing, and tugs-of-war before a crowd of 30,000.[34] The winners of these events, rather than being given gold medals, were awarded small American flags.

To McGee, anthropology's special areas of professional knowledge were evolution, biological development, and social progress. Anthropology explored "mankind as an assemblage of varieties or races, and as social creatures united by language and law and organized in families, communities, societies, commonwealths, and nations." He sought to introduce fair visitors to his social vision through an evolutionary multifaceted living and static exhibit that would implicitly end with the historic sections (especially American pioneers settling the St. Louis area) and highlight the civilization buildings at the fair. In the 40-acre anthropology area, visitors would see "the advances of human culture, in its lower stages" and would implicitly compare them to the displays from the industrial world.[35] In short, McGee wanted to display his "improved," highly complex (and often convoluted) model of how the world was ordered and demonstrate visually that comparison, a central methodology of evolutionary anthropology, was useful and met society's needs for placing incredible cultural diversity into an understandable hierarchical order.[36]

McGee's ordering developmental scheme attempted to classify people into a combined model of biologically based "race-types" and "culture-grades," or "culture-stages," that accounted for those peoples who seemed to evade simpler racial or cultural anthropological explanations. These types and grades were intertwined: The development of manual dexterity accompanied the development of thought, physical appearance, gesture, and artifact. McGee recognized that simply classifying the world's populations into five races allowed anomalous groups to fall through the cracks; an example were the Japanese, who were an "ethnological puzzle if not a distinct race." McGee believed that, beyond racial definitions, people also fell into a hierarchic structure characterized by what they produced, industrially and socially, or "what they DO as human creatures rather than what they merely ARE as animal beings." Expanding on this model, he contended: "As the world's peoples and tribes were classed by race and culture jointly, it was soon seen that the types of culture really represent grades or stages in development, and also that the exercise of function and organ [sic] attending culture is a material factor in development; and hence that the course of human progress is not that of vital evolution alone but one affected increasingly through the ages by activital [sic] forces arising in and with man himself."[37]

One of McGee's goals was to visually synthesize the work of evolutionary theorists and to classify specific cultures in four principal types or stages "according to the degree of their advancement" in the activities of the arts, industries, laws, languages, and philosophies, as well as to advance his own theories and provide evidence for emerging research problems, especially the role of the environment in the development of culture and specific cultural manifestations.[38] Whether speaking in terms of race-types or culture-grades, McGee placed all of humanity on a universal hierarchic scale of physical-cultural development, positioning the Caucasian or white race-type at the top. Because the fair itself was a manifestation of the products of the enlightened, American Caucasian culture-grade, McGee organized the ethnology section of his department to illustrate the lower non-Caucasian race-types in their different levels of culture-grades as a foil for the industrial displays. In this sense, the Cocopa were to illustrate the emergence from the "Law of the Maternal Family," as sparsely populated groups "living largely in a state of nature, i.e., small and isolated tribes of too low intelligence to recognize paternity or organize confederacies, to devise economic systems or to realize humanitarian motives and institutions."[39] To McGee, these were "the conditions under which all early men must have lived." McGee summarized his conceptualization for the native villages succinctly in an article for *The World's Work:* "The peoples, living in skin tents, dugouts, and thatched huts, outside, picture in their daily life different stages in these lower strata of development. In brief, one may learn in the indoor exhibit how our own prehistoric forbears lived, and then see, outside, people untouched by the march of progress still living in similar crude manner."[40]

Native Peoples in St. Louis: Populating the Indian Village

Native peoples were seen all over the fairgrounds, working in various venues as entertainers. But McGee had a more grandiose plan: to systematically assemble thousands of people under a scientific paradigm for the touristic gaze. McGee proposed to gather in St. Louis representatives of native peoples from all over the world, including parts of Japan, South America, Asia, and Africa, while he focused especially on the American Indians who lived in the lands considered a part of the original Louisiana Purchase Territory. Each of these peoples were selected to fill McGee's racial-cultural evolutionary matrix. In addition, each had special scientific or cultural interest. The Kwakiutl, for instance, were to be "living examples of the dominant influence of environment on primitive life." The Cocopas, Pygmies, Negritos, Ainus, and Patagonians were to represent one of the world's "least known ethnic types," a group "least removed from the subhuman or quadrumane form."[41]

When the LPE Corporation's Executive Committee learned of the expenses involved and the number of expeditions it would take to bring families from hundreds of different groups to St. Louis, as well as the expense of housing and feeding them, the scope of evolutionary progress was reduced to a few native communities that represented the "least-known ethnic types."[42] The focus was still on the Plains and the Prairie region with a heavy dose of the Greater Southwest. Representatives eventually came from a small but significant number of American Indian societies: "Apache," Arapaho, Cheyenne, Chippewa, Chiricahua Apache, Cocopa, Comanche, Crow, Jicarilla Apache, Kickapoo, Kiowa, Kwakiutl, Laguna, Maricopa, Muskwaki, Navajo, Nez Perce, Osage, Pawnee, Pima, Pomo, "Pueblo," Santa Clara, Rosebud Sioux, and Wichita families spent many weeks in St. Louis demonstrating activities for tourists and serving as living examples of cultural progress.[43] Zuni demonstrators were unable to attend because of unexpected bad weather, so McCowan arranged for a small group of San Juan and Acoma people to represent Puebloan culture, although there is no clear indication that these groups actually came.[44] Special efforts were made to bring native peoples who lived within the area of the Louisiana Purchase Territory and, to fill specific niches within McGee's racial-cultural scheme, those who built distinctive types of houses. For reasons elaborated upon shortly, the Cocopa were labeled foreign natives, not American Indians, and were thus placed in a unique status with regard to the Bureau of Indian Affairs (BIA) and exposition authority and control; $2,500 was allocated separately for the Cocopa exhibit in January 1904.[45] The Indian village or "Indian reservation" was situated on a tract west and south of the intramural railway in the west-central portion of the grounds on what is now the campus of Washington University. The village was on sloping land between the anthropology and the government buildings, near a lagoon (called Arrowhead Lake), and across from the Filipino village. The village surrounded the parade grounds, where "the transformed boys and girls of the Government Indian schools perform[ed] their evolutions."[46] The village stretched out in what McGee believed would reflect an authentic setting as well as his evolutionary paradigm. The Indian school was located at the top with the Ainu and Patagonian encampments at the base. The Cocopa were placed near the Patagonians.

Each tribe had a specific locale that quietly mirrored McGee's evolutionary matrix. Along the three sides of the parade ground, the visitor encountered a Rosebud Sioux encampment with thirty-five individuals, Apache wickiups, Jicarilla Apache tipis, and Pueblo adobe houses. "A Wichita group, dwelling in grass huts, are next to the brilliantly clothed Pawnee braves, endlessly giving a war-dance to the sound of cacophonous drums in the faintly smoky interior of the commodious lodge," as McGee described the scene. Moving up the hill visitors could enter a large Arapaho wattled stockade, a Cheyenne dance ground, and three Navajo hogans where weavers and silversmiths worked. Finally, the visitors encountered camps of seven Pima-Maricopa, two Pomo, and twenty Chippewa individuals. The tour ended at the "apex of civilization" for the village, the Indian school.[47]

McGee hoped that the native village would be a moral example of harmonious living: "The special object of the Department of Anthropology is to show each half of the world how the other half lives and thereby to promote not only knowledge but also peace and good will among nations." Native residents were expected to perform peaceful daily activities, such as cooking food, dancing, singing, or producing pottery, tools, baskets, and textiles, to show the nature of their work, customs, habits, and ultimately their personalities. This required that they bring utensils, tools, and raw materials from their reservation homes. In addition, residents participated in special events and parades, competed against each other in various games and sporting events, and performed "exotic" ceremonies, songs, dances, and rituals. In exchange for this work, they were promised transportation to and from the fair and rations as well as the opportunity to sell their art and obtain money from photographs, or in the case of Geronimo, from his autograph and handmade bows and arrows. The native performers and artisans were not paid a wage; McGee and the other exhibit organizers felt that the money they would receive from selling arts and crafts would supplant any other form of compensation.[48] Individuals were chosen to participate, with the help of BIA officials, "either for the prominence of the chiefs or for the faithfulness with which they portray[ed] aboriginal habits and customs."[49] By this, McCowan and McGee meant that the Indians they sought for the exhibit would embody what they considered characteristics of traditional "Indianness." That is, they worked in "primitive" methods of manufacture without having adopted what were considered Western techniques and styles and tried to live in the "old way" as it existed before the reservation period.

The Cocopa Come to St. Louis

McGee selected the Cocopa to illustrate the consistent maintenance of what he called a physical or ethnic type "in which the stature [of] the two sexes is strikingly different—the males being among the tallest of our aborigines and the females among the shortest of our native women." The

Cocopa were also chosen to illustrate a distinct type of culture, an idea that for McGee had two meanings: They were a unique people with an interesting way of life and they represented the "barbarian" stage of development. McGee believed that the Cocopa's flood-plain agricultural methods had remained unchanged since before contact so that they could illustrate "such native lore and legend as those embalmed in Hiawatha." "They still cultivate pre-Columbian corn and beans by pre-Columbian methods; they are our finest archers, and perform significant ceremonies of devotional character, attesting [to] the close interrelation between early man and their natural surroundings." In addition, McGee portrayed the Cocopa as having some of the "most extravagant known mortuary customs, in which the goods of the descendent are distributed to non-relatives while his house and his body are burned together, so that the people are perpetually impoverished and prevented from gathering in communities; and their marriage and puberty rites are elaborate, while the tribal law is in a state of transition from that of the maternal family to that of the paternal family."[50] In short, for McGee the Cocopa were scientifically important; culturally exotic; individually unique; and nice, quiet, "peaceful folk." They were also obscure to the American public, and McGee and others believed that their lives required professional training to understand and interpret. According to one newspaper reporter:

> These Indians are among the greatest puzzles that scientists have met with. The men are remarkably large for that latitude [,] few of them being under six feet. The women are about 5 feet 6 inches. They inhabit the lowlands of the Colorado valley, despite the fact that every year they are driven out by floods. They are a tribe of undoubted antiquity, but scientists have never been able to trace their origin. They inhabited the Colorado River valley when Cortez came to America and their mode of life is now the same as it was then. The race is rapidly dying out.

McGee often reinforced the notion that the Cocopa's participation was timely: "Their early extinction seems inevitable; and it would seem probable that they will have the distinction of melting away through voluntary adoption of unfit Caucasian customs without the aid of church or state."[51]

In his press releases, McGee prepared visitors for their encounters with the "timid and home-loving" Cocopa. They would not be like what people expected, and McGee felt this was one of their special merits. The Cocopa would demonstrate that not all Indians were the same: They were very different from the warriors of the northern Plains or other stereotypical portrayals of American Indians. Describing his idealized version of Cocopa personality and athletic ability, McGee told potential fairgoers that

> No Cocopa Indians have ever before been induced to leave their homes. They are shy and gentle, and their children are the happiest of all the little "barbarians." They roll about on the ground, play marbles and other games—their brown eyes flashing with interest—and they shoot arrows at a mark with unerring accuracy. One day, Indian games were held. Of four Indians whose arrow struck the bull's eye, one was a Sioux and three were Cocopa. If a visitor to their encampment set up a coin for a mark, every Cocopa boy turns as quickly as a flash; there is a whiz of arrows, and the coin goes spinning into the air.[52]

It had not been easy to arrange for Cocopa participation. Even though McCowan and the local BIA agent were to select American Indian participants and arrange their transportation, McGee oversaw the quest for Cocopa cooperation.[53] McGee had a personal and professional stake in their participation. He had visited the Cocopa briefly in 1900 as part of an aborted BAE research expedition to the lands of the Seri and Tohono O'odham people. Working with one band briefly and quizzing them especially about their subsistence methods, he made vague plans for an in-depth fieldwork project because the Cocopa had never been studied by ethnographers. McGee was intrigued by what he considered their traditionalism; DeLancey Gill, the BAE photographer who accompanied McGee, found that many of the women wore willow bark skirts as well as shirtwaist calico dresses and the men loincloths in summer as well as shirts and cotton pants.[54] McGee had previously used Seri and Tohono O'odham material he had obtained in the winters of 1894 and 1895 as the centerpiece of the BAE-Smithsonian exhibit at the 1896 industrial exposition in Atlanta; Cocopa material culture from the 1900 expedition was used in the BAE exhibit at the Pan-American Exposition at Buffalo in 1901.[55] Although McGee never published much on his Cocopa fieldwork, he did deliver one paper on January 22, 1901, to the Anthropological Society of Washington comparing Seri and Cocopa culture and another on March 12, 1901, outlining Cocopa agricultural techniques.

Even more than Cocopa participation, McGee wanted the Seri to come to St. Louis, in part because to McGee they represented in his scheme "true savagery." As he described them in a letter to the editor in 1901, the

Seri from Tiburon Island in Sonora were important because they were "reputed cannibals, . . . of gigantic stature, and so swift of foot as to capture deer by the hands alone." In addition, the Seri would have complemented the Patagonians, being "of nearly equal stature and superior strength and swiftness though of less weighty frame, the supposed type of Swift's Brobdignagians, and the most savage tribe of North America." McGee also hoped to bring the famous runners of northern Mexico, the Tarahumara, the "Papagos" [Tohono O'odham] of the international border, and a community of Yucatan. He later lamented that these groups could not attend but noted that "the difficulties and dangers of the expedition prevented the carrying out of the contract."[56]

The Cocopa lived at the base of the Lower Colorado River with homes in Sonora, Mexico, Baja California, and Arizona Territory.[57] Many were placed under the loose jurisdiction of the U.S. federal and state governments in the mid-nineteenth century when treaties dissected their traditional lands. They were not federally recognized until 1917, when two small reservations were created for them near Yuma and Somerton. The U.S. government labeled many Cocopa as "Mexicans" at the turn of the century, although members of the Mat Skrui band had been in Arizona Territory living near San Luis and the Hwanyak band had lived near Somerton since the Gadsen Purchase in 1853.[58] In Sonora, Wi Akwir and Kwakwarsh Cocopa lived on private land owned by a land-grant patron, in neighborhoods near Mexicali, along the railroad, or in small *ejidos* and *colonias.* In each case, the Cocopa lived and moved in extended family groups. McGee wanted a contingent from Sonora, because he considered them less assimilated than those living in Arizona. As such, McGee labeled the Cocopa "foreign aborigines" rather than Indian wards of the United States. Thus, he did not place them under the direct supervision of McCowan, as he had other Indian groups.

Each native group was placed under the immediate guidance of a special agent. McGee hired Edwin C. Cushman Jr. of St. Louis to bring the Cocopa extended family, and hopefully a Seri family, from Sonora.[59] In November 1903, McGee noted that press dispatches indicated that a party of Seri had been imprisoned in Mexico for supposed "depredations" in western Sonora.[60] Because the expedition was international, McGee provided Cushman with papers of introduction to important Mexican government officials, explaining his purpose and that of the fair. As the "most primitive group in North America," McGee was originally more interested in Seri participation than Cocopa at the fair. The papers referred to a group of Seri that McGee suspected were "in the employ of the Government in or about the capital city."[61] For the Seri, "in the employ" actually meant "in captivity"; they had been placed in work camps, in the employ (loosely defined) of patrons. It was McGee's hope that these patrons would help Cushman locate a Seri family and persuade them to travel more than 2,000 miles to St. Louis. Cushman, however, was unable to locate any Seri "held in captivity or in any other capacity in Mexico." This was a situation similar to what McGee had encountered in his own fieldwork: The Seri had all escaped captivity and were hiding in remote areas, as far away from government officials and ethnologists as possible. Ramon Corral, Mexico's Minister of the Interior, confirmed Cushman's conclusion: "I regret to inform you that it will not be possible to obtain the Seris [sic] Indians you wish for the Exposition in St. Louis, as those who were prisoners have been given their freedom by the Government. In order to obtain others, we would have to make a [military] campaign which would be very costly." McGee never succeeded in enticing any Seris to the fair.[62]

McGee decided to concentrate on the Cocopa as the next-best example of "primitivism." He asked Herbert Brown, superintendent of the Arizona territorial prison in Yuma and first director of the Arizona State Museum in Tucson, to assist Cushman in finding Cocopa demonstrators.[63] McGee told Brown that Cushman's ostensible purpose was the continuation of McGee's earlier ethnographic work, undertaken in 1901. He downplayed his quest for native people to bring to St. Louis, but he did mention an opportunity for some "sophisticated" Cocopa to travel: "should [Cushman] find two or three of the more responsible chiefs or head men of the tribe desirous of attending the exposition in person, . . . he may be able to afford them facilities in the way of transportation from Yuma." To Cushman, however, McGee gave more explicit instructions that stressed the importance of bringing an entire group of Cocopas to the fair; without them his grand conceptual scheme would be incomplete: "while all the letters [of introduction] expressed, just as your conversation should, the idea that the research factor is the conspicuous one in your work, you should constantly have as a mental background the primary motive of bringing a good group of those Indians to the Exposition. This is the mariner's compass below and behind all the bunting and salvo and cheering that normally attend the sailing of a new ship. Pray let this be your deepest conviction."[64]

McGee particularly wanted to convince Chief Pablo Colorado, whom he had met on his earlier field trips. He sent a letter and a Chinese silk handkerchief to Colorado as "Head Man of all the Cocopa Indians." McGee invited Colorado "to visit the World's Fair next summer and see with your own eyes the greatest productions of all nations." McGee argued that this was a once-in-a-lifetime opportunity for a man who had never been away from the Lower Colorado River Valley area. Cushman met with Colorado and his group in mid-January 1904 and delivered McGee's letter. It is unknown exactly what Cushman told them or the other groups he visited repeatedly, those of Captain Manuel and Captain Tomas, but it must have included a request that the Cocopa would remain in St. Louis for at least three months, if not for the entire six-month run of the exposition, bring their families, demonstrate, and perform some appropriate activities. Although Cushman did not offer them wages or compensation for their time and effort, he did proffer transportation and food, and he gave several small gifts of money, tobacco, and food. His expense accounts for February and March noted $2.25 for handkerchiefs for the Indians as gifts and $20.00 and $31.00 "paid to Indians."[65]

It appears that the Cocopa men were not enthusiastic about the proposed undertaking. Colorado dictated a letter to McGee through an interpreter expressing ambivalence both about traveling to St. Louis, which he said was a very long distance away, and about staying for an extended period of time.[66] Three other men in the band told Cushman that they also had problems with the plan. First, they objected to the length of the stay, noting that the fair would interfere with their agricultural cycle (especially planting and harvest). Leaving their fields unattended, they would not be able to survive the next winter, and no plan had been devised to compensate them or to purchase the necessary winter supplies. Second, they did not think it appropriate to bring women, fearing that they would not be treated kindly or courteously. Several of the men thought that they should go without their wives. Cushman stated that he was firmly committed to bringing women, explaining that only families could go and "that we were doing them a great favor in bringing them at all."[67] Cushman was not sure that he could convince any to come for more than three months.

It appears from exposition records and correspondence that the negotiations with the Cocopa were the most difficult of any group that came to St. Louis. Cushman continued to discuss the issues with three headmen and their families, using Mrs. Annie Flynn as his interpreter, at their camps and in Yuma. He lived in their community, which they called "The Colony," during January and February, while gathering basic ethnographic information on social organization, agricultural techniques, and industrial methods for McGee and continuing his negotiations.[68] His letters to McGee speak of his consternation and optimism. McGee, in turn, told Cushman that a relatively small representative gathering of Cocopa families in St. Louis for only three months was acceptable, but he preferred a stay of six months; like McCowan, who arranged for many of the other Native American demonstrators, he did not want a large contingent but rather one or two "outstanding" families. McGee wanted enough adults so that they could perform their "collective ceremonies"; twelve to fifteen adults and four or five children were sufficient for McGee.[69] Negotiations continued for another two months, during which time Cushman continued to live in the community. But the Cocopa remained skeptical. Only after what he described as a hard fight did Cushman feel relatively confident that a group of fifteen to twenty individuals were willing to go to St. Louis. Captain Tom, who was the leader of "a typical group," agreed to come by early March.[70]

Cushman had still not convinced Pablo Colorado, but was hopeful that a new negotiating strategy would be successful. Informing McGee of the problem, he reported, "I don't think Captain Pablo wants to come. He says that his place is with his people, and that he cannot leave them, but I think he is trying to see if he can't work me for some money. He is a foxy old fellow. I took him down a bit the other day when I informed him that the Americans didn't care whether he went to the fair or not, in fact I thought it would be better if he didn't go. Since then he has been more meek, and I should not be surprised to have him come and ask to be taken." Colorado still held out. By late March 1904, however, he had agreed to go, without a salary, as did the principal subchief, Tom Moore, but with remuneration for their expenses and board. Cushman reported to McGee that "it has been a hard fight to gain their confidence and overcome their many superstitions." Cushman did pay Annie Flynn, a "half breed Cocopa woman," $25 a month to accompany the group as translator and promoter. Her job was to "induce the Indians to give their different ceremonials on the grounds" over the course of the summer.[71] This they appear not to have done, but they did perform other cultural activities for the general public.

Living in Full View of the Public

The fair opened on April 30, 1904, but the Indian encampment was not ready. Fair organizers were to have cleared and graded the tract and provided pathways, water, and toilet facilities, but inclement weather during March and April turned the land into a quagmire. The official opening of the ethnology exhibit was postponed until June 1 and of the Indian school for mid-May.[72] Nevertheless, McGee wanted some of the native peoples to participate in the opening ceremonies; as a result, the native peoples were scheduled to arrive and expected to stay the entire six months. Groups trickled in. McGee had Cushman keep the Cocopa in Yuma for a few extra days because he thought that the cold and rainy St. Louis weather would make them ill and uncomfortable.

On April 24, 1904, St. Louis newspapers announced that the Cocopa, the fair's "antique Indian tribe," would begin their journey the following Monday.[73] The cost of transportation and other expenses was around $300; the railroad underwrote part of this with half-price "limited first class" tickets for all Native Americans. But Monday came and the Cocopa remained in Yuma. There were delays because railroad authorities had not arranged for a separate car for the delegation and their building materials, as requested, and because McGee had not sent funds in a timely manner. There was also continued disagreement over the number of Cocopa who would attend. McGee and the railroad settled on twelve, but according to Cushman, eighteen, nineteen, or twenty-one people now wanted to go (the figure varied daily in telegrams). After weeks of frustration and miscommunication, the contingent, along with food that the Cocopa provided for their own journey, finally left Yuma on April 27, 1904.[74]

Apparently the delegation arrived in time to participate in the opening ceremonies for the anthropology program and for the fair. A photograph shows McGee and Cushman with twenty-one individuals: seven adult men, five adult women, two adolescent males, four boys, one girl, and two babies.[75] McGee's final report on the fair noted the following twenty-four individuals traveled to St. Louis: Pablo Colorado and his wife; Thomas Moore (Captain Tomas, second in authority to Colorado), his wife, and two grandchildren; subchief Artuckero and his wife; Annie Flynn; Shokee, "a stalwart man in his prime"; "Cherry," with his wife and two children; Chinyun Sacup, with his wife and three children; three unmarried young men, Pahup, Ilpuk, and Skick; Ecusheput, an unmarried young woman; and an unnamed ten year old girl. A boy or man named Chizi was also listed in the "savage" Olympics list.[76] It is likely, although there is no conclusive evidence, that all participants were members of the Hwanyak band who lived around Somerton at this time.[77] Cushman remained with them on the grounds until the end of July, when failing health compelled him to resign and seek admission to an Adirondack sanitarium.

The Cocopa had brought building materials to erect their own housing, as well as materials to produce art. The housing material, in preparation for its eventual rail delivery, had been collected by the local BIA agent prior to April 13 and was transported to Yuma from Somerton in two big wagon loads.[78] The tule or brush houses they built had wood frames of willow saplings and were thatched with tule along the walls and on their flat roofs. On top of each were placed storage baskets designed to hold grain. Some were square with lids, whereas others were shouldered jars. Straw was placed on the ground both inside and in front of the structures. Tables and benches were placed under a ramada. A single fence of two-by-fours was erected around the 100-foot by 120-foot compound to prevent the crowds from overrunning the houses.[79]

The Cocopa men and women dressed in their normal attire, rather than in costume. These were not fancy outfits (i.e., special-occasion attire) such as those donned by the Sioux in the Wild West Show or by the Puebloans performing secularized dances. Cocopa men wore dungarees and boots; long-sleeved, collarless, cotton shirts; neck handkerchiefs; and no suspenders or belts. Older men wore plain dark vests and light colored shirts. Young men and boys wore dark colored cotton shirts without vests. The only items that distinguished the Cocopa men from other residents of the Southwest were their bead necklaces; these long, special, T-shaped necklaces made by the women were highly prized. The men were also distinguished by their hairstyle: long free-flowing hair, parted in the middle with thick bangs for some individuals.

Women wore typical pioneer-style shirtwaist dresses that buttoned up the front, in striped or plaid calico. Their skirts were full and floor length and the women generally went barefoot. Women covered their dresses with short shawls, either elaborate silks from eastern Europe or plain pieces of wool. Women's hair was cut like the men's and in the photographs only one young woman wore a bead necklace. McGee felt somewhat disappointed that the Cocopas' attire was not as exotic as that of some of the other natives, but he felt that they were of interest because of their "copper-tinted" skin and the "luxuriance of [their] hair."[80]

Like most of the other groups, the Cocopa lived as an extended family grouping with children, theoretically following their accustomed pursuits.[81] McGee noted that Colorado "much enjoyed the comparative leisure of life at the Exposition, and still more greatly the lengthy and ceremonious councils with the special agents and other officials." Generally there were harmonious relations within the Cocopa delegation, but one of the group members, Shokee, caused problems and was sent home in July. McGee considered Shokee the most "picturesque member of the group."[82] Several Cocopa complained to Cushman about Shokee, stating he had made himself objectionable to the women. "On three different occasions," they said, "he had used violence in attaining his ends upon the person of one of the younger women of the tribe, and had even attempted assault upon the person of a young girl not more than ten years old."[83] The Cocopa leaders and women wanted him sent home in disgrace for his own family to punish. The Cocopa made this decision using their own code of ethics; Cushman and McGee respected their wishes. On July 7, Shokee, who could not speak English, was placed on a train with $2 to purchase coffee and food and a letter of introduction and transmittal to the railroad conductors, who would assist him in changing trains.[84] McGee described Shokee during his departure as "submissive but weeping."[85] Shokee made it safely to Yuma and Somerton a few days later. Upon his arrival, Cocopa leader Frank Tehano sent a letter to Captain Tomas and Pablo Colorado in St. Louis asking for clarification about the problem that had prompted Shokee's expulsion. There was skepticism about Shokee's rendition of the affair.

The Cocopa attempted to earn money and supplement their diet in different ways. Native performance and work were combined at the fair; people were paid for their activities, both formally and informally. Fair organizers felt that the sale of handmade artifacts by native artists who were dressed in their native attire, working in front of exotic dwellings or in the Indian school, and conversing through sign language or pidgin would be a great attraction to visitors as well as economically beneficial for the participants. Several Cocopa made money during their stay in St. Louis. One of the main sources of income for women was beadwork, which they made as demonstrations of their manual dexterity and creativity. We have no indication that any Cocopa artisan had a booth or room in the Indian school; however, they very likely erected a sales bench in front of their dwelling, near their garden. The delegation brought with them native seeds and tools such as digging sticks and harvesting baskets.[86] Although fair records do not show what foods were grown, they were likely corn, beans, and squash. The Cocopa had to have adapted their floodwater irrigation methods to a St. Louis garden, and we have found no explicit reference to the success or failure of their attempts.

One of the reasons McGee wanted the Cocopa to participate in the exposition was so that they could perform their old-style girl's puberty ceremony and demonstrate for the American public their talents in face tattooing. Cushman collected materials for this ceremony and also for tattooing, especially for use in a "marriage ceremony." He informed McGee before the start of the fair, however, that the Cocopa had discontinued, at least as far as ethnologists and other outsiders were concerned, the elaborate ceremonies he wanted performed: "they content themselves now with simply tattooing the chin, and having a festival of feasting and song."[87] Although Annie Flynn expressed confidence that she could convince the contingent to perform the entire old-style ceremony, she appears not to have been successful. Nor do the Cocopa appear to have earned money from any other sort of dances and ritualistic performances, as did the Nootka, Sioux, and Kwakiutl. They met the touristic gaze and McGee's quest for primitivism on their own terms.

The Cocopa also obtained wages from Cushman prior to their arrival at the fair and from other means. In several expense reports, there are notes that Cushman paid individuals substantial amounts of money; unfortunately, he never indicated what the sums were for. While waiting for the Cocopas to agree to travel to St. Louis, he paid in one instance $20 for work done in camp and in another $31.[88] Cocopas also charged tourists and professional photographers 25¢ per shot to take their pictures. They made a good deal of money from this activity, at least when photographers honored the rule that all native peoples had to give their consent before photographs were taken. Many tourists, of course, did not honor the rule.[89] Marksmanship was another area where Cocopa men excelled as competitors and performers. One Cocopa won $1 as the second prize in the archery contest during the sports and field games that were part of the Indian exhibit opening ceremonies on June 1.[90] Archery also provided another means by which the Cocopa could finagle money straight from the tourists' pockets: nickels and quarters provided by visitors were used as archery targets to demonstrate eyesight, dexterity, and hunting (or military) ability. The archer, upon hitting the coins, could keep the money. In other cases, boys from different tribes competed for coins furnished by visitors. McGee reported that the Cocopa usually won these informal competitions.[91]

Representatives from all the ethnic groups also performed in special public programs. While we have not located any specific lists of individual participants, it is very likely that some Cocopa participated in many of these events. For example, on July 15 the native peoples participated in a program on Plaza Saint Louis that was attended by 15,000 people and "proved a satisfactory feature—except that on completion of the program most of the gathering ushered in for closer inspection of the aliens [i.e., native peoples], who were extricated only with difficulty." More elaborate programs were held on July 23 and July 30 for even larger crowds. On Transportation Day, 50,000 visitors watched various groups demonstrate the use of canoes, travois, and wagons. Native children participated in events on the fair's Model Playground. The ethnology staff also tried to stage special features in the encampments, "but these events like most others arranged for the primitives were found to involve serious risk to the people and their custodians by reason of the overwhelming crowds brought together and the irresistible crushes [that] sometimes developed."[92]

Boredom and monotony were a major problem, although field representatives and newspaper reporters liked to say that the native demonstrators were happy and only occasionally homesick.[93] McGee acknowledged that "one of the greatest difficulties met by the Department was that of keeping alive the spirit and interest of the primitives under the (to them) deadly dull monotony of Exposition existence."[94] To alleviate this problem, the special agents provided guided outings both within and outside the grounds. These were usually on Sundays following a church service under the direction of an Episcopal minister, the Reverend Doctor Scott Charging Alone, a Sioux from South Dakota, which all the Indian participants were encouraged to attend. Many of the American Indians were particularly fond of one afternoon outing, attending Cummin's Wild West Show.

Poor Living Conditions, Illness, and the Return to Arizona

Life in the fair villages was difficult for reasons other than being under constant public scrutiny. The budget for the Anthropology Department had been cut repeatedly before the fair opened: There was only $10,000 to pay for all the expenses of the American Indians and for the salaries of the non-Indians who assisted them. Anthropologist James Mooney, who organized the BAE exhibit at the fair around a Kiowa camp circle as a symbol of the Indian past, was appalled by conditions when he arrived on June 8. He advised McGee to cancel the exhibit and send the Indians in residence home immediately because the exhibit had deteriorated into a "glorified medicine show." He found the area for the encampments too small and barren. There was no grass, trees, or running water, and the sanitation facilities were extremely poor. Most of the Indians were dissatisfied and more than a third had left after only six weeks of residency.[95]

The poor living conditions in the exhibit caused inevitable illness among the native people. Inclement weather had turned the grounds to mud. There was not sufficient drinking water. As Mooney noted, the Indian village was filthy; open sewers ran through it, which prompted many native demonstrators to return home early. McGee complained to the exposition's Department of Works and Exhibits several times throughout the summer about the unhealthy conditions. By June, almost all of the Ainu had malaria and several Sioux had been sent home.[96] McGee himself developed typhoid during the fair and never completely recovered. He was constantly plagued by fever.[97] Reporting to exhibit director Frederick J. V. Skiff in his monthly report for July 1904, McGee stated that whereas other groups were ill, "the Cocopa group have fared tolerably well despite the wet weather which has prevented proper arrangement of household facilities, clothing, etc.; yet they, too, have constantly attracted surprising attention in view of the unsuitability of their surroundings and the impossibility of permitting exhibition of the most distinctive tribal characteristics."

In early September, Pablo Colorado's wife grew seriously ill, suffering from a relapse of tuberculosis, a disease she had contracted before she came to St. Louis. Thinking that she would soon die, McGee decided to rush her back home so that she would not die on the fairgrounds or under his care. For McGee, her death could have posed a serious international problem and would have given his department bad publicity. The Anthropology Department had already received some bad press because of the unsanitary conditions.[98]

Pablo Colorado decided to accompany his wife, as did Pahup and Ilpuk. To hasten the ill woman back to Yuma, McGee called upon his administrative assistant, C. E. Hulbert, who left with great anticipation and "an exceeding great relief from the dull, almost ambitionless slavery of St. Louis."[99] Hulbert, a recent anthropology graduate of the University of Chicago, was ill-prepared for the task. Expenses for the journey to Arizona were probably around $250, and Hulbert had to wire McGee for additional money to return to St. Louis near the end of the trip.[100] For lodging, Hulbert and the Cocopas slept on the train; as for food, Hulbert and Pablo Colorado secured only enough for the group's journey to Yuma, barring any delays or mishaps.

Unfortunately, after the travelers left on October 8 they encountered "trouble on top of trouble."[101] The trip started out well: Hulbert reported to McGee on October 12 that they had reached La Junta, Colorado and then Trinidad by easy stages, with the kind assistance of the Fred Harvey Company and railroad personnel. They slept on the train and ate their own food, apparently mingling little with other travelers. Hulbert's wife, Esther Linn Hulbert, remembered the subsequent misadventures in 1952 and insightfully contextualized the diplomatic implications.

When the US Government had borrowed the Indians from the Mexican government it had agreed to return them safely to their homes. So when the grave illness was discovered my husband was given the job of accompanying the Cocopah back to Mexico. In those days the only transportation was by Santa Fe train to Yuma, Arizona! They started off expecting to arrive in Yuma in three days! They got as far as La Junta Colorado and were held there for *3 weeks* on account of washouts on the railroad ahead! Mr. Hulbert took as good care of the Cocopah as he could, a physician saw the woman every day and, although they had not been on the first train to be held up, Mr. Hulbert made arrangements to be put on the first train out—he got the Cocopah on the train and went back to make final arrangements in the station and when he came out the train had gone with the Indians and nobody to see that they had food or anything. He telegraphed ahead that they should be put off at Albuquerque and got the second train out. Got to Albuquerque to get the Indians and found that through some mistake they had been put off at Lamy Junction. He had to wait for a train to take him back there and by the time he got to Lamy Junction the poor Indians had nothing to eat for two days! The first thing he saw to give them was some cantaloupes and they were so hungry that they ate rind and all! Finally he got them to Yuma where he bought a big scow and started them off down the Colorado River. The Indians arrived home the second day and the woman lived only three weeks after they arrived. So was avoided an "incident" between the US Government and the Mexican Government, even at that time the two Governments were on the verge of trouble, stirred up by the American mining people and the bandits under [Pancho] Villa.[102]

Mrs. Hulbert did exaggerate the length of time the travelers were stranded in Colorado. Hulbert wired McGee on October 19 from Deming, New Mexico that the Indians had started downriver in good shape the previous day. The travelers also encountered other problems that Mrs. Hulbert either did not know about or failed to recollect: half of the railway station at Trinidad, Colorado where they were stranded had been "cut clean in two by the water as by a huge knife" but luckily the Harvey Hotel where they all stayed was on high ground. It does not appear from Hulbert's correspondence that the Cocopa were denied hotel rooms or food service at this juncture, at least when they were with Hulbert. Hulbert insisted that the Cocopa "were traveling as first class passengers" and "that they be given every privilege." However, there were some problems later in the journey concerning food, for Hulbert told McGee that he was "making every effort to have the Indian[s] store enough away of the abundance provided [food provided in St. Louis] to last through to Yuma as they have practically exhausted the supply brought with them."[103] Despite the difficulties they encountered, the Cocopas eventually made it home safely, although the safe return obviously did not insure Mrs. Colorado's health.

Mrs. Colorado, of course, had a more difficult trip than anyone else. Hulbert acknowledged in his correspondence that he did not realize how sick she was when they left and that he was not prepared to care for her adequately nor deal with her death, if this unfortunate event should occur while she was in his charge. Mrs. Colorado grew steadily weaker after they left St. Louis, Hulbert reported to McGee, but the unexpected troubles in Colorado probably helped her survive the journey. She "was in pretty good shape at La Junta so long as we were lying still, but the motion of the train doesn't seem to agree with her very well, though she appears to pick up immediately when we stop." Hulbert also speculated as to the benefits of the Fred Harvey Company restaurant food: "Perhaps, too, the good food has helped, for I am quite sure the group never had such good fare as they are getting here."[104] Hulbert had originally thought that being stranded at such a high altitude would have made her plight especially difficult, but this later did not appear to Hulbert to be a problem. Mrs. Colorado did improve somewhat during the trip, in part due to the ministrations of a doctor, but she relapsed and then died a month after returning home.

The remainder of the Cocopa contingent stayed in St. Louis until the middle of November, when the gray skies, rain, and chilly winds made them long for "the perpetual sunshine of their habitat." McGee considered the cold, dreary weather impossible for peoples raised in desert and tropical environments. Hulbert also accompanied this Cocopa contingent; they reached Yuma and Somerton safely and without incident several days later. Although we have no firsthand accounts by the Cocopa of these journeys, there are indications that the close working relationship changed Hulbert. Reflecting on his journeys, Hulbert wrote to McGee: "It is a genuine treat to feel that you are doing something to make these poor simple people a little happier. I never realized before that they are human beings, a great deal like ourselves, with real human feelings, real emotions and real sensibilities." The people with the "picturesque physiques," "primitive industries," and "shy disposition" had taught a degree of cultural tolerance to at least one middle-class American.[105]

Conclusion

The St. Louis fair "offered a once-in-a-lifetime opportunity" for anthropologists and visitors because "no previous international exposition had brought together so many people from so many foreign countries."[106] Native peoples were used by fair and exhibit organizers as scientific specimens and tools to explain technological progress and to justify their subjugation and conquest through a self-celebratory rhetoric to an eager population of American tourists. McGee estimated that more than 3 million visitors came through the Indian school, making it one of the most crowded exhibits on the fairgrounds.[107] Even more tourists visited or walked past the native villages. Through the purchase of art, crafts, and photographic images as souvenirs, these visitors preserved their encounters with and memories of native peoples in a commodified state.

The anthropology exhibit at this fair marked a vortex of nationalism, imperialism, capitalism, and scientific racism on an unprecedented scale. Native peoples represented for the fair organizers the world's earlier stages of cultural development and the past of the nation and the territory encompassed by the Louisiana Purchase. For McGee, it was a unique opportunity "to show our half of the world how the other half lives; yet not so much to gratify their untrained curiosity which leads even the child to look with wonder upon the alien as to satisfy the intelligent observer that there is a course of progress running from lower to higher humanity and that all the physical and cultural types of man mark stages in that course."[108]

The Cocopa entered the fair with ambitions of their own. Cocopa around Somerton and Yuma worked for local farmers and lived in camps on or near the farmers' land. They did not have permanent *rancherias* of the size and complexity as those in Sonora.[109] They constructed irrigation ditches and leveled the land for early agribusiness. But the early twentieth century was also a time of great transition for the Cocopa. In 1905, Americans diverted the course of the Colorado River to California's Imperial Valley, making the Cocopa's delta lands unfit for farming. While many families tried to continue some agriculture, others shifted to unskilled wage or temporary farm labor.

The fair became an opportunity for the Cocopa, although it was a risky one. As the Cocopa case demonstrates, native peoples were not merely exploited. They were neither unwittingly fooled by anthropologists or fair agents nor completely trusting of them. The Cocopa thought long and hard about attending the fair, negotiated the conditions of their participation, controlled how their members acted (including sending one man home in disgrace), and left when they thought the situation was becoming exploitative. Living and performing at the fair was a form of work for which the Cocopa were paid. To speculate for a moment, the Cocopa probably did not fully understand what they were getting into, but neither did other native and nonnative fair participants, McGee, McCowan, or other organizers. Some were probably disoriented, some had a good time, some were homesick, and some loved to travel. In short, the Cocopas who attended the fair were sophisticated men, women, and children who had a rare adventure—they entered a strange land and truly met some strange people.

Notes

1. McGee, "Strange," 5185. McGee always used WJ, without periods, in his letters and publications.

2. See Macdonald and Fyfe.

3. Quoted in McGee, "Report," 115.

4. Bennitt and Stockbridge, 443–45; "The Inspiring," 5176.

5. Walker, 615.

6. Quoted in Breitbart, 30.

7. Francis, 531.

8. Breitbart, 31.

9. Quoted in Moses, *Wild,* 151; Rydell, 155; *St. Louis Sunday Republic.*

10. Breitbart, 13.

11. Quoted in Rydell, 155; quoted in Rydell, 160; Breitbart, 5.

12. Rydell, 157.

13. Quoted in *St. Louis Sunday Republic;* "The Overlord."

14. Native peoples were the center of attention for much of the time they were at the fair, often too much attention. Like celebrities of today, tourists followed their every move, often invading their privacy and taking unwanted, unsolicited, and inappropriate photographs. Many photographers, of course, worked

with the approval of their subjects. For members of marginalized communities, such intense scrutiny was simultaneously flattering, profitable, annoying, and an invasion of privacy. It highlighted a tourist problem still prevalent, especially in Indian country: the lack of good manners on the part of tourists toward their hosts.

15. Lehman to Francis. The 1904 anthropology exhibits were also the most extensive of any world's fair. They were commented on frequently in the press and served the corporation's goal of drawing in tourists through their novelty.

16. McGee was a self-taught naturalist, meteorologist, botanist, and geologist who was gradually steered into ethnology by John Wesley Powell. He was a noted land surveyor and topographer who had studied law (1871–1876) and excavated (i.e., pot hunted) mounds in Iowa. He also held several patents on farm implements and had for a time worked as a farmer and a blacksmith. After his death, his sister described him in a very celebratory manner as fastidious, methodical, hardworking, very ambitious, systematic and painstaking, a good organizer who wanted things kept in their place, extremely loyal, eccentric, proud to a fault, and an individual with a commanding presence. He was a man who attracted attention to himself in all situations and who held boundless energy and indomitable determination (see E. McGee). In 1903–1904, he was also president of the American Anthropological Association.

17. Hinsley, 255. McGee accepted the position on 31 July 1903, after having worked for the BAE for ten years and the U.S. Geological Survey since 1883 (*St. Louis Globe-Democrat;* McGee "Report"). LPE President Francis expressed concern over McGee's blemished reputation in the executive committee minutes of 14 February 1903. McGee did have considerable fair experience, however. He had worked on Smithsonian exhibits at the Atlanta, Nashville, Omaha, and Buffalo expositions (see LPE Files).

18. McGee, "Report," 1.

19. McGee, "The Anthropology," 683.

20. McGee, "Strange," 5188.

21. McGee, "The Anthropology," 683.

22. To date, we have not located any of the field notes or student papers on the Cocopa. There appear to have been no publications resulting from this scholastic exercise.

23. McGee, "Remarks." Like his colleague William Holmes, McGee considered displaying living peoples an exhibition technique superior to the period-room or life-group techniques that were emerging in history and natural history museums. According to Holmes, living groups were superior to static displays because "the real family, clothed in its own costumes, engaged in its own occupations, and surrounded by its actual belongings" best illustrated a people (201).

24. More than 1,000 Filipinos were part of the State Department's exhibit in the government building that was located next to the anthropology building.

25. McGee, "The Anthropology," 683.

26. McGee, "Strange," 5188. This was an unusual placement. Generally, the BIA exhibits were part of the federal government exhibits and housed in separate buildings. The Smithsonian Institution's anthropology exhibits were not part of the corporate-sponsored Anthropology Department. These government exhibits contained more of the natural history and history display approaches, such as the use of period rooms, dioramas, and material-culture displays.

27. McCowan was a long-term employee of the BIA and had served as a superintendent of the government schools on the Rosebud Reservation and at Fort Mojave, Albuquerque, and Phoenix. He moved to Chilocco in 1902 at the age of thirty-eight. He was firmly committed to government assimilation programs and felt that traditional cultures had to be destroyed for individuals to be saved (Trennert, "A Resurrection," 275). McCowan was made second in charge of the Anthropology Department and oversaw the welfare of all Indian groups except the Cocopa. He was assisted by Miss Emma Johnson, a native kindergarten teacher from Sacaton, Arizona.

28. McGee, "Strange," 5188.

29. Quoted in McGee, "The Anthropology," 683.

30. McCowan, "Resume," 119.

31. Children ranged from kindergartners to eighth graders and were chosen for their oratorical, musical, or artistic proficiencies or because they excelled as potentially successful models of the government programs (Trennert, "Selling," 215). There were no Cocopa children in this group, nor were the children of the native family groups invited to participate in any of the school activities.

32. McGee, "Strange," 5185; McCowan, "To the Commissioner." Benham owned Benham Trading Companies and was one of the nation's largest entrepreneurs specializing in American Indian art. He had retail outlets in Albuquerque, Los Angeles, New York City, and Phoenix and trading posts near the Navajo Reservation in Thoreau and Farmington, New Mexico. Benham contacted McCowan in 1903 and asked to be appointed McCowan's assistant; McCowan eventually agreed "because Benham offered to loan the government a large quantity of Indian goods for display and decoration, including traditional pieces that McCowan had been unable to secure from the Indians" (Trennert, "A Resurrection," 284). Benham was given an official appointment as "reservation trader" from the LPE Executive Committee and was also allowed to sell native-produced goods without the 25 percent exposition markup.

33. McGee, "Strange," 5187; Ibid.; M'Carty.

34. According to a list of native participants, many Cocopa competed: Artuckero, Chinyan Sacup, and Skik participated in the 100-yard run (won by George Mentz, Sioux, running in 13 seconds); Chief Pablo Colorado, Cherry, Artuckero, and Chizi performed in the shot put; Artuckero and Nethab ran in the 440-yard

run, Cherry and Chizi in the running broad jump; Cherry, Artuckero, and Ilpuk threw the baseball; Colorado, Cherry, and Moore threw a 56-pound weight; Skik, a young Cocopa boy, won the archery competition (McGee, "Report," 181–90).

35. McGee, "Report," 1; "Strange," 5185.

36. Rydell discusses the national need for order in this period and how the various components of the exposition came together to form a symbolic universe that "ritualistically affirmed fairgoers' faith in American institutions and social organization, evoked a community of shared experience, and formulated responses to questions about the ultimate destiny of mankind in general and of America in particular" (3).

Boundaries as a need for order [handwritten margin note]

37. McGee, "Report," 5; Ibid., 7; Ibid., 7, 8. McGee named his five races of the world as: (1) Caucasian or White race; (2) Mongolian or Yellow race; (3) Malayan or Brown race; (4) African or Black race; and (5) Amerind or Red race ("Report," 5).

38. Ibid., 8.

39. Ibid., 16.

40. Ibid., 16; "Strange," 5186.

41. "Strange," 5187; Francis, 527.

42. McGee, "Report," 18. The estimated initial cost for the anthropology exhibits was $3 million (Lehman). Only $200,000 was actually allotted in 1903 to the Anthropology Department, which was placed under the Division of Exhibits; $100,000 of this was allocated for collecting expeditions, including the bringing of native peoples to the fair (Skiff, "To David R. Francis"). This amount was further reduced to $60,000 on 2 April 1903, supplemented by $40,000 from the federal government for the Indian school and the expenses of bringing Indian groups to the fair (Missouri Historical Society). The budget cutbacks continued even beyond this point. At all times McGee felt that participation by the Cocopa (and hopefully the Seri) was crucial for his educational scheme. At one point he even told the LPE Corporation's Executive Committee that if he could only bring two groups it would be the Cocopa and the Ainu ("Report," 52). Matilda Coxe Stevenson had been arranging the Zuni delegation. The Pueblo and the Navajo elders worked in the Indian school.

43. McCowan, "Resume"; McGee "Strange"; "Family Register." No complete list of the participants or their cultural affiliations seems to exist. Of the listings that do exist, each source states that different people participated at the fair and provides different numbers. Other groups are mentioned in individual letters dealing with specific logistical problems (McGee to Frederick J. V. Skiff, 12 January 1904, Department of Anthropology Files, LPE, Missouri Historical Society, St. Louis). The number and cultural heritage continues to change if one counts state and commercial exhibitions. Moses states that fifty-one tribes were represented, although he does not provide a source list (*The Indian*, 157). His compilation may

come from an edition of *The Piker* that lists the following in addition to the aforementioned: Assiniboine, Blackfoot, Brule Sioux, Cayagua [*sic*], Crow Creek Sioux, Flathead, Fox, Gros Ventre, Hopi, Iowa, Jicarilla Apache, Lower Brule Sioux, Mescalero Apache, Mohawk, Mojave, Oglala Sioux, Ojibway, Omaha, Onadaguia, Oneida, Oto, Piegan, Pipeclay Sioux, Ponca, Porcupine Sioux, Pottawatomie, Pueblos, San Carlos Apache, Santee Sioux, Sauk, Seneca, Shoshone, Tuscarora, Winnebago, White Clay Sioux, White River Sioux, and Wounded Knee Sioux (see "Cummin's"). Other scholars have made a few unintentional errors regarding cultural designations of native participation, however. For example, Breitbart fails to distinguish the Cocopa and the Maricopa in photographs and text. The peoples designated as Maricopa are clearly Cocopa, based on their attire, hair, and jewelry, as well as from documentary evidence in the McGee Papers in the Library of Congress and the Missouri Historical Society. By this time, the Maricopa had moved to the Pima Reservation and would have come to the fair with the O'odham contingent. They were not encamped with the Cocopa. Another problem is that most photograph captions found in the archives do not give names, except for celebrities like Geronimo, and in many cases groups performing on the midway are differentiated by the name of the tribe the promoter wanted, not the actual cultural affiliation of the participants. McGee planned a Zuni exhibit, but this scheme was abandoned in April 1904 when negotiations broke down ("Report," 53). Although some sources state that Hopi (or "Moqui") individuals participated, this identification is questionable, because Hopi was often the default category for all Puebloan peoples.

44. McGee, "Report," 110.

45. McGee to Frederick J. V. Skiff, 1 August 1904, Box 16, McGee Papers, Library of Congress, Washington, D.C. (hereafter cited as MP).

46. McGee, "Strange," 5187.

47. Ibid.; McCowan, "Resume," 118.

48. Quoted in Buel, vol. 5, i–ii; McGee, "Report," 40. Indian celebrities like Geronimo and Quanah Parker, along with their families, were expected to bear their own transportation costs, although the Anthropology Department agreed to cover their per diem expenses while in St. Louis. The reasoning was that they would profit substantially due to their celebrity status.

49. McCowan, "To WJ McGee."

50. McGee, "Strange," 5187; "Report," 22. McGee was heavily influenced by Louis Henry Morgan's schemes of stages of development. For examples of his work, see *League* and *Ancient*.

51. "Antique Indian Tribe"; McGee, "Report," 105.

52. McGee, "Strange," 5187.

53. McGee also took responsibility for groups living outside the United States, arranging for anthropologists, missionaries, and other interested parties to

accompany each group and serve as cultural liaison while they remained at the fair (McGee to Frederick J. V. Skiff, 21 May 1904, Chilocco Papers, National Archives, Southwest Region Branch, Fort Worth, Tex.).

54. Tisdale, 84–85; Williams, 101–103.

55. McGee's fieldwork on these expeditions leaves much to be desired, even according to the different standards of the period. He drew sweeping conclusions based on nonexistent data; he stated in his publications that he visited a score or more of Seri rancherias and found them all abandoned (see *The Seri*). In his publications, McGee romanticized his own bravery and the danger he felt during his excursion among the Seri, whom he portrayed as extremely wary and hostile individuals. Like McGee's theoretical paradigm for the fair, his publication on the Seri was another instance of his making facts fit into his unilinear evolutionary theories (Fontana, xvii). McGee had returned to Cocopa territory in the fall of 1901 to survey archaeological sites along the eastern part of the Lower Colorado River.

56. McGee, "Letter to the Editor"; McGee, "Report," 20. McGee also regretted not securing Seri or Australian Aborigines because both groups exemplified what he described as "the lowest known types of law and faith" ("Report," 22).

57. The Cocopas are members of a category anthropologists refer to as River Yumans. Other cultures in this complex group include the Halchidoma, Halikwamai, Kamia, Kohuana, Maricopa, Mojave, and Quechan (Kroeber, 475).

58. Tisdale, 121–22.

59. Cushman was not a university-trained anthropologist. In his letter of application to McGee, he noted that he had worked on several of the Wetherill family's archaeological expeditions between 1893 and 1897, including those at Mesa Verde (9 August 1903).

60. McGee, "Report," 60.

61. See "To Barlow," 23 November 1903; "To Clayton," 23 November 1903; "To Chavero," 23 November 1903; "To Leon," 23 November 1903; and "To Ramon Corral," 23 November 1903, Box 14, MP. It should be remembered that at this time concerns over the international status of native peoples themselves as sovereign entities were not prevalent. Also, considering McGee's conservative political stance, his evolutionary theories, and his feelings about the "white man's burden," it is doubtful that he would ever have accepted the argument that Indian societies held any status equivalent to a nation-state.

62. Cushman, "To McGee," 1 December 1903; Corral, "To WJ McGee," 1 December 1903. A fair visitor asked McGee why there were no Seris at the fair, indicating that McGee had made a public statement somewhere about trying to obtain Seri demonstrators. We have not been able to locate this publication. In responding, McGee tried to instill a sense of danger and convey the problems of the collecting expedition: "there were just two men living who might be trusted to

perform the difficult mission of bringing these savages to Saint Louis; one of them was tied up by the administrative duties in this Department [referring to himself]; the other (Charles Meadows, or 'Arizona Charlie,' of Yuma) was ready to undertake the task, but when the critical moment arrived his crew decided that they 'hadn't lost no Seri Indians' and deserted the colors" ("To C. M. Ginther," 27 September 1904, Box 15, MP). In his final report, McGee also noted that Meadows had convinced some Seri "direct from the range" but that at the last moment they decided not to go ("Report," 64).

63. On 5 January 1904, McGee also wrote to Eduardo J. Andrade, owner of the land grant that contained the "traditional" Cocopa rancherias in Sonora.

64. "To Herbert Brown," 5 Jan. 1904, Box 20, MP; "To E. C. Cushman," 11 Jan. 1904, Box 20, MP.

65. "To Chief Pablo Colorado," 5 Jan. 1904, Box 14, MP; "Expense Account."

66. Colorado also stated that he found Cushman an honorable man and that he would like to see McGee again and talk to him personally.

67. Cushman, "To McGee," 26 January 1904. Other native groups who were asked to participate had similar objections. Charles Newcombe reported to Dorsey and McGee that he had tried to get Makah and Haida families to participate, but that they had declined because they did not believe that they could make enough money from the sale of crafts and performance to make up what they would lose from fishing and food gatherings (Newcombe, "To George Dorsey"). Likewise, the Patagonians agreed to come only if they were given horses to ride. According to one newspaper account, the fair field representative agreed to provide them with white horses ("Patagonian").

68. This community was probably in the Andrade grant, according to a letter of introduction for Cushman that McGee sent to Señor Eduardo J. Andrade of Yuma, a gentleman McGee had met during his own research trip three years earlier. The land had been sold to the Imperial Cattle Company. Cushman also paid a Cocopa, "Indian Frank," to assist him on his trip.

69. McGee reasoned thus: "So far as I am aware, the Cocopa ceremonies are somewhat peculiar in that they do not necessarily require the cooperation of numerous individuals but may be confined to particular clans or family groups. Pray exercise your judgment in this matter, remembering that economy as well as ceremony are primary conditions" ("To E. C. Cushman," 16 April 1904, Box 20, MP). McCowan tried to attract skilled and trustworthy native artisans rather than individuals who would perform ceremonies. He rejected any individuals suggested by BIA agents who had a reputation for drinking, rowdiness, laziness, or unreliability (Trennert, "Selling," 215). One can assume that McGee and Cushman had the same personal requirements for the Cocopa.

70. Cushman, "To McGee," 3 March 1904; "To McGee," 28 March 1904.

71. Ibid., 3 March 1904; 28 March 1904. McGee acknowledged Cushman's efforts and his negotiation problems in a letter discussing transportation arrange-

ments: "You have had a long and hard siege, yet I doubt not that the first-hand information you have gained will fully recompense you and at the same time fully justify me through the increased excellence of the exhibit in prescribing so long a probation. So far as I can foresee, the Cocopa group will be the best understood native assemblage on the grounds. Of course, your troubles are not over, but I trust the difficulties of transportation to Yuma and the passage thence to St. Louis will not prove serious" ("To E. C. Cushman," incomplete letter, probably April 1904, Box 20, MP).

72. McGee, "Report," 36. Proper preparations were never completed and caused significant hardship for the participants throughout their tenure (Troutman).

73. "Antique Indian Tribe."

74. The separate car was needed so that the delegation could carry the materials for their houses with them. McGee and Cushman feared that putting the housing material in freight could result in its loss or it not arriving on time. Next, it appeared that the railroad refused to take houses as baggage. McCowan had arranged for all the Native American groups to travel by a special reduced passenger cost along with their tools and houses (McGee, "To E. C. Cushman," 16 April 1904, Box 20, MP). For some reason the railroad passes were held up and the group stayed in Yuma for several days. The problem may have been due to too few passes and transportation funds not being wired from St. Louis. Although McGee had authorized twelve passes, Cushman insisted that at least eighteen were needed. McGee agreed to pay for nineteen passes including those for children (Western Union telegram, "To E. C. Cushman," 13 April 1904, Box 19, MP). McGee tried to placate Cushman about the situation and rationalized that it was all for the best: "weather here too cold and wet for Indians if they can be held few day without demoralization" (Western Union telegram, "To E. C. Cushman," 26 April 1904, Box 19, MP). Field agents were expected to get as many of their supplies as possible from a merchant at the point of departure and supplement them with coffee as needed from the railroad eating stations en route, although this required wiring the station in advance.

75. McGee, "Report," 63; Breitbart, 6.

76. McGee, "Report," 63, 105, 188.

77. Kelly, 13.

78. Cushman, 13 April 1904. George A. Dorsey, curator at the Field Museum in Chicago, had been commissioned by McGee to oversee the construction of the Indian dwellings in the camp during April and May.

79. Skiff, 28 September 1903.

80. McGee, "Report," 109.

81. The exception to this living arrangement appears to have been the translator Mrs. Flynn. Cushman had negotiated special arrangements for her participation, reflecting her more elevated social position: "She is a woman of some educa-

tion, and is highly thought of here in Yuma. She will not live as the Indians do on the grounds, but will be with them constantly. [She] has enormous influence, in fact they obey her implicitly in all things. I have thought that perhaps she might have a small room in the Indian School building. Her meals we can easily arrange for" (Cushman, "To McGee," 13 April 1904).

82. McGee, "Report," 106. Archival materials are inconsistent on whether Shokee went home by himself or was accompanied by any other Cocopa.

83. Cushman, "To McGee," 7 July 1904.

84. McGee also wrote a letter to Herbert Brown, his contact in Yuma and an important territorial official, who represented the main judicial authority in the Cocopa area south of Yuma, explaining the assault. It is unknown if Shokee ever gave this letter to Brown.

85. McGee, "Report," 106.

86. Cushman, "To McGee," 28 March 1904.

87. Ibid., 13 April 1904.

88. Ibid., 27 February 1904; 3 March 1904.

89. McGee asked the Jefferson Guard to protect the Indians from intrusions into their privacy. This did not always work. The Cocopa were involved in at least one confrontation with an obnoxious tourist and confiscated his camera. Although the Jefferson Guard did not support their action, McGee did (Flynn; McGee "To H. P. Kingman," 21 July 1904, Box 20, MP).

90. Yellow Hair, head to the Sioux contingent, won $2 for first prize ("Indian Exhibit").

91. McGee, "Report," 106.

92. Ibid., 89; Ibid., 89–90.

93. According to one reporter, " 'Our Indians are having the time of their lives,' said E. Mattox, who is looking after the various tribes in the Indian reservation. 'I was born among the Sioux in Nebraska and I know them. When you see an Indian look at everybody and half smile you know that he's happy. He grunts and you may think he's trying to speak, but he's only grunting his satisfaction' " ("Indians Fond").

94. McGee, "Report," 90.

95. Moses, *The Indian,* 155–57. McGee had wanted Mooney to run the Indian encampments at the exhibit to make sure that they did not turn into a Wild West show (Moses, *The Indian,* 156).

96. McCowan, "To Isaac S. Taylor."

97. E. McGee, 84. Given the poor climate and conditions, it is surprising that more people did not become ill and die. According to his sister Emma, McGee went back to Cocopa country in Arizona after the fair closed and he had finished his paperwork. McGee felt that the arid desert was the only place to cure his typhoid. He stayed there for several months accompanied by a Cocopa friend named José. They lived in the Tinajas Altas Mountains to the east of Yuma. In

1907, McGee returned to St. Louis and became the first director of the St. Louis Public Museum. McGee died of cancer on 5 September 1912.

98. See Troutman.

99. Hulbert, 11 October 1904. Hulbert later worked for the Fred Harvey Company in Albuquerque.

100. McGee, "Report," 54.

101. Hulbert, 11 October 1904. Hulbert also told McGee in the same letter that he had "enjoyed every minute" of the trip, for it was "a rare pleasure to meet real difficulties and over come [*sic*] them." Without knowing more about Hulbert, it is impossible to conclude whether he was being ironic or was grateful for his assignment.

102. E. L. Hulbert.

103. Hulbert, 12 October 1904; 11 October 1904; 11 October 1904; 12 October 1904. Hulbert was rather paternalistic toward the Cocopa, considered them naive, and felt that they would have been taken advantage of by unscrupulous Anglos: "I am not surprised at Cushman's affection for them; they are so helpless, and withal, so patient and (apparently) grateful for kindness that no trouble seems too great to take to make them a little happier" (11 October 1904).

104. Hulbert, 12 October 1904; 11 October 1904.

105. McGee, "Report," 106–107; Hulbert, 11 October 1904; McGee, "Report," 106–107.

106. Breitbart, 18.

107. McGee, "Report," 116.

108. Ibid., 39.

109. Tisdale, 123.

Works Cited

"Antique Indian Tribe Leave Monday for Fair." *St. Louis Post-Dispatch,* 24 April 1904, n.p., Box 32, MP.

Bennitt, Mark, and Frank P. Stockbridge, eds. *History of the Louisiana Purchase Exposition.* St. Louis, Mo.: Universal Exposition Publishing, 1905.

Breitbart, Eric. *A World on Display: Photographs from the St. Louis World's Fair, 1904.* Albuquerque: University of New Mexico Press, 1997.

Bruner, Frank. "The Hearing of Primitive Peoples." Special issue of *Archives of Anthropology* July 1908.

Buel, J. W., ed. *Louisiana and the Fair.* 10 vols. St. Louis, Mo.: World's Progress Publishing, 1905.

Colorado, Pablo. To WJ McGee, 20 January 1904, Box 20, MP.

Corral, Ramon. To WJ McGee, 1 December 1903, Box 14, MP.

"Cummin's Wild West Show and Indian Congress." *The Piker* 1, no. 2 (1904): 16.

Cushman, Edwin C., Jr. To McGee, 9 August 1903, 1 December 1903, Box 14; 26 January 1904, 27 February 1904, 3 March 1904, 28 March 1904, Box 19; 13 April 1904, 7 July 1904, Box 20, MP.

Department of Anthropology Files, Louisiana Purchase Exposition. Missouri Historical Society, St. Louis.

"Family Register of Indians at World's Fair Exhibit." Box 28, MP.

Flynn, Annie. To Cushman, 21 July 1904, Box 20, MP.

Fontana, Bernard. "Introduction." Pp. xvii–xxi in *The Seri Indians,* by W. J. McGee. Glorietta, N.M.: The Rio Grande Press, 1971.

Francis, David R. *The Universal Exposition of 1904.* St. Louis, Mo.: Louisiana Purchase Exposition, 1913.

Hinsley, Curtis M. *The Smithsonian and the American Indian: Making a Moral Anthropology in Victorian America.* 1981. Reprint, Washington, D.C.: Smithsonian Institution Press, 1994.

Hoffman, Phil. "A Study of the Feet of Barefooted Peoples for the Purpose of Comparison with Those of Shoewearers." Unpublished manuscript, n.d., Box 16, MP.

Holmes, William H. "The Exhibit of the Department of Anthropology, Report on the Exhibits of the U.S. National Museum at the Pan-American Exposition, Buffalo, New York, 1901." Pp. 200–218 in *Annual Report of the U.S. National Museum for 1901.* Washington, D.C.: Government Printing Office, 1903.

Hulbert, C. E. To WJ McGee, 11 October 1904, 12 October 1904, Box 20; Western Union telegram to McGee, 19 October 1904, Box 20, MP.

Hulbert, Esther Lynn. To Oral Etter, 28 August 1952, Louisiana Purchase Exposition Corporation files, correspondence of C. E. Hulbert, 1904–1907, Appendum Series III, Subseries XI, Box 30, File 1, Missouri Historical Society, St. Louis.

"Indian Exhibit Formally Opens: Progress Which Red Man Made under Government Supervision Displayed in Many Ways." *St. Louis Republic,* 22 June 1904, n.p., Box 32, MP.

"Indians Fond of Compliments; E. Mattock Explains Some of the Traits of the Aborigines." Newspaper clipping, n. source, n.d., Box 32, MP.

"The Inspiring Display of the States." *The World's Work* August 1904: 5164–78.

Kelly, William H. *Cocopa Ethnography.* Anthropological Papers of the University of Arizona, no. 29. Tucson: University of Arizona Press, 1977.

Kroeber, Alfred L. "Yumans of the Lower Colorado." *University of California Publications in American Archaeology and Ethnology* 16, no. 8 (1920): 475–85.

Lehman, F. W. To David R. Francis, 31 August 1901. Louisiana Purchase Exposition Corporation Executive Committee minutes, Missouri Historical Society, St. Louis.

Louisiana Purchase Exposition Corporation Executive Committee. Minutes, 14 July 1903, Missouri Historical Society, St. Louis.

Louisiana Purchase Exposition Files. Missouri Historical Society, St. Louis.

Macdonald, Susan, and Gordon Fyfe, eds. *Theorizing Museums: Representing Identity and Diversity in a Changing World*. London: Blackwell Publishers for the Sociological Review, 1996.

M'Carty, W. C. "The Tribes [*sic*] Last Stand: Remnants of Many Once Powerful Indian Tribes, Headed by Noted Chieftains Will Be Featured at the World's Fair under the Supervision of Experts from the United States Government's Indian Bureau." Bridgeport, Conn. *Herald,* 6 December 1903, n.p., Box 32, MP.

McCowan, S. M. "Resume of Government's Indian Exhibit." Pp. 117–31 in "Report" by W. J. McGee.

——. To Isaac S. Taylor, 10 June 1904, Chilocco Papers, National Archives, Southwest Regional Branch, Fort Worth, Tex.

——. To the Commissioner of Indian Affairs, 2 January 1904; To WJ McGee, 20 April 1904, Chilocco Papers, National Archives, Southwest Regional Branch, Fort Worth, Tex.

McGee, Emma. *The Life of WJ McGee*. Farley, Iowa: privately printed, 1915.

McGee, W. J. "The Anthropology Exhibit." Printed essay, n.d., Box 16, MP.

——. "Expense Account." February and March 1904, Box 19, MP.

——. "Letter to the Editor." Unnamed St. Louis newspaper, 19 August 1901, n.p., Louisiana Purchase Exposition Corporation Executive Committee minutes, Missouri Historical Society, St. Louis.

——. Letters. Due to the numerous correspondence from W. J. McGee cited, full citations appear in the notes.

——. "Monthly Report." 1 July 1904, Box 16, MP.

——. "Remarks." *World's Fair Bulletin* August 1903: 29.

——. "Report of the Department of Anthropology to Frederick J. V. Skiff, Director, Universal Exposition of 1904, Division of Exhibits." 10 May 1905, Louisiana Purchase Exposition files, Series III, Subseries XI, Missouri Historical Society, St. Louis.

——. *The Seri Indians*. Seventeenth Annual Report of the Bureau of American Ethnology to the Secretary of the Smithsonian Institution, 1895–1896. Washington, D.C.: Government Printing Office, 1898.

——. "Strange Races of Men." *The World's Work* August 1904: 5185–88.

Morgan, Louis Henry. *Ancient Society*. 1877. Reprint, Tucson: The University of Arizona Press, 1985.

——. *League of the Ho-dé-no-sau-nee, or Iroquois*. Rochester, N.Y.: Sage and Brother, 1851.

Moses, L. G. *The Indian Man: A Biography of James Mooney*. Urbana: University of Illinois Press, 1984.

——. *Wild West Shows and the Images of American Indians, 1883–1933*. Albuquerque: University of New Mexico Press, 1996.

Newcombe, Charles F. To George Dorsey, 13 April 1904, Anthropology Department, Field Museum of Natural History, Chicago.

"The Overlord of the Savage World." *St. Louis Post Dispatch,* 14 July 1904, n.p., Box 32, MP.

"Patagonian Giants Object to Camera." *St. Louis Republic,* 15 April 1904, n.p., Box 32, MP.

Rydell, Robert W. *All the World's a Fair: Visions of Empire at American International Expositions, 1876–1916.* Chicago: University of Chicago Press, 1984.

Skiff, Frederick J. V. To David R. Francis, 2 December 1902, 28 September 1903, Louisiana Purchase Exposition Corporation Executive Committee minutes, Missouri Historical Society, St. Louis.

St. Louis Globe-Democrat. Untitled article, 14 August 1903, n.p., Box 32, MP.

St. Louis Sunday Republic. Untitled article, 6 September 1903, n.p., Box 32, MP.

Tehano, Frank. To Captain Tomas and Pablo Colorado, 29 July 1904, Box 19, MP.

Tisdale, Shelby J. "Cocopah Identity, Indian Gaming, and Cultural Survival in the Lower Colorado River Delta, 1850–1996." Ph.D. diss., University of Arizona, 1997.

Trennert, Robert A., Jr. "A Resurrection of Native Arts and Crafts: The St. Louis World's Fair, 1904." *Missouri Historical Review* 87, no. 3 (1993): 274–92.

———. "Selling Indian Education at World's Fairs and Expositions, 1893–1904." *The American Indian Quarterly* 11, no. 3 (1987): 203–20.

Troutman, John W. "'The Overlord of the Savage World': Anthropology, the Media, and the American Indian Experience at the 1904 Louisiana Purchase Exposition." M.A. thesis, University of Arizona, 1997.

Walker, John Brisbeen. "The Pike: Chapter XIII of the World's Fair." *The Cosmopolitan* 37, no. 5 (1904): 615–20.

Williams, Anita Alvarez de. "Cocopa." Pp. 99–112 in *Handbook of North American Indians.* Vol. 10, *Southwest,* ed. Alfonso Ortiz. Washington, D.C.: Smithsonian Institution Press, 1983.

2

Command Performances

Staging Native Americans at Tillicum Village

KATIE N. JOHNSON AND TAMARA UNDERINER

As you cruise to Blake Island State Park, the ship's captain will describe
the activities in one of the world's busiest seaports. With its lush forests
and open beaches, Blake Island offers the perfect setting for Tillicum's
"longhouse," styled in the fashion of the ancient dwellings of the
Northwest Coast Indians. Upon entering our building, you will see
fresh Pacific salmon being prepared on cedar stakes over alder fires,
using a traditional Northwest Coast Indian method. . . . As you finish
your meal, the lights dim and the myth and magic come to life in the
spectacular stage show, "Dance on the Wind," produced by world-
famous Greg Thompson Productions.[1]

AS EARLY AS 1493, when Columbus brought Native Caribbeans back to
Isabella's court, Native Americans have been featured in various spectacles
of empire. This 500-year tradition of displaying the Other to white audiences has been one way, Eugene Jones argues, of justifying the physical
and cultural conquest of indigenous peoples, perceived as obstacles to the
"New" World.[2] Ethnographic displays and dioramas have functioned as
both trophies of conquest—command performances of Manifest Destiny—
and as carefully bounded representations that allowed this difference to be
sampled from a safe distance.

In the United States, tourist attractions can function as the modern
equivalent of such displays and dioramas—sometimes, but not always, with
the consent and participation of Native Americans themselves, whose cultures are thus reenacted for paying, predominantly non-Native audiences.
This chapter relates our recent experiences, as white tourists and research-
ers, with Tillicum Village, a four-hour spectacle of Northwest Native
Americans performed in a state park a short ferry ride from downtown

Seattle, a tourist performance in which culture is, quite literally, consumed.[3] Part cultural display, part dinner theatre, the event raises questions that are not easily answered: Is Tillicum Village a recent example of a long and lamentable history of Natives appearing as cultural artifacts on the (white) stage? Or is there more to Tillicum Village than meets the tourist gaze (theoretically informed as it may be)? Certainly, as Jones and others remind us, the historical context from which Tillicum Village emerges is too politically charged to be dismissed.[4] Given this history, how might we accommodate the increasingly global nature of tourism, in which perceiving groups as Others might occur along axes of privilege as well as ethnicity? And finally, how are we to approach the participation of the Native Americans themselves in this event? In this chapter, Tillicum Village functions as a sort of prism through which we explore a more general question, one that has become increasingly important in the current climate of border exploration: To what extent is such tourist art a sharing of culture, and to what extent is it a form of cultural commodification, appropriation, and consumption? Are these identifications mutually exclusive?

A Visit to Tillicum Village

Visitors approach Tillicum Village through a series of frames ("reiterated frames," to use Robert Cantwell's phrase), which helps to structure the tourist experience.[5] Tillicum Village's ferry departs from the Seattle waterfront amid a collection of other attractions like Ye Olde Curiosity Shoppe (an overcrowded marketplace of knickknacks and curios from all over the world); numerous seafood restaurants trading on Seattle's Nordic heritage; and a trolley to the Seattle Center, which features Seattle's most famous attraction, the Space Needle. The stage is thus set before the ferry leaves the dock: There are sights to be seen, "cultures" to be sampled here. Indeed, the utterly eclectic mixing of cultures in this tourist economy has the troubling effect of suggesting that all cultures, from Norwegian to Native American, are equally consumable, providing one has the economic wherewithal to take advantage of these offerings.

Once aboard the ferry to Tillicum, visitors are given a tour of the Seattle harbor area, a busy place where freighters from all over the world come to disburse their wares. Thus, trade becomes another trope around which tourists, who are also multinational, can organize their experience.[6] As a reiterative frame, trade is perhaps fitting, for "Tillicum" means "friendly" in the Chinook dialect, which was a trade jargon employed by tribes who otherwise did not share a language. Yet the notion of trade, associated historically with the project of westward expansion, goes uncontested in this event. Trade, like tourism, is both naturalized and celebrated, as tourists in the boat are dwarfed by massive cranes and shipping crates on shore. Moreover, this trip to Blake Island situates modern (i.e., "advanced") technology of the mainland against the simpler ("primitive") world of the island. We sail back in time (another trope about which we will have more to say later). For visitors who are interested, Bill Hewitt, who founded Tillicum in 1962, still makes the trip on most weekends and is available to talk about its history as a family business enterprise.

The notion of consumption is equally fitting when examining how Tillicum originated. From our interview with Bill Hewitt and various Tillicum press releases, we discovered that Hewitt began his career as a caterer. He was especially fascinated with salmon prepared "potlatch style," which Hewitt learned about from a State Department of Fisheries employee, Milo Moore. Soon, this method became a specialty of Hewitt's Catering Service.[7] The salmon dinner was so popular that Hewitt drafted a plan to build a restaurant in the style of an "Indian" longhouse. Hewitt chose Blake Island and drafted plans to open his restaurant in time for the 1962 World's Fair in Seattle. As we discuss in more detail below, Tillicum Village is connected to the legacy of the world's fairs both temporally and thematically, particularly in regards to ethnographic displays from the turn of the century. Despite many years of financial struggle, Tillicum Village grew, adding Native American dancing as part of the experience. Initially, these dances were performed by Boy Scouts, presumably non-Native; some years later, Native Americans began performing the dances, as well as working on the staff. As a 1995 brochure explains: "Employees of the attraction are members of local Indian tribes. They serve, they entertain, and they prepare a delectable salmon feast cooked on cedar stakes over alder wood, just as their ancestors did." Although much of this is true, the commercialized context of Tillicum Village makes it very different from how Native ancestors prepared their salmon and practiced their dances.

After a half-hour ride, the ferry docks at Blake Island, in front of a spacious lawn filled with totem poles and other carved statues that are flanked by the large longhouse and dancing house (figs. 2.1 and 2.2). Employees, some dressed in replicas of traditional outfits, welcome and direct visitors to the steaming kettles of clam broth served in plastic cups on the lawn. This disjuncture of the nostalgic "Native" clothing and modern pragmatism of plastic cups is just one of the many tensions between the

FIGURE 2.1. Blake Island State Park, home of Tillicum Village. (Photograph by Kevin Morris)

urge to recreate the Native American past within a postmodern tourist moment at Tillicum Village.

Once inside the longhouse, the frame becomes briefly exhibitional. The inside walls are decorated in murals with traditional Native American motifs. Historical nostalgia is once again marked with representational excess, which one could read as postmodern irony (although we doubt it was intended as such), as these symbols are juxtaposed with color photographs of President Clinton's 1993 Asia Pacific Economic Cooperation forum. This 1993 event was so highly publicized that Tillicum Village promoters created a new slogan, "Where Leaders Meet," designed to attract conference planners. (They also redesigned their 1994 brochure cover so that a photo of Clinton and the Asian leaders replaced the former photo of a Native American staff member baking salmon—but the salmon itself reappears in the new version.[8] Here the trade trope frames, if not jettisons, Native American identity, while the salmon remains central.) Meanwhile, a video of Edward Curtis's 1914 *In the Land of the War Canoe* is shown in a corner of the longhouse. This silent film is his controversial effort to document the Kwakiutls of Vancouver Island, with obviously staged scenes. It is unclear how this video is meant to be perceived—as educational, or as a

Figure 2.2. Tamara Underiner (left), other tourists, and a staff member at the dock entrance to Tillicum Village. (Photograph by Katie N. Johnson)

reflective reference to the complicated history of ethnography, particularly ethnographic film. Regardless of intent, the video frames the tourist experience within a kind of "first-contact" moment, a nostalgic tribute to a bygone age.

In the main hall, visitors are funneled past employees engaged in crafts such as woodcarving and beadwork. That this itself is a staged performance is clear from the separation that exists between the crowd passing by and the employees working on a raised platform to their right. This reminder of ethnographic displays from the world's fairs of the late nineteenth and early twentieth centuries is troubling, not only for its exhibitional, living-museum aspect, but also for the way it tends to reify the distance—and thus power imbalance—between the observers and the observed, rather than to invite exchange.[9]

With extreme efficiency, the queue proceeds to the buffet tables, behind which salmon are prepared over pit fires. A sign reads "Watch your salmon being prepared Indian style." (Recipes are available in press packets.) There is much spectacle in this preparation: It takes place in front of a huge mural of a salmon skeleton, painted in a Northwest Native American style, that forms the backdrop to the alcove in which small fires glow. The salmon are split and mounted vertically on cedar stakes, which are then planted

FIGURE 2.3. A staff member prepares salmon on cedar stakes over alder-wood fires. (Photograph by Kevin Morris)

into the "ground" around the alder-wood fire pits (fig. 2.3). Here, as in the woodcarving and beadwork displays, the employees wear street clothes, which again presents an ambiguous code: Is this meant to preserve the magic (not to mention the physical condition) of the costumes these same employees will later don for the show or to subtly intervene in the otherwise relentless message that the world of Tillicum Village is an "ancient" one? As with so much about Tillicum Village, it is a matter of perspective, of reception as well as intent.

Once baked, the salmon are ceremoniously carried to the buffet tables, where they are smothered in lemon butter and served with standard American fare: tossed salad, sauteed potatoes, bread and butter, all on plastic platters designed in the shape of a fish. At the risk of reading too much into this culinary text, we now see it as an anticipatory metaphor for what we later see on stage: the thrill of the new, cushioned by the safety of the familiar. At the time, we were all too conscious of our participation—and our enjoyment—in consuming the packaged culture set before us. Vexed as this process was, the salmon was undeniably delicious. While chewing over these contradictions, we awaited the show.

Inside the dancing house are scores of tables that seat ten to twelve people, perpendicularly arranged to a proscenium-style stage on which are visible the scenic elements of the production. Tent cards with excerpts from Chief Seattle's famous speech (which will eventually conclude the performance) are on the tables. As we dine, we are served beverages by the people who will later perform, in the perhaps uniquely American tradition of dinner theatre, where often the actors are also waiters. Toward dessert (a bit of salmon-shaped chocolate), the lights dim and a hushed and hushing voice announces that in a moment, the performance of "Dance on the Wind" will begin.

"Dance on the Wind" is a production full of visual spectacle, cowritten by Mark Hewitt (Bill Hewitt's son) and Greg Thompson and produced by "world-famous" Greg Thompson Productions, a company known for its Las Vegas extravaganzas. Although the promotional literature never mentions Thompson's connections to Las Vegas (we learned this through Bill Hewitt, who clearly views this production as belonging to the same genre), a travelwise spectator could probably detect it. Sophisticated lighting design and a variety of special effects complement a forestlike set, on which several myths and excerpts from tribal dances are performed to taped narration (fig. 2.4). At times, a small discovery space is revealed from behind two sliding rock panels, providing a frame-within-a-frame for some of the action. The performance itself is a tightly structured, thirty-minute piece that provides a pastiche of information: background on the various tribes in the area, potlatch customs, mask traditions, blanket work, legends of the Terrible Beast and of the Raven, and dances performed between bits of narration and pantomime. The narration itself is somewhat general in nature, but despite what we might have expected, it acknowledges that the generalizations it deals in are based on distinct traditions from different northern and southern coastal tribes, which it names. Another disjuncture

FIGURE 2.4. A scene from "Dance on the Wind" by Greg Thompson Productions. (Photograph by Kevin Morris)

emerges—a show with commercial polish during which the Native American performers never speak.

Cultural Exchange or Cultural Appropriation?

As Coco Fusco notes, "The contemporary tourist industries and cultural ministries of several countries around the world still perpetrate the illusion of authenticity to cater to the Western fascination with otherness."[10] In catering to this fascination of otherness, does Tillicum Village also perpetuate appropriation, as do so many commodified cultural events? Or, is something else occurring? For art historian Deborah Root, cultural appropriation "signifies not only the taking up of something and making it one's own but also the ability to do so. People have always shared ideas and borrowed from one another, but appropriation is entirely different from borrowing or sharing because it involves the taking up and commodification of aesthetic, cultural, and, more recently, spiritual forms of a society. Culture is neatly packaged for the consumer's convenience."[11] The Pacific Northwest is rife with examples of appropriation, such as the frequent use of totem poles and Native iconography to grace business establishments rarely patronized by Natives themselves. In many circumstances, "appropriation" can be equated with "theft," which occurs when Natives are not consulted about the use of their aesthetic, cultural, and spiritual materials and when financial gain is the primary motive for the appropriation. As noted, the appearance of Native Americans on stage for non–Native audiences is hardly a new phenomenon. Historically these performances have worked to help such audiences not only assert their superiority over the "primitive" world, but also to effectively control and limit their knowledge about that world.[12]

Residents of the Pacific Northwest have long used the "primitive" as a natural resource for mining and display. In her study of Native American performance on the Northwest coast, Mary Elizabeth Fullerton observes that the "construction of the cultural other" occurs at the price of "the exclusion of the native speaker," a symbolic erasure linked to programs of physical exclusion and genocide in the service of westward expansion.[13] Jones agrees: "Despite their long history in vaudeville and circus, however, Indians, like other ethnic performers, did not appear as intelligent speaking performers in stage productions before the mid–twentieth century."[14] Equally important for this discussion, Fullerton points out that historically, this construction has almost always framed Native American performance in terms of the subjugator's theatrical tradition. She argues that such performances (like ethnographic displays at world's fairs) are "reified by and culminate in the Western theatre narrative."[15]

Fullerton's insights achieve a contemporary resonance in the case of the "Dance on the Wind," in which rituals and entertainment normally conducted in the open air or in dimly lit longhouses for a surrounding circle of spectator-participants are here framed by a double proscenium in a very Western-style production for an audience literally fenced off and enjoying after-dinner coffee. Moreover, here the disembodied wisdom of a legend is heard not in the soul of the seeker, but over a loudspeaker system from a prerecorded tape written by two white men.

"Rarely, if ever," reads a 1992 press release announcing the new Thompson production, "have the legends and dance of Northwest Native Americans been combined with the theatrics of the stage in such a remarkable way, while at the same time enhancing the ethnic and cultural heritage of these exceptional people." This short paragraph reveals the ambivalent heart of the matter, allowing history to resume its mirrored mask: It would seem that the heritage of an indigenous people is only enhanced when it is framed by and for European conventions and taste.   ZACATECAS CHURCH

The performance at Tillicum Village appears to be an interaction between those who Peter Stallybrass and Allon White have called the "high" (i.e., those who have access to power or who, to use Raymond Williams's term, subscribe to "the inherent dominative mode") and the "low" (those who have been consigned to the margins). The inevitable tensions between high and low are characterized by a dialectic of contempt and desire. As Stallybrass and White put it,

> The primary site of contradiction, the site of conflicting desires and mutually incompatible representation, is undoubtedly the 'low.' Again and again we find a striking ambivalence to the representations of the lower strata . . . in which they are both reviled and desired. Repugnance and fascination are the twin poles of the process in which a political imperative to reject and eliminate the debasing 'low' conflicts powerfully and unpredictably with a desire for this Other.[16]

The fascination with Tillicum Village for the tourist audience—themselves ethnically diverse, but sharing economic privilege—could be read as the kind of desire Stallybrass and White articulate. At the same time, the tourist's confrontation with the material realities of the low remains conveniently deferred. This is why, for example, references to contemporary Native American culture are hidden at Tillicum Village in nostalgic visions of an untroubled past. The history of the colonization of land, traditions, and people is never mentioned, yet the entire enterprise seems underwritten by that history.

At Tillicum Village, Native culture is indeed neatly packaged for tourist consumption, and it is difficult to avoid employing a metaphor of consumption and commodification in describing what occurs there. In addition to the dinner and dances, there is also a gift shop in which souvenirs made by the communities represented are available for sale. As if to embody the many paradoxes of Tillicum Village, also for sale are more obviously souvenir-type trinkets made by non–Native artists. In all, the cost of the day can easily exceed $50 per person.[17] The question of profit in this process of commodification therefore becomes important. As a private business, obviously the owners are the key beneficiaries, but this in turn raises other questions that implicate the larger economy within which Tillicum Village operates. Inequities in the job market remain in the Northwest, and it is ironic that while "culture sells" in the tourist economy, in the larger arena, the people who practice their culture do not always profit financially from it.

Nevertheless, the Native American participants of Tillicum Village have always exercised a degree of control over what is presented of and by them and are compensated both for their participation and for the handicrafts they sell in the tourist market there. Importantly, the dances are "owned" by family members of the various tribes represented in the performance, and permission to dance them must be granted by tribal elders; it should be noted that over the years a few have withheld that permission. As discussed earlier, the performance was originally danced by Boy Scouts whose troops had been authorized by the tribes to do so, and until 1992 they were danced on a bare stage. According to Marcel, a Haida dancer with whom we spoke, the performers all dance the dances they have either learned from their own families or from other Tillicum dancers (fig. 2.5). (Mark Hewitt is also authorized to teach new employees the dance steps.) Thus, given that the tribes have granted permission to teach and perform the dances, it becomes difficult to categorically dismiss this exchange as another act of appropriation. Yet, the economic disparity, as discussed above, leaves us dissatisfied.

However, if the Native Americans control the dances, they cannot fully control the subtle messages inherent in the way they are promoted and presented. The dancers themselves come from a variety of different tribes (from as far away as Idaho and Oklahoma—and in one case, from Vietnam). In fact, promotional literature is careful to list this tribal representation, but this fact itself is problematic.[18] On the one hand, it does represent an attempt to call attention to the tribal diversity among Tillicum participants. On the other, it manifests the "unmarked" status of those participants who are not Native American. For example, Hewitt told us that one staff member was part Mexican, one Vietnamese, and one African Ameri-

FIGURE 2.5. A Tillicum Village dancer demonstrates the use of a Northwest mask after the show. (Photograph by Tamara Underiner)

can; presumably they pass as Northwest Native Americans. Yet the fact that Tillicum Village's founders are white is never mentioned. Therefore, what is non–Native, and particularly what is white, is invisible. To ignore whiteness—and the privilege it inherits—not only marks the Other as different, ethnic, and exotic; it also denies the power, politics, and historical legacy of colonial discourse. This problem of the invisibility of whiteness is caught up in the illusionary search for "authenticity" in the Other. Multicultural theorist Trinh T. Minh-ha writes that this search for origins leads us to false identifications of the "real":

> *Authenticity* as a need to rely on an "undisputed origin," is prey to an obsessive *fear:* that of *losing a connection.* Everything must hold together. . . . The *real,* nothing else than a *code of representation,* does not (cannot) coincide with the lived or the performed. This is what Vine Deloria, Jr. accounts for when he exclaims: "Not even Indians can relate themselves to this type of creature who, to anthropologists, is the 'real' Indian."[19]

In fact, Tillicum Village presents a relatively undifferentiated picture of the cultures it displays, despite whatever degree of sensitivity to these differences may exist on the part of its creators. As Paul Rathbun warns, "any homogenized expression of Native sentiment or worldview can only be distorted."[20] Not only is the distortion the result of juxtaposing different cultures in one performance space, but also of compressing (or ignoring) temporal parameters as well. Tillicum Village's tourist brochure and press packets suggest that its creators have bought into what Root calls the "salvage paradigm," the assumption that the societies that have produced the culture therein promoted are now dead.[21] These promotional materials rely for their appeal on a time when "ancestral traditions" were alive and well along the Northwest coast (as though they are no longer). Press releases, for example, describe Tillicum as follows: "Imagine leaving Seattle on a journey back in time, arriving at a gathering place once used by Northwest Coast Native Americans as a fishing camp"; "nestled on the shore of Blake Island State Park, stands a huge cedar longhouse styled in the fashion of the ancient communal dwellings of the Northwest Coast Indians"; and, finally, "muralled walls and the mingled aroma of alder smoke and cedar create the perfect atmosphere to display the culture that flourished here for thousands of years."[22] Citing First Nation writer Marcia Crosby, Root outlines the danger of such an approach: "Predicated on the concept of a dead or dying people whose culture needs to be 'saved,' those doing the saving choose what fragments of a culture they will salvage. Having done this, they become both the owners and interpreters of the artifacts or goods that have survived from that dying culture, artifacts that become rare and therefore valuable."[23] This kind of selective collection is precisely what Tillicum offers to the tourist, who is invited to travel "back in time" to a place where Native Americans "display the culture that flourished here for thousands of years." Thus, Tillicum Village consciously offers a nostalgic quotation of the past, a culture frozen in time, "performing" tasks "just as their ancestors did." Or so they would have us believe.[24]

Having said all this, we are still vexed by the timbre of our experience at Tillicum Village. Despite the historical valence of such cultural productions, we came back with the clear impression that Native American subjectivity could and did find expression here, although that impression was not uncomplicated. There is something at work in Tillicum Village that prevents an easy dismissal on the grounds of cultural appropriation. For us, it was rooted in the physical presence of the dancers, who cannot be consigned to some easy classification scheme that has them innocently internalizing their own oppression. Diana Monsegur, for example, who has worked there for fifteen years, told us that the opportunity to "share their culture" with a larger world is one of the reasons certain tribes have granted permission for their dances to be performed. She joked that in the annual Canadian potlatches that she was familiar with, the dancers tired of presenting their dances to the same people year after year.[25] Marcel is another, younger performer who first learned his dance when he was two years old and parlayed his performing experience into several appearances on the television show *Northern Exposure.* Alexander Joseph has a more nuanced attitude, difficult to articulate, which we call "making wedges." Like the carving tools he uses to coax form from huge blocks of cedar, in his responses to tourists and in his sense of presence, Joseph attempts to chisel away the ground from under facile expectations. One of us, interested in the sources of his artistic inspiration, asked him what the whale he was carving "started out as." Joseph's response was, simply, "a tree." This response can be read in at least two ways: as the most literal and material response and as a subtle way of declining, in his way, to enter into the same system of tourist discourse that we were trying to initiate. With two words, Joseph introduced a wedge into the interaction and into our consciousness as well.

In such moments, we see a hybrid variety of what Barbara Babcock calls "symbolic inversion," subtle moments of active resistance wedged into an overall scheme of cultural exchange. Such moments seem to diffuse, if not entirely erase, the problem of cultural commodification and appropriation that at first glance seems to govern Tillicum Village.[26]

After many hours of reflection that our visit to Tillicum Village prompted, we cannot say that it does not participate in a larger circulation of stereotypical images of Native Americans, promulgated through acts of exhibition and display that have been with us since the fifteenth century. But does Tillicum Village represent an act of "cultural appropriation" in Root's sense? We are not so sure. To say so would deny the long hours of consideration and deliberation among tribal elders regarding the authorization of the dances to Tillicum Village. These dances are meant for non-Native consumption and were not taken from the tribes without their permission. To label the performance as "appropriation" also denies performers' enthusiasm for and commitment to their work.

As a bundle of contradictions, the kinds of cultural interaction occurring at Tillicum Village may be more dialogic and collaborative than current theory indicates. As Ana M. López points out in her analysis of

Hollywood's cultural colonialism, what is needed is a retheorization of the producer's role in representing others (in this case, Tillicum Village), using recent shifts in ethnographic theory as a model. Replacing Hollywood with Tillicum Village in this paradigm, then, would be to think of it *not* as

> a simple reproducer of fixed and homogenous cultures or ideologies, but as a producer of some of the multiple discourses that intervene in, affirm, and contest the socioideological struggles of a given moment. To think of Hollywood [Tillicum Village] as ethnographic discourse is to affirm its status as an authored, yet collaborative, enterprise, akin in practice to the way contemporary ethnographers have redefined their discipline. James Clifford, for example, has analyzed the discursive nature of ethnography "not as the experience and interpretation of a circumscribed 'other' reality, but as a constructive negotiation involving . . . conscious politically significant subjects."[27]

By honoring the Native American dancers and elders as "conscious politically significant subjects," we wish to open up a freer theoretical space in which they can be seen as coproducers (although perhaps not yet equal) of this cultural experience. While much remains uncertain, our visit confirms the need in critical discourse to incorporate a more dialogic approach, which includes Native subjectivity along with the vexed colonial frame. In this, Alexander Joseph's succinct eloquence provides a guiding light.

Notes

We are grateful to Sarah Bryant-Bertail and the members of the Theatre and Anthropology Seminar at the University of Washington for their insights and critical responses. An earlier version of this essay was given at the 1996 American Society for Theatre Research Conference in Pasadena, California.

1. Excerpt from a 1994 Tillicum Village promotional brochure.

2. For a history of Native Americans on stage, see Jones. For an interesting overview and analysis of displaying Native Americans to non-Natives, see Fusco.

3. We visited Tillicum Village in February 1995.

4. In addition to Jones and Fusco, see Fullerton.

5. By "reiterated frames," Cantwell refers to the various ways cultural representations are staged, or framed, to train viewers, audiences, and/or consumers in how to perceive and interpret the representation. In the case of Tillicum Village,

the tourist frame begins in Seattle's dockside souvenir shops, which is then reiterated through the harbor ferry tour and multiplied in the exhibitional frames-within-frames of the visit itself, until one arrives at the literal proscenium frame of the dancing house for the after-dinner performance.

6. According to promotional materials, Tillicum Village attracts more than 100,000 tourists annually.

7. Hewitt, 5.

8. From a 1994 Tillicum Village promotional brochure. Their current brochures no longer feature the 1993 Asia Pacific Economic Cooperation forum.

9. Ironically, Tillicum Village was intended to open in time for the 1962 Seattle World's Fair, but financial difficulties prevented this. For a general study of how world's fairs participate in imperial discourse, see Rydell. For an in-depth discussion of these exhibitions relative to Pacific Northwest Native Americans, see Fullerton.

10. Fusco, 147.

11. Root, 70.

12. Fusco, 143–67.

13. Fullerton, 18.

14. Jones, 121.

15. Fullerton, 18.

16. Stallybrass and White, 4–5.

17. We were treated to a reduced ticket price of $12 by Roberta Greer, Senior Vice President of Public Relations for Tillicum Village. As graduate students, we were particularly grateful for this discount. Prices in the year 2000 are $55.25 for adults, with reduced prices for seniors and children. For current information, visit the website at www.tillicumvillage.com.

18. Promotional literature from 1993 lists the lineage of the dancers and their "homelands" as the following: West-Tsartlip (Canada); Chu-Chua (Canada); Tlingit (Angoon, Alaska); Tshmshian/Tlingit (Ketchikan, Alaska); Haida (Ketchikan, Alaska); Nuu-Cha-Nult (Coast Salish from Ahosht, Tse-shaht, and Ditidaht, Canada); Navajo-Flathead (Coeur D'Alene, Idaho); Quinalt (Tahola, Washington); Nez Perce/Cherokee (Idaho); and Nez Perce (Kiowa, Oklahoma).

19. Trinh, 94.

20. Rathbun, 10.

21. Root, 74.

22. Undated press release from Tillicum Village.

23. Root, 75.

24. Nor do the promotional materials or the dance production itself mention any of the material realities attending life on the reservations since they were created by official mandate. Although we are not arguing that a privately funded tourist attraction is ultimately responsible for portraying a completely balanced picture, along with its darker historical side, we do believe it can be held responsible for the

NEW AGE

perpetuation of stereotypes. There is little in the experience of Tillicum Village to direct the interested visitor to more information from which to draw a contemporary picture, and to all appearances, these traditions are promoted rather as relics of a bygone age.

25. Because our interviews with the dancers were brief and informal and our ethnographic expertise minimal, we unfortunately did not obtain all the dancers' last names. We have since realized that this omission, juxtaposed with our use of Bill Hewitt's full name, replicates the regrettable mistakes of early anthropology, where the subjects (or, perhaps more precisely, the objects) of study remain nameless, whereas the white people are named. Similarly, Tillicum Village promotional material does not list the dancers or staff by name at all.

26. Babcock, 14.

27. López, 405.

Works Cited

Babcock, Barbara, ed. *The Reversible World: Symbolic Inversion in Art and Society.* Ithaca, N.Y.: Cornell University Press, 1978.

Cantwell, Robert. *Ethnomimesis: Folklife and the Representation of Culture.* Chapel Hill: University of North Carolina Press, 1993.

Fullerton, Mary Elizabeth. "Reception and Representation: The Western Vision of Native American Performance on the Northwest Coast." Ph.D. diss., University of Washington, 1986.

Fusco, Coco. "The Other History of Intercultural Performance." *The Drama Review* 38, no. 1 (1994): 143–67.

Hewitt, Mark. *The Story of Tillicum Village: The Myth and the Magic.* Seattle, Wash.: Tillicum Village and Tours, Inc. 1989.

Jones, Eugene H. *Native Americans as Shown on the Stage, 1753–1916.* London: Metuchen, 1988.

López, Ana M. "Are All Latins from Manhattan?" Pp. 404–24 in *Unspeakable Images: Ethnicity and the American Cinema,* ed. Lester Friedman. Urbana: University of Illinois Press, 1991.

Rathbun, Paul. "Native Drama in History." *Native Playwrights' Newsletter* 1 (Spring 1993): 10–11.

Root, Deborah. *Cannibal Culture: Art, Appropriation, and the Commodification of Difference.* Boulder, Colo.: Westview Press, 1996.

Rydell, Robert. *All the World's a Fair: Visions of Empire at American International Expositions, 1876–1916.* Chicago: University of Chicago Press, 1984.

Stallybrass, Peter, and Allon White. *The Politics and Poetics of Culture.* Ithaca, N.Y.: Cornell University Press, 1986.

Tillicum Village Employees. Interviews by Katie N. Johnson and Tamara Underiner, Seattle, Wash., February 1995.

Tillicum Village Press Packets and Promotional Literature, 1991–1994. Seattle, Wash.: Tillicum Village and Tours, Inc.

Trinh, Minh-ha T. *Woman, Native, Other: Writing Postcoloniality and Feminism.* Bloomington: Indiana University Press, 1989.

3

Savage Desires

The Gendered Construction of the American Indian in Popular Media

S. ELIZABETH BIRD

THE SCENE IS A POPULAR DRUG store, anywhere in the United States. In one direction is a display of cartoon images of Pocahontas, the voluptuous Indian princess. On another wall, a bright poster features a noble, Indian elder gazing toward a setting sun. A doe-eyed maiden, in flowing white buckskin, smiles enticingly from her home among the "collectable" art prints. Meanwhile, the shelves of romance novels display bare-chested, love-lorn warriors among the pirates, cowboys, and regency dandies. In contemporary popular culture, American Indians have become potent cultural symbols, and more specifically, Indian men and Indian women have come to fill separate and different places in the popular white iconography.

In this chapter, I wish to trace the development of this gendered imagery by addressing male, then female, construction. Moving from historical origins to contemporary media manifestations, I suggest that to understand the way American Indian imagery functions in contemporary white culture, we must consider how American Indian men and women have become both sexualized and desexualized, not in relation to each other, but in relation to the white gaze. I begin with an overview of the way American Indians have been represented.

Constructing the Indian: The Role of Anthropology

It is not new to point out that mass-culture images of American Indians are images created by white culture, for white culture.[1] In earlier times, that alien image was feared and hated, fed by and feeding a popular culture that mythologized the massacre of whites by savage, uncontrollable Indians. The "captivity narrative," in which honorable white women and children were degraded and destroyed by lustful savages, became a staple of popular journalism and fiction in the eighteenth and nineteenth centuries and echoed on into the twentieth.[2] Alongside that image, of course, has been a parallel narrative of the Indian as the noble, spiritual keeper of the land and wisdom. Whichever narrative is in the ascendancy, Indians themselves have little voice in the story. Their role is to be the object of the white gaze and the focus of white myth.

Current media representations of American Indians are understandable only if seen as the legacy of a complex mesh of cultural elements, including formal history, literature, material artifacts, folklore, photography, cartoon, art, mass media, and anthropological discourse. The work of early anthropologists among Native American peoples was crucial in codifying the idea of the Indian as Other. Their ethnographic descriptions became the core of museum exhibits, world fairs, Wild West shows, and early silent films, ultimately leading to current popular depictions.[3] The anthropological convention of the timeless "ethnographic present" effectively placed Native cultures into a kind of time warp, from which, in the white consciousness, they have not emerged. From nineteenth-century tourist displays to contemporary movies, television, and romance novels, white audiences have found pleasure in the traditional clothing, nobility, and sacred rituals that anthropologists and early photographers first portrayed.

Traditional American Indian cultures are among the most thoroughly studied anywhere; overwhelmingly, these ethnographies have been of the classic, objective type, providing a wealth of detail about costume, customs, myths, and rituals, but very little sense of the people *as* people. This is especially true of the huge wave of "salvage ethnography" that swept across the Great Plains at the end of the last century, inspired by Franz Boas—the work of anthropological pioneers like Clark Wissler, Alfred Kroeber, Paul Radin, and Robert H. Lowie. Their goal was not primarily to understand contemporary Native cultures, but to record them before they were lost. As Dippie writes, "Ethnography was the anthropological equivalent of wilderness preservation. It drew upon the belief in the Vanishing American and substantially reinforced it."[4] Volumes of American Indian ethnographies produced accounts of peoples programmed by cultural rules, calmly going about their (ultimately doomed) business.

Many American Indians have complained that they do not recognize themselves in these ethnographic descriptions. This sense of misrepresentation is at the core of the distrust of anthropology that is so pervasive among contemporary Native Americans, epitomized by the anger of Vine Deloria:

"behind each policy and program with which Indians are plagued . . . stands the anthropologist. The fundamental thesis of the anthropologist is that if people are objects for observation, people are then considered objects for experimentation, for manipulation, and for eventual extinction."[5]

Thomas Biolsi uses the career of anthropologist Haviland Scudder Mekeel, noted for his 1930s' work with the Lakota, to illustrate the role of anthropology in constructing the Lakota as "primitive," as Mekeel searched for "authentic," full-blood Indians to study.[6] While Lakota people were more interested in debating treaty rights and coping with change, anthropologists like Mekeel were looking for untainted primitivism. Similarly, Whiteley argues that standard descriptions in introductory anthropological textbooks have been important in confirming the image of American Indians as fundamentally different from whites and as representing past, "primitive" cultures. Speaking of popular portrayals of the Hopi, Whitely writes: "So, (we) self-righteous anthropologists can be appalled by Smokis, art collectors, or New Agers, while conveniently blinding ourselves to a family resemblance with our own representations of Hopi culture."[7]

Perhaps most important, as Renato Rosaldo observed, "classic" ethnographic techniques had the effect of distancing the observer from the people studied, literally "objectifying" them. Individual ethnographers may have had close personal ties with the people they studied, but the conventions of ethnography prevented such closeness from showing. Bataille and Sands point out that whereas traditional anthropologists did employ techniques like autobiographies, they used these accounts simply as indicators of cultural patterns, rather than as ways to present their informants subjectively. The importance of this practice is that these ethnographies, and the white cultural products that spun from them, have continued to define popular conceptions of American Indians, even though ethnography itself has been transformed and problematized within the field of anthropology.

For example, a central stereotype of Indians is their stoicism and lack of emotion, conditioned by a century and a half of stern, unsmiling photos and descriptions of people behaving with programmed ritualism. As Rosaldo puts it, "the general rule seems to be that one should tidy things up as much as possible by wiping away the tears and ignoring the tantrums."[8] "Objective" ethnography produced accounts of people devoid of human emotion, because to write of emotion was "unscientific," not to mention uncomfortable. Current popular culture perpetuates this image. Thus, Kimberley Norris, an Indian woman who had a small role in the 1980s' television miniseries *Son of the Morning Star*, reports how she was told to redo a scene in which she wept for the slain leader Crazy Horse. Instead of her tears, she was told, "Let's do it again and just take it with that dignified stoicism of the Indians."[9] As Norris commented, "That was a real quick lesson in their perception of how we don't have those natural human emotions."[10]

My recent work on audience response to the television show *Dr. Quinn, Medicine Woman,* which features a post–Civil War Cheyenne village on a regular basis, indicates that the different responses of Indian and non-Indian audiences often hinged on their acceptance or rejection of the classic unemotionalism of the Cheyenne characters. Thus, a white woman remarked approvingly on the stoicism exhibited by an imprisoned Cheyenne: "You know, they can be very intense emotionally but able to suppress it and not show it."[11] Another agreed, saying that stoicism was "a Native American value, and that's being true to your word and being willing to go to death."[12] Yet American Indian viewers were especially angered by this very same story, arguing that "his manhood was suppressed," "his dignity was violated," and the character was not allowed to show normal emotions. "I could have seen anger, but he just . . . put his head down, made him look pitiful."[13] Whereas white viewers generally found the portrayal of the Cheyenne positive and accurate, the Indian viewers did not: "They're caricatures and they're not human beings with their own language, their own thoughts, their own feelings."[14] Similarly, JoEllen Shiveley, in comparing male Indian and Anglo responses to a classic Western, *The Searchers,* found that although both groups enjoyed the film and both identified with the hero, played by John Wayne, the Anglo viewers also thought the film was generally authentic in its portrayal of the Old West, whereas the Indian men did not. Shiveley's conclusion, like mine, is that white viewers have tended to naturalize the popular, objectified imagery of Indians and accept it as "authentic," whereas Indian viewers resist the dehumanizing they see as central to the imagery.

Therefore, it was not surprising to see perhaps the most elaborate, recent incarnation of white mythological construction of Indians, a 1995 major theatrical movie now doing the rounds of the video stores. *Last of the Dogmen* postulated a "lost tribe" of Cheyenne, who, having escaped the 1864 Sand Creek massacre, hid in the mountains of Montana for more than a century. A cynical mountain man (Tom Berenger) finds them and reports them to (who else?) an anthropologist (Barbara Hershey). An archaeologist by specialty who understands Cheyenne culture through the study of ancient artifacts, she accompanies him to visit the band and finds that her anthropological expertise in nineteenth-century Cheyenne culture enables her to understand and be accepted by this noble, idyllic people. The message is clear: The Cheyenne are dead, and only by some wonderful miracle do we find them, pure and unchanged, offering themselves up for study to the enchanted anthropologist, who never returns to the corrupt twentieth century. The marriage of anthropological and popular imagery is complete.

The denial of American Indians' sexual identities in relation to each other has been an important element in the objectification of the Indian. Anthropology has also had a role in this. Just as emotions tend to be purged from the ethnographic record, so does sexuality. The classic ethnography contains information about incest and marriage rules, but it provides little sense of people who are active sexual beings. Frequently, Indian sexuality was classified as somehow inferior or more primitive than the refined expressions of Western love. For example, Lewis Henry Morgan, in his classic work on the Iroquois, wrote, "of that passion which originates in a higher development of the powers of the human heart, and is founded upon a cultivation of the affections between the sexes, they were entirely ignorant. In their temperaments, they were below the passion in its simplest forms."[15] The apparent denial of sexuality among ethnographic subjects reinforced a cultural tradition of viewing Indian men and women (separately) as the sexualized objects of the colonialist gaze.

The Objectification of the Indian Male

THE DOOMED WARRIOR

As Berkhofer points out, depending on the era, the Indian male has usually been seen as either the "noble savage" or his alter ego, the "ignoble savage."[16] What Berkhofer does not emphasize is that in both guises, the male image has always had a strong sexual dimension. During times of conflict between whites and Indians, Indian males became sexual threats, epitomized most clearly in that most pervasive of myths—the captivity narrative. The captivity narrative is clearly a major cultural tradition in North America that confirmed the notion of Indian as Other, whether that Other is evil or noble. As June Namias points out, the Indian, whether male or female, was not only noble and savage, but also both exotic and erotic, and all those dimensions were present even when Indian males were demonized. Part of the conception of the "primitive native" has been an often-repressed awareness of "animal sexuality." In the colonial period, Indians were seen as wild, passionate, alluring, and blessed with a "dark beauty": "The concoction of the noble, the wild, and the exotic appeared to whet the English sexual appetite, at the same time inspiring trepidation among several white captives."[17] Rape of white captives appears to have been rare in the colonial period; captive Elizabeth Hanson, for example, writes that "the Indians are very civil towards their captive women, not offering any incivility by any indecent carriage."[18] Nevertheless, Puritans like Cotton Mather quickly came to equate Indians with the Devil, with sexual predation taking an increasingly larger role in the image.

After the 1820s, as whites encroached further upon Indian lands, the image of the sexual brute capable of every kind of excess became more and more prevalent.[19] As Namias points out, anthropological arguments for the existence of superior and inferior races helped to justify exploitation and destruction, and "proven" sexual brutality bolstered further the rationale for destroying the Indian, who appeared in endless dime novels as a huge, highly sexualized figure. In 1867, Henry Tuckerman, speaking about Erastus Dow Palmer's 1859 sculpture *The White Captive,* commented that "No more suggestive incident can be imagined for either poetry, romance, or art, than the fair, youthful, and isolated hostage of civilization surrounded by savage captors."[20] Captivity narratives such as Mary Jemison's, which described the love of a white captive for her Indian husband, were unusual and often required editing or glossing for publication. Jemison writes of her first husband Sheninjee: "The idea of spending my days with him, at first seemed perfectly irreconcilable to my feelings; but his good nature, generosity, tenderness and friendship towards me, soon gained my affection; and strange as it may seem, I loved him!"[21] She also loved her second husband, Hiokatoo, yet in the 1856 edition of Jemison's story, editors added material that made him appear brutal and murderous. Jemison had been married to him for almost fifty years and had written not only that "he was a man of tender feelings in his friends," but also that "he uniformly treated me with tenderness, and never offered an insult."[22] The tone of the narrative frequently changes, as the editor steps in to describe events that Jemison could not have experienced personally; during these episodes, Indians become "savages" and their cruel deeds are described enthusiastically.

This is not to deny that white captives were sometimes raped and mistreated by Indian captors; however, the captivity narrative became the most pervasive vehicle for standardizing particular images of Indian males. During the nineteenth century, the same episodes of sexual savagery were repeated again and again in both "true" and "fictional" accounts of captivity, truly producing a mythical "reality." The infamous narrative about the torture and death of Maria and Christina Manheim, captured by Senecas in 1779, ends as "these helpless virgins sunk down in the arms of their deliverer, death," and was endlessly copied and embellished upon in the years to come.[23]

The fear of the blatant sexuality of the Indian male continued into the era of cinema. Gary Edgerton describes the 1920 Maurice Tourneur and Clarence Brown version of James Fenimore Cooper's *The Last of the Mohicans*, in which Wallace Beery as the evil Magua "stabs Cora repeatedly during the final rebuke at the cliff, after leering at her in uninhibited ways for much of the picture."[24] In the 1936 George Seitz version, the white heroines continue to be terrorized by the evil, lustful Hurons, as Magua tries to force Alice to be his "squaw." However, it is the "good" Indian, Chingachgook, who voices the stereotypical vision of Indian lust for white women: "Pale face squaw no good Mohican. Fair hair make heart of Uncas weak like water."[25]

Nevertheless, alongside the brutal savage, the erotic appeal of the male Indian body was never deeply buried. As the "Indian problem" grew less pressing in the middle of the nineteenth century and into the 1890s, the noble and often eroticized savage gradually ascended, as the physical appeal of the imagined Indian body grew increasingly overt. Whereas the African-American male has been stereotyped exclusively as a sexual predator (at least until very recently), an important dimension of the objectification of the Indian male has long been an acknowledgment of his erotic appeal, even if that appeal is forbidden. From first European contact, much was made of the physical nature of the natives of America—their nakedness, their fine physical development, and so on. As Berkhofer writes, describing sixteenth-century engravings of newly "discovered" Indians, "Such pictures as this one of a 'prince' established the muscular handsomeness and athletic virility of the Noble American Savage. . . . The lack of clothing and the careful distribution of artifacts upon and about the prince's body only enhanced the image."[26] For years, depictions of Indians tended to show them almost naked, even if the cultures concerned actually did tend to wear more clothes. As long as Indians were not a threat, their physical beauty was often admired and their "innocent" enjoyment of their nakedness was even envied; "even when presented in the guise of moralizing, appreciation of the unclothed body of Native Americans has a long history."[27] Popular literature of the nineteenth century continued the appreciative gaze of the male body, often comparing the Indian with a classical sculpture: an

Apache "so perfectly formed that he would make Apollo envious."[28] William Gerdts describes the popularity of male Indian figures in neoclassic sculpture: "The Indian figure suggested a general aura of romance and nostalgia, but the male Indian often came to express a certain sexual prowess that the white man could not. He was usually depicted as a powerful physical being, frequently semi-nude, while Caucasian males were almost invariably clothed, except for adolescent or youthful types . . . a symbol of primitive virility."[29] Striking in these images is a sense of the Indian male as an object of desire, presented as exposed and available, as only white women, not men, could be. Cooper, in *The Last of the Mohicans,* has the beautiful Alice gazing at Uncas "as she would have looked upon some precious relic of the Greek chisel . . . while Heyward . . . openly expressed his admiration of such an unblemished specimen of the noblest proportions of man."[30]

June Namias points to the strong nineteenth-century undercurrent of eroticization of the Indian male in both art and popular culture. Chauncy B. Ives's sculpture *Willing Captive,* first produced in 1862 and reproduced several times since, portrays a young woman clinging to her Indian abductor, while her mother begs her to return to the white world. As Namias points out, "If there were Indians who looked like this one, no wonder there was a need for stories of tragic sexual unions," in which those who defied convention could only suffer for their choice.[31] African-Americans were pure sexual threat, but American Indians, although also often characterized as animal-like, at the same time carried associations of pristine "first American" purity. They might actually be objects of white desire—their savagery and nobility being schizophrenically expressed in their sexual personae. The sexualized Indian male apparently appealed to both white men and women. We might hypothesize different reasons for this: Perhaps there was a forbidden fantasy appeal for women who read captivity narratives voraciously in a culture that rigidly repressed female sexuality. Although there is arguably an element of homoeroticism in the white male gaze, I believe the core of the attraction for white men lies in the powerful "going-native" myth that has long been entrenched in American culture. As Robert Baird notes, the going-native narrative plays on the fantasy identification of the white man with the free, "natural" American Indian, who is simultaneously noble and yet able to allow free reign to his "wild" sexuality. For both white men and women, fear and fantasy are two sides of the same coin.

These noble Indians, although attractive and exotic, were highly Europeanized in appearance, indeed often painted and sculpted as classical figures. Often the beauty of the Indian body was coupled with a romantic nostalgia, with the rise of the "doomed Indian" stereotype—the Indian who knows his time is past, but accepts it with honorable resignation. Thus, in Thomas Crawford's famous 1855 sculpture, *Dying Chief Contemplating the Progress of Civilization,* a muscular, naked (except for his headdress) Indian "brave" sits, pondering the extinction of his people. An 1870 critic admired "the bowed head, the clenched hand, the stoical despair of this majestic figure."[32] Two other sculptural images that have become cultural icons are Cyrus Dallin's 1908 *Appeal to the Great Spirit* and, most significantly, James Fraser's 1915 *End of the Trail.* In different ways, each portrays a noble, defeated, scantily clad Indian warrior, emblematic of the end of the race. Van Lent suggests that the resonance of these images, which have been copied endlessly in popular imagery, is rooted at least in part in the sheer physical appeal of the figure: "Even at the end of the trail, the fearless warrior, with all his depressive weariness, is irresistibly appealing."[33] Although to call these early images "sex objects" would be stretching a point, we see the appeal of the exhausted, victimized warrior returning more explicitly later. Striking about all these images, whether verbal or visual, is that the representation is always of Indian men either alone, as the object of the white gaze, or in relation to white women. The Indian woman is absent—the very conception of Indian men and women interacting together in some real, cultural world is simply not part of the construction.

This has continued into contemporary mass culture. The physical attractiveness of the "noble" Indian male, as I suggest above, has not been unnoticed in early popular culture, although it has been repressed and condemned. As early as the 1920 version of *The Last of the Mohicans,* the allure of the "good" Indian to white women was acknowledged. Cora admires Uncas to the British Captain Randolf: "Surely among his own people he is a prince!" Randolf is suitably disgusted: "You! The daughter of Colonel Munro! Admiring a filthy savage!"[34] This mutual attraction was developed in subsequent versions of the film. Later Hollywood productions like *Apache* (1964) allowed white stars like Burt Lancaster to bare their bodies far more than they could in "white" roles.

Turning to the romance novel, we find that in the 1990s, the wild, rapacious beast has been replaced by a kinder, gentler version of savage. In a recent study of male Indian imagery in film, romance novels, and other popular media, Peter Van Lent convincingly shows that the image of the

Indian male has become a cultural icon in the 1990s. Perhaps in response to cultural uncertainties about "correct" male roles, the Indian man, usually placed in a safe, "dead" historical context, has finally become a thorough-going sex object.[35] Young Indian men are handsome and virile, with the potential for decisive action when pressed, yet tender, loving, and vulnerable, in a way that white action heroes rarely are. Thus, Indian or mixed-blood men prove incredible lovers for white women in romance novels, while Indian women are invisible. The Indian heroes are strong, yet tender, as in a typical scene from a 1996 romance, *Too Tough to Tame:* "His arms were bands of steel and velvet around her, powerful but gentle. . . . She felt as if she were a feather, floating in his arms" (fig. 3.1).[36]

The captivity narrative has proven to be a resilient myth that can be interpreted and reconstructed to fit the times—collapsing fiction, history, and folklore into a continuing, malleable narrative. In this mythical realm, the Indian male becomes anything the current white culture wants him to be and so does his sexuality. In romance novels, the captivity narrative moves on to a new stage of development, providing the framework for almost all examples of the genre. Romance author Cassie Edwards, for example, won the *Romantic Times* "Lifetime Achievement Award for Best Indian Romance Series," for her continuing "Savage Series." These books range across nineteenth-century Indian country, where beautiful white women are captured with regularity. "Searching the wilds of the Wyoming Territory for her outlaw brother, Rebecca Veach is captured by [Blazing Eagle,] the one man who fulfills her heart's desire" *(Savage Secrets);* "Alone in the Kentucky wilderness . . . Pamela and Strong Bear share a forbidden love forged in a breathless rapture of mounting ecstasy" *(Savage Eden);* "[In] the lush forests of Minnesota . . . she is his captive. Yet even as she trembles before his masterful gaze, Jeanine's ripe young body begins to smolder with a newfound desire . . . his gleaming, bronzed chest and hard-muscled arms ensure her surrender" *(Savage Splendor).*[37]

Significantly, although these Indian men are strong and virile, they are also vulnerable. As Van Lent points out, a common characteristic of Indian heroes is that they are often victimized, forced to suffer, lose their culture, and even die. The romance hero Storm, in Deborah Camp's *Too Tough to Tame,* begins the book severely wounded, and the heroine nurses him back to life; other heroes have to accept the reality of the impending doom of their people. In a 1994 television movie, *Cheyenne Warrior,* the romance also begins with the near-death of the hero, followed by a growing attraction between him and his nurse / lover. Eventually they separate, and the warrior

FIGURE 3.1. An example of the Indian romantic hero. (Copyright HarperCollins/Avon Books)

rides off to a fate as inevitable as that of the doomed lover Uncas in *The Last of the Mohicans.* The pathos of the *End of the Trail* is an integral part of the attraction of the wounded Indian lover. Feminist critics have pointed to the seemingly perverse attraction that women often have for suffering men. As Kirkham and Thumim put it, "the penetration of wounding and its consequent invalidity . . . places the male in the position of the female and allows for female recognition, empathy and the acknowledgment of sexual attraction. . . . The physical and psychological wounding of the male marks him as vulnerable, in the manner of the wounded Christ—an ultimate symbol of male vulnerability."[38] Handsome Indian men fit the "wounded" role perfectly—not only are they often personally victimized, but, carrying the resonance of the *End of the Trail* with them, they represent the tragedy of their vanished race.

Chelley Kitzmiller, author of several Apache romances, conducted a survey of on-line Indian romance readers. She summarizes the "allure" of the genre as "the stoic Indian brave with his long, black hair, riding bareback across the plain . . . the half-naked warrior fighting to preserve his home, his family, his people and his way of life against the greedy White Eyes . . . [and] the forbidden love factor of the handsome young brave and his white female captive."[39] According to her survey, readers enjoy rooting for the outsider, the honorable "underdog." They "see the Apache hero as an honest man, a truthful man—a man who is strong in mind and body and who will fight and die for what he believes in, his people and his way of life." She quotes one reader: "The archetypal view is strength, protection, honesty, love of the land, animals, and God. A very romantic archetype, I think!"

Of course, these romantic Indian or half-Indian heroes are always inexorably drawn to white women. The romance hero Storm is wounded because he was discovered in bed with a white woman. He laments: "White women. Would he ever learn to stay away from the pale-haired witches?"[40] Naturally Storm fails to learn and falls in love with the heroine, "a moon maiden with golden hair and alabaster skin kissed here and there by the sun."[41] In the publicity blurb for Cassie Edwards's *Savage Spirit,* we learn that Apache chief Cloud Eagle is helpless: "Her snow-white skin makes him tremble with longing; her flame-red hair sets his senses ablaze." Indian women are presented as Squaws, who put up with the fact that once their men have laid eyes on a white woman, their own women lose all their appeal. The prevailing view of Indian women in the books is summarized in *Comanche,* a book purportedly written by model Fabio. The heroine is discussing the fate of white women in history who have been captured by the Indians, never to return: "Agnes had disappeared to become another faceless squaw and breeder among the People."[42] In some of these books, "squaws" will put up with drudgery and abuse from their men, accepting the need to "service" any man who wants them, while the proud white captive refuses to submit.

The Indian romance novel has moved to the screen fairly successfully. *Cheyenne Warrior* drew from the genre, as did a 1995 movie, *Follow the River,* based on a captivity tale. In that film, the handsome, sensitive Indian captor (Eric Schweig, who also played Uncas in the 1992 version of *Last of the Mohicans*) falls in love with his white captive (Sheryl Lee), whom he abducts along with her children, but never wins her. She is clearly drawn to him in several erotically charged scenes, but does not succumb and eventually escapes. In the final scene, the honorable Indian brings her children back to her, in a gesture of selfless love. The 1995 theatrical release *A Good Day to Die,* starring Sydney Poitier, features a young, orphaned Indian named White Wolf (Billy Wirth), who is raised by a white Indian agent and falls in love with the man's daughter. The father forbids the romance, but the two eventually run away together, with tragic consequences—White Wolf has killed the woman's abusive husband, and he dies in a hail of vengeful white gunfire. The 1992 Michael Mann version of *The Last of the Mohicans* lovingly displays the physical attractions of both Eric Schweig, as Uncas, and Daniel Day-Lewis, as Indian wanna-be Hawkeye, although of course only the white hero survives to enjoy the love of a white woman.

The full-blown Indian captivity romance moved to television in a 1997 CBS movie of the week, *Stolen Women, Captured Hearts.* This production, "based on a true story," traced the romance of Anna Morgan (Janine Turner), who was captured in 1868 by Lakota Chief Tokalah, played by Cree actor Michael Greyeyes.[43] The love story follows the now-standard pattern of the captivity romance. At first, she refuses to cooperate, while the arrogant chief tries to make her bring him food and behave as an Indian woman should. Meanwhile, she sneaks furtive glances at his seminaked body and gazes from the tepee at an eroticized scene in which Tokalah dances at the campfire. She finally escapes, but is caught, at which point the couple have an angry scene that culminates in their passionate embrace, followed by a night of lovemaking. It emerges that Tokalah had long ago had a vision in which he saw Anna as his destiny, a common motif in Indian romance novels. Their happiness is shattered when General George Armstrong Custer is dispatched to retrieve the captured women, which he does through an exchange of prisoners. Anna, however, is unable to adjust to life with her unloved husband, so she rides off to her lover, whom she finds broken and weeping around the smoking wreckage of his village. The final shot of the film shows them embracing, nothing certain except the un-disputed fact that love conquers all. The movie was a success, finishing twelfth in the ratings that week, and it has since been rerun at least once.

Anna Morgan's story seems an odd choice for such a retelling, given that there is ambiguous evidence, at best, that her capture ended in love for her captor, unlike the experiences of Cynthia Ann Parker and Mary Jemison. Morgan, who was captured along with Sarah White, may indeed have married a chief, "but whether she willingly consented to the marriage is doubtful."[44] She gave birth to a son, conceived during her captivity, who died at age two, and there is some evidence that "she was placed in a home for the feeble-minded in Topeka, where she died."[45]

Even in these thorough-going romances, however, the brutal savage still lurks. In many, possibly the majority, of romance novels, the hero is described as having white blood, which tempers his savagery with a touch of civilization. Even if he is full-blood, he is often seen as more rational and realistic than other men of his tribe, who have a tendency to raid, pillage, and fight among themselves when not listening to his wise advice. The hero is frequently seen as the voice of progress, who realizes change is coming. In other words, the Indian hero is a wonderful fantasy figure for the white reader—just wild enough to be exciting, while still "civilized" enough to be acceptable.

What these romantic young Indian men have in common is relative powerlessness. They are physically strong, of course, but structurally impo-tent. Constantly, they represent a dying culture, even when not dying themselves, as they are loved by more powerful white women or serve as the sidekick for more powerful white men. They evoke admiration and pity, but they are not a threat. This, especially in the past, was the key to being able to view them as exposed, naked, and objectified, in a way that white men could not be viewed.

THE WISE ELDER

In addition to the young, romantic hero, there is another male Indian type. Indian men, more than women, were the focus of the wave of fascination with things Indian that first crested in the 1960s and 1970s when the counter-culture embraced Indians as purveyors of ancient wisdom and spiritual knowledge.[46] Once again, this image of the Wise Elder was not new; nineteenth-century advertisements often portrayed images of "old sachems," or "wise chiefs," hawking patent medicines and herbal remedies, along with their Princess daughters. Daniel Francis writes of the careers of two men, "Grey Owl" and "Chief Long Lance," who gained international fame as writers in the 1920s and 1930s. Long Lance claimed to be Cherokee; in his autobiography he wrote words of wisdom about the "old ways," and he later appeared in movies. Eventually, he was exposed as a fake who was raised as Southern black or "colored" and whose writings were entirely imaginative. Grey Owl, who became a spokesperson for wildlife and nature, turned out to be an Englishman named Archie Belaney; he has just become the subject of a new movie Grey Owl, starring Pierce Brosnan. Their importance to the Wise Elder stereotype is that the admiring acceptance of people like Grey Owl by white audiences was not so much because of what they said, but because they "spoke with the accumulated wisdom of the people who had inhabited the eastern woodlands for thousands of years."[47] In other words, being a "real Indian" was crucial. The same "authenticity" was central to the taking up of the largely reconstructed 1854 speech of Chief Seattle by environmentalists in the early 1970s and the enormous success of Carlos Castaneda's "Yaqui Medicine Man" Don Juan during the same period.[48] A widely popularized image of the Wise Elder was the famous 1972 advertising campaign featuring actor Iron Eyes Cody, apparently gazing at the environmental havoc wrought by white culture, a single tear forming in the corner of his eye. Powerfully playing on the stereotype of the stoic Indian, this image suggested that the defilement of nature was perhaps the only thing that could move an Indian to tears. Ironically, it now turns out that Cody was not a "real" Indian either, but an Italian-American named Espera DeCorti, who lived out a lifetime fantasy of being Indian.[49] The Indian Elder who is close to nature and wise beyond white understanding began to appear in films like Little Big Man (1971) and One Flew Over the Cuckoo's Nest (1975) and returned in force after Dances with Wolves (1990).

The fascination with a largely invented notion of Indian spirituality subsided somewhat in the 1980s, although the Indian "wanna-be" phenomenon was gaining momentum, with the fascination rising again in the 1990s, this time in a more mainstream, ecologically minded form.[50] In the 1990s, as never before, Indians were chic—mystical, wise, earth-loving, and tragic. New Age culture appropriated Indian religious practices, clothing, music, and myths, while Indian-inspired art and design became all the rage.[51] In this trend, Indian culture is yet again commodified and made the object of white consumption, as it has been for centuries. The new mystical Indian man is in late middle age, gray haired, somber, and wise. He is represented on greeting cards and popular art, clad in buffalo robes and feathers. Unlike his younger counterpart, he is rarely scantily clad, and he is definitely *not* a sex object. Unlike the young Brave, the Wise Elder has power; he communes with the spirits and passes on his wisdom, usually to white people. Whereas the young Warrior represents the pathos of a doomed race, the Wise Elder represents the way the wisdom of the lost race can be incorporated peacefully into the modern world. In period pieces like *Dances with Wolves* and *Little Big Man,* elderly chiefs speak wisely about the inevitability of white domination, while younger hotheads protest. In movies set in more recent times, these older men provide a spiritual dimension in films like *Free Willy* (1993), *Legends of the Fall* (1994), and even *Natural Born Killers* (1994).

These Wise Elders are usually isolated from other Indians—they are mysterious loners whose role in the film is to advise the white heroes. *Legends of the Fall* is a classic example of Indian identity being appropriated to add mystery and resonance to white characters' life problems. The film is narrated by Gordon Tootoosis as a Cree elder with no family and no apparent goal in life other than to frame the life of hero Tristan Ludlow (Brad Pitt) in terms of an epic, spiritual identification with the Bear. On television, the stereotypical "mystical wise man" pops up in action adventures such as CBS's *Walker, Texas Ranger,* where the supposedly part-Native hero (Chuck Norris) is advised and inspired by his Indian uncle and mentor on a semiregular basis. Once again, the mentor is disassociated from any tribal context of his own. The Wise Elder appears regularly in popular television shows of all kinds; for instance in a 1996 episode of the CBS series *Touched by an Angel,* the Judeo-Christian guardian angels enlist the help of a wise Navajo elder (Russell Means) to help a young Jewish archaeologist repudiate his godless ways and find spiritual redemption. Even the fluffy syndicated series *Baywatch,* reportedly the most popular series in the world, gave its nod to Indian spirituality in an episode featuring a tribal elder's wish to die on a beach and the legal fight for him to do so.[52] When he actually dies, surrounded by chanting Indians, the audience is treated to a slow-motion image of an eagle ascending the sky, apparently representing his departing spirit.

Rather unusually, *Dr. Quinn, Medicine Woman* has flirted with both stereotypes embodied in the same character. The series began with its only major Cheyenne character, medicine man Cloud Dancing (Larry Sellers), married and a member of a village. However, no other Indian characters were ever fully developed, and most, including his wife, were killed off. Once alone, Cloud Dancing became the epitome of the stoic, strong, noble male Indian, who suffers horrendous personal losses with dignity and forgiveness. However, after the destruction of his village at the infamous "battle" of Washita, his rare appearances focused on a rather unlikely romance with a middle-aged white woman, and he became the sole representative of Indian cultures, shifting uneasily from Wise Elder to Warrior Stud.

With this odd exception, the Indian Elder is uniformly desexualized, in that he appears not to have a family or an identity himself. His culture is only relevant in so far as it serves the white hunger for spirituality. And like his younger, sexier counterpart, he assuages white guilt. The Warrior's fight was noble, but of course futile, whereas the Wise Elder recognized the inevitable and now uses his power only to aid white culture. Whether he is eroticized as a sex object or coopted as a spiritual resource, the sexuality of the Indian male is successfully contained and the existence of sexuality among Indian people is erased.

Princess or Squaw: The Objectification of the Indian Woman

As Albers and James note, popular imagery of Indians has tended to be focused on males. They trace, for example, the tradition of portraying Indian women on postcards, which usually took the form of photographs of anonymous women, unlike the male images, which usually named the "chiefs" and "warriors" they portrayed. Whereas Indian men appear in white mythology as named individuals—Crazy Horse, Sitting Bull, Geronimo—women are represented only by Pocahontas, Sacagawea, and nameless artisans or "squaws." Just as male imagery traditionally alternated between nobility and savagery, so female Indian imagery is bifurcated, although equally objectified, and contains the same mixture of erotic fascination and revulsion. From early times, a dominant image was the Indian Princess, represented most thoroughly by Pocahontas, the seventeenth-century sachem's daughter who, according to legend, threw herself in front of her tribe's executioners to save the life of colonist Captain John Smith. Even before this, the Indian Queen image had been used widely to represent the exoticism of America, evolving into the dusky Princess who "continued to stand for the New World and for rude native nobility."[53] The imagery of the American land as an Indian maiden was tenacious. Roger

Fischer describes a centerfold article in an 1889 issue of *Puck* magazine, welcoming Washington, Montana, and the two Dakotas to statehood, and "portraying the older states as white debutantes in gowns, Montana as a pioneer lass in buckskin, and Washington and North and South Dakota as beautiful, bronzed but thoroughly Caucasoid Indian maidens."[54] The Maiden or Princess is the female counterpart of the "noble savage" portrayed by the early colonists and artists, although significantly the two images are rarely seen together as part of a representation of an Indian culture—each is presented separately for white perusal. After all, if the Princess represents the virgin land that will be possessed by the white man, it would be somewhat inconvenient if she already owed her allegiance to a native Prince.

As Robert Tilton describes it, the Pocahontas/Princess myth became a crucial part in the creation of a national identity: The Indian Princess became an important, nonthreatening symbol of white Americans' right to be here, because she was always willing to sacrifice her happiness, cultural identity, and even her life for the good of the new nation.[55] Endless plays, novels, and poems were written about Pocahontas, extolling her beauty and nobility. The prevailing view of the Princess was that she was gentle, noble, nonthreateningly erotic, virtually a white Christian, yet different, because she was tied to the native soil of America. As Tilton explains, the Pocahontas/Princess story enabled the white United States, but especially the South, to justify its dominance, providing a kind of origin myth that explained how and why Indians had welcomed the destiny brought to them by whites.

The sexualized Indian Princess stereotype thrived in the nineteenth century. As Rayna Green points out, "the society permitted portrayals to include sexual references (bare and prominent bosoms) for females even when tribal dress and ethnography denied the reality of the reference."[56] Scherer mentions the tradition of "cheesecake" photographs of half-naked Indian women; sculptures, such as Joseph Mozier's 1859 *Pocahontas,* portrayed bare-breasted, classical-looking figures, glancing demurely down from the white gaze. Daniel Francis describes the late-nineteenth-century success of author and poet Pauline Johnson, the daughter of a Mohawk chief. Dressed in a "polyglot" costume of ermine tails, knives, and beads, the "Mohawk Princess" declaimed melodramatic tales of doomed love between Indian women and white men.[57]

Even as the noble Indian Maiden was exotic and desirable, nineteenth-century white society was still uneasy about the implications of that desire.

Popular tales abounded of the fate that befell white men who married Indian women, but especially the women themselves, epitomized by Ann S. Stephens's dime novel *Malaeska: The Indian Wife of the White Hunter* (1861). In that story, Malaeska married a white man and gave birth to a son, who eventually rejected her and killed himself when he learned his mother was Indian. Malaeska died, "the heart broken victim of an unnatural marriage."[58] As Namias points out, the Indian women who married white men, although often doomed, were generally seen as noble, selfless, and willing to sacrifice themselves for love. Often carefully described as unlike their more degraded sisters, they sometimes turned out (quite logically) not to be Indians at all, but enculturated white captives. In this way, the white man's exotic fascination with the Indian woman could be indulged, yet tamed in "the dream of finding the dark woman of his dreams, who was a kind of white girl next door with whom to settle down and love happily ever after."[59] Like the later romanticized male Indian or half-blood heroes, these noble Indian maidens or exotic white captives have all the trappings of exciting "Indianness," but usually side with whites and aid their white lovers against the intemperate savagery of their compatriots.

As with males, the lustful and inhuman savage is but the other face of the Maiden or Princess. And Indian women have endured the burden of both racial and gender stereotyping; just as popular imagery defined white women as either good or bad, virgin or whore, so it forced images of Indian women into a similar bipolar split. According to Rayna Green, the Indian Princess is defined as one who helps or saves a white man, but if she actually has a sexual relationship with a white or Indian man, she becomes a "squaw," who is lower even than a "bad" white woman.[60] The Squaw is the other side of the Indian woman—a drudge who is at the beck and call of her savage Indian husband, who produces baby after baby, who has sex endlessly and indiscriminately with whites and Indians alike. This image, like the romanticized Princess, had its roots in the very earliest accounts of Native American cultures. Vespucci's *Mundus Novus,* published around 1504, describes Native women as "tolerably beautiful and cleanly," yet they are "very libidinous," and drawn inexorably to white men: "When they had the opportunity of copulating with Christians, urged by excessive lust, they defiled and prostituted themselves."[61] John Lawson, writing in 1709, declared that "those Indian girls that have conversed with the English and other Europeans, never care for the conversation of their own Countrymen afterwards," which was no doubt convenient, because white traders "find these Indian girls very serviceable to them."[62] The use of Indian women by white men was often justified by essentially dehumanizing them—claiming that they were not capable of the same emotions as white women, even to the extent of neglecting their children. Thus, according to the 1764 captivity narrative of Henry Grace, Indian women "seem almost void of natural Affection, being more careless of their Offspring than Brutes."[63] In many such narratives, Indian women are portrayed as bloodthirsty, lazy, filthy, and prone to drunkenness, the occasional acts of kindness being interpreted as out of character or abnormal for Indian women.

Clearly, some relationships between white "squaw men" and Indian women were caring partnerships, but the overwhelming image of the Squaw is indeed that of a sexual convenience. Rayna Green documents the sad history of this image in popular songs and tales of the nineteenth century, and it lives on today in the "squaw" jokes that circulate among non-Indian people.[64] As D'Emilio and Freedman write, in the nineteenth century, "sexuality continued to serve as a powerful means by which white Americans maintained dominance over people of all races. . . . At a time when middle-class morality rested heavily upon a belief in the purity of women in the home, stereotypes of immoral women of other races contributed to the belief in white superiority."[65]

The inescapable fact about this dual imagery of Indian women is that the imagery is entirely white defined. From early contact, white observers brought their own categories and preconceptions to indigenous American cultures, and "authoritative" sources, including ethnographies, defined the role of the Indian woman in ways that bore little relationship to reality. Thus, James Hall and Thomas McKenney (who was the chief U.S. administrator of Indian affairs from 1816 to 1830) wrote in 1844: "The life of the Indian woman, under the most favourable circumstances, is one of continual labour and unmitigated hardship. Trained to servitude from infancy and condemned to the performance of the most menial offices, they are the servants rather than the companions of man."[66] No actual Indian culture saw women in these limited terms; in fact, the range of Indian cultures offered a variety of roles for women, many of them holding a great deal of honor and prestige.[67] The complexities of these roles rarely appeared in ethnography, mainstream history, or popular culture because they were not understood by white cultural observers. Thus, as Green argues, stereotypes of male and female American Indians "are both tied to definition by relationships with white men, but she (woman) is especially burdened by the narrowness of that definition."[68]

As popular media evolved, imagery of Indian women remained narrow.

The popularity of the Western genre has kept Indians locked in the past, as film and television endlessly relived the myth of the late-nineteenth-century frontier. During the "golden age" of Western film, from the 1930s through the 1950s, actual Indian characters were surprisingly rare, appearing mostly as yelling hordes, scenery, or in occasional bit parts. And, as Jane Tompkins notes, the Western is overwhelmingly male, dealing with male quests and challenges. Indian men appear as savage warriors, scouts, and occasional expendable sidekicks. Indian women disappear or surface as minor plot devices.[69]

Thus, during the height of the cinematic Western, the Squaw was the most common image of Indian women. At the same time, the sacrificing Princess stereotype was still salient. Marsden and Nachbar describe the Princess image in such early films as the 1903 *Kit Carson,* when an Indian woman helps Kit escape and is killed by her own chief. Although Pocahontas herself is portrayed in many movies, others replay the theme in other guises: *The Squaw's Sacrifice* (1909), *The Heart of the Sioux* (1910), *The Indian Maid's Sacrifice* (1911), *The Heart of an Indian* (1913).[70]

From the 1920s to 1940s, the portrayal of the Princess declined. She returned with the "sensitive" Westerns of the 1950s and beyond, led especially by director Delmer Daves's *Broken Arrow,* released in 1950. This film told the story of a white man (James Stewart), who, in the course of setting up a peace accord with Apache Chief Cochise (a prototype Wise Elder), falls in love with and marries Sonseeahray, or Morning Star (Debra Paget), an Apache woman who is, naturally, a princess. Sonseeahray dies after being shot by a white man who is breaking the peace. But, as always, her death is not in vain. As the Stewart character speaks over the final scenes in the film, "The death of Sonseeahray put a seal on the peace." The Princess figure again went into decline in the 1960s, seeming outdated and of less importance to white culture. Although the graphically obscene dimension of the Squaw rarely translated into the movie era, the remnants of it remained in the few, tiny roles for Indian women in Westerns from the 1950s onward. Without the Princess stereotype, white culture had only the Squaw, and she was by definition unimportant and uninteresting.[71]

Like her Princess predecessor, the newer Squaw was devoted to a white man, but she had even less importance to the plot and was easily sacrificed if necessary. None of the famous "Indian" movies of the early 1970s had substantial roles for women. In the going-native fantasy *A Man Called Horse* (1970), the English protagonist Morgan marries the chief's sister, Running Deer, played by Corinna Tsopei, a Greek actress. Running Deer is generally the sexual aggressor, and the film suggests throughout that Indian women are naturally attracted to white rather than Indian men. Running Deer dies, of course, as does the mute Indian wife in *Jeremiah Johnson* (1972), as well as Indian wives in *The Man Who Loved Cat Dancing* (1973) and *Little Big Man* (1971). Later, the 1991 film *Black Robe,* although lavishly praised by critics for its accuracy, misrepresented the important role of Iroquoi women in political decisionmaking, as Ward Churchill points out. Worse, perhaps, the film resurrected the Squaw in Annuka, a young Algonquin woman portrayed by Sandrine Holt, who is Eurasian, not Native American. Churchill comments on "Annuka's proclivity, fair and unmarried maiden though she is, to copulate voraciously with whatever male she happens to find convenient when the urge strikes. More shocking, she obviously prefers to do it in the dirt, on all fours."[72] Only when she falls in love with Daniel, a young Frenchman, does she learn how to enjoy love and the civilized "missionary position." Once again, the message is that sexuality among Indians is casual and animal-like, although an Indian can be uplifted by a real love relationship with a white.

American Indian women are even less apparent on popular television than Indian men—there is no standard female figure comparable to the Wise Elder who can be grafted as guest star onto a range of different shows. Network television went some way in expanding the imagery of Indian women in the CBS series *Northern Exposure,* which ran from 1990 to 1995. *Northern Exposure* was set in contemporary Alaska, and the creators seemed to consciously set out to break stereotypes through all its characters. As part of an ensemble cast, the show included two Native Alaskan characters, Ed Chigliak (Darren E. Burrows) and Marilyn Whirlwind (Elaine Miles). Like all the characters on the show, neither was simple and one-dimensional, but rather displayed idiosyncratic, quirky characteristics. Ed was neither a stud nor an elder, but a classic film buff and would-be shaman, while Marilyn was a physician's receptionist who in many ways was wiser than the physician, Joel Fleischman. She was, perhaps, the Wise Elder transmogrified into female form, yet she was allowed to be sexual without being portrayed as "loose" or "squawlike." In the long term, it will be interesting to see if *Northern Exposure* has any impact on mainstream portrayals of Indians. The show was so distinctive, dreamlike, and "unrealistic" that it may be remembered as a unique and nonrepresentative moment in television. Yet when I asked Indian viewers to contrast *Northern Exposure* and *Dr. Quinn,* which is ostensibly presented as more "realistic," they all agreed that *Northern Exposure* was more "real," reflecting a sense of identification with the Native

Alaskans as human beings, rather than cardboard characters.[73] In that respect, *Northern Exposure* was in a different class from any television show, before or since.

Aside from *Northern Exposure,* the only show that includes Indians as regular characters is the aforementioned *Dr. Quinn, Medicine Woman.* Generally despised by critics, *Dr. Quinn* has proved especially popular with women, and one reason for this is its essentially feminist point of view.[74] Created and produced by Beth Sullivan, the show takes many of the standard Western formulas, such as the hero battling for justice, while transforming the hero into a woman. It is especially striking, then, that the show has failed to produce a strong Cheyenne female character. Over the five years of the show's run, the Wise Elder character of Cloud Dancing has become the sole focus of Cheyenne representation. Even before she was killed off, Tantoo Cardinal as Cloud Dancing's wife Snowbird had little to do but offer smiling advice to her husband, just as she did as Kicking Bird's wife in *Dances with Wolves* and as a nondescript wife in *Black Robe* and *Legends of the Fall.* Other Cheyenne women drift around the village, smiling and carrying babies. Cardinal must have had shows like *Dr. Quinn* in mind when she commented, "Native people are not brought into the foreground, or even accepted as an everyday part of life, not anywhere in the American media. It is rare, rare, rare that you see anything about Native people as human beings."[75]

In one episode of *Dr. Quinn,* the show displaced Indian women completely, while trying to use their cultural experience to make a 1990s' moral point. It focused on a woman who is the sole survivor of an Army raid on her Cheyenne village. She is brought to town, where she faces the ignorance and racism of the local people and meanwhile proves to be a temporary rival for hero Sully's affections. This story offered a chance to develop a Cheyenne female character more fully, and yet this is avoided—it turns out the woman is white and was merely raised Cheyenne. She fits perfectly into the pattern of white female Indian adoptees that we have seen in movies from *Soldier Blue* to *Dances with Wolves.* In this context, the white woman essentially stands in for the Indian woman, apparently making the character more interesting for white viewers. Just as with the nineteenth-century white man/white captive romances, the audience can vicariously enjoy "going Indian" without having to see a real Indian woman as an engaging individual. At the end of the 1994–1995 season, the producers seem to have found the strain of incorporating Indian characters too much and killed off most of them, including Snowbird. Her dying words to Dr. Quinn are typically designed to assuage white guilt: "One day, perhaps many seasons from now, my people and your people will come to understand each other and no longer be afraid."

In the mid-1990s, living, breathing Indian women have become largely invisible and irrelevant in mainstream popular culture. In fact, the most prominent Indian icon of the decade was, perhaps fittingly, a cartoon. In spite of being touted as a feminist rendering of the tale, Disney's 1995 animated feature *Pocahontas* clearly echoes the old imagery. Pocahontas persuades her father to make peace, even though it is not clear why it is in her best interests to do so. She rejects the Indian man chosen for her in favor of the Nordic John Smith. And even though she eventually loses her lover, Pocahontas learns to recognize the inevitability of "progress," an important, guilt-reducing element in the white image of Indians. In the cartoon, Disney tells us also that Pocahontas taught John Smith respect for nature, implying that she had a profound impact on how the nation developed—a sentimentalizing of the way things actually happened and a kind of collective fantasy that recalls the sentimental image of Pocahontas embraced in the nineteenth century. Disney's version harks back to Victorian imagery in other ways. The cartoon character is notably voluptuous and scantily clad, as were the earlier images; the film even echoes Victorian conventions in showing Pocahontas as lighter skinned than the men of her tribe.

This *Pocahontas* is still a white fantasy, a point emphasized in another recent rendering of the tale, a 1995 television movie/video release, *Pocahontas: The Legend.* Cowritten and directed by Daniele J. Suissa, the film stars Eurasian Sandrine Holt as Pocahontas, with Gordon Tootoosis as her father Powhatan, a classic Wise Elder. Standard plotlines for male captivity narratives are played out to the letter, as Pocahontas is irresistibly drawn to John Smith (Miles O'Keefe) from the moment she sees him. When he is captured, she ministers to him, bathing him and helping him heal, before falling into his bed. The young warrior Kocoum (Billy Merasty) is treacherous and evil, betraying his own people through his lust for guns and power, underlining further the purity of Pocahontas's love and the wisdom of her quest for peace. As Tilton writes about the Pocahontas tale generally, "We might argue that if one were to formulate the narrative from an Indian perspective, Pocahontas would have to be presented as an extremely problematic character."[76] Naturally, we have seen no dramatizations that seek to do that.

And the Disney-led revival of the Pocahontas story has breathed new life into an Indian Princess stereotype that never really disappeared. The image lives on in local legends about Indian maidens and princesses who leaped to their deaths for love of a handsome brave or a white man.[77] It makes occasional forays into romance novels, such as Cassie Edwards's 1997 *Savage Longings*. Indian heroines in romances are rare, partly because they would not fit easily into the captivity structure—the power relations between a white male captive and an Indian female captor would be too uncomfortable. Instead, *Savage Longings* follows the pattern of the white hero who brings an Indian bride home, although in the 1990s the end result is happiness. Indian women in the story are drudges or worse, with the exception of the heroine, Snow Deer, a "Cheyenne Princess," who lives with her father, Blazing Eagle, and his white wife, Rebecca, the central couple in one of Edwards's earlier *Savage* novels. Years before, Blazing Eagle's Indian wife (and Snow Deer's mother), "a cruel, spiteful woman," had deserted her husband, and Snow Deer was reunited with her father as a young child.[78] Fortunately, Rebecca's influence has enabled Snow Deer to learn English and acquire a certain level of civilization: "My mother brought her book knowledge to not only her family, but also our people."[79] Snow Deer is thus well-prepared to meet and fall in love with the handsome Charles Cline, who makes her heart beat in a way no man has before. He, of course, is entranced by her sweet innocence and perfect beauty: "He did not want to let his eyes linger on how her wet buckskin dress clung to her shapely figure so tightly, revealing her beautifully rounded breasts, her tiny waist, and her tapered thighs."[80] After various travails, the couple marry, and Snow Deer learns to become a perfect white wife and mother, changing her name to Mame. Meanwhile, her brother also marries a white spouse and leaves the village to live with his wife. Strikingly, no successful Cheyenne-Cheyenne marriages appear in the book.

With a few exceptions, however, the romance with an Indian heroine has not been widespread or popular, undoubtedly because targeted readers are white women. The Maiden or Princess is still around, however, on Pocahontas-inspired merchandise, "collector plates," and so on. Just as the Wise Elder has become an important symbol of ancient wisdom and harmony with nature, so has the Indian Maiden, although more frequently in graphic art rather than television and movies. Gift shops abound with "artworks" of round-eyed Indian maidens in fringed white dresses; "princesses" named "Little Flower" or "White Dove" gaze provocatively from the cover of greeting cards. The design on a typical recent "collectable" plate, entitled "Native Harmony," shows a very Caucasian-looking Indian woman, with flowing hair, beautiful buckskins, and an entourage of wolves: "A beautiful young maiden greets the long lost wolf brother she raised from a pup and set free."[81] Barbara Babcock points to the long-standing place of the female Pueblo body in the white appreciation of Southwestern arts and crafts: "An Indian mother shaping Mother Earth and gracefully carrying her burdens was and is indeed something of a bourgeois dream of an alternative redemptive life."[82] In whatever representational context, the Indian Maiden is almost always seen alone—not as the partner of the Warrior, who, of course, prefers white women.

Challenging the Imagery

Although mainstream popular culture offers little subjectivity to the Indian, male or female, the impetus for change is mounting. Independent Indian filmmakers are producing their own movies that speak about who they are, and there are more Indian people in production roles in Hollywood.[83] Nevertheless, in 1995, Leuthold wrote that no major feature film had as yet been directed by an American Indian.[84] Since then, Sherman Alexie and Chris Eyre have made *Smoke Signals,* a critically praised film that premiered in 1998, but even this film has not received the wide distribution given to major Hollywood "Indian" movies.[85] As always, resources for large, mainstream productions go where money can be made, and as long as Indians are not considered marketable in their own right, change will be slow.

When the conventional wisdom is challenged, it is usually by independent producers. In documentary filmmaking, American Indians have made great strides in gaining control over their own representation.[86] In the area of features, the National Film Board of Canada has produced many films, including a 1986 series of four one-hour television movies called "Daughters of the Country." These features told four different stories of Indian or Metis women, from the eighteenth century to the present. They were unusual in that they used a mostly Native cast, but the films were extraordinary in that they told their stories from the point of view of the women who were their central figures, as *Smoke Signals* did. Instead of movies that gaze at Indians through the eyes of white settlers, soldiers, or trappers, we see those whites as interlopers, whose ways are strange and alien. Life in the Ojibwa village is simple, mundane, and the characters concentrate more on survival and everyday tasks than on mystical ceremonies. The lead roles, such as Hazel King as Ikwe or Mireille Deyglun in the title role of *Mistress*

Madeleine, are neither voluptuous princesses nor dumpy squaws, but ordinary women who face human dilemmas that are not defined by their ethnicity.

In the more commercial arena, we saw a hopeful sign in the Turner Broadcasting series on *The Native Americans,* which attempted to dramatize historic moments in Indian history in a series of feature-length television films made in the mid-1990s. Although *Geronimo* and *The Broken Chain* were dismissed by at least one Indian critic as "feeble," the same writer had kinder words for *Lakota Woman: Siege at Wounded Knee,* a dramatization of the autobiography of Mary Crow Dog, who took part in the 1973 American Indian Movement (AIM) siege at Wounded Knee.[87] The movie was made with a 90 percent Indian cast, and 40 percent of the crew were Indians, offering unprecedented opportunities for Indian people to gain experience in filmmaking techniques. Executive Producer Lois Bonfiglio described the filming as "an extraordinary spiritual and emotional experience" for everyone involved. Indeed, the movie proved exceptional in that, like the smaller-budget Canadian films, it told the story from the point of view of Mary Crow Dog, played effectively by Irene Bedard (the voice of Disney's Pocahontas). The film does not glamorize Indian women: Mary is seen sinking into a life of alcoholism and promiscuity before being transformed by the message of AIM. But neither does it stereotype her as a degraded Squaw; she is simply a human being, dealing with a set of problems and issues, many of which confront her because of her ethnic heritage. Although some may be cynical that Ted Turner and Jane Fonda were merely jumping on the Indian bandwagon, *Lakota Woman* does offer a step in the right direction.

Finally, it will be interesting to watch the further development of the career of Graham Greene, the Canadian Oneida actor who first came to prominence as Kicking Bird in *Dances with Wolves.* The character of Kicking Bird was neither a Warrior Stud nor a Wise Elder, but a quirky, intelligent individual who defied stereotypes, even being allowed a sexual relationship with his wife. Greene went on to play another, nonstereotypical character in *Thunderheart* (1992), although the film as a whole fell frequently into New Age–type mysticism about Indians. Most recently, and surprisingly, Greene appeared in *Die Hard III* (1995), a Bruce Willis action movie, portraying one of Willis's police colleagues. The role was not written as "Indian," and indeed no mention of Greene's ethnicity was made. Although even he seems doomed always to be the sidekick for a white star, Graham Greene may be the only Indian actor to have transcended the standard "Indian" role, perhaps because he is neither young and handsome nor elderly and wise-looking—just a competent and engaging performer.

Conclusion

The fact that these stereotypes have been around so long demonstrates the way they have become entrenched in white mythology. Where personal knowledge is lacking, media have additional power as agents of enculturation, and in many parts of the country non-Indians never see or encounter a real, living Indian person. In JoEllen Shiveley's study, whites saw Westerns as historically accurate, whereas Indians did not. The point is that Westerns, even family television ones like *Dr. Quinn,* feel "authentic" to white audiences—a myth that is "an affirmation of their own social experience."[88]

At present, with the popular infatuation with things Indian, there are probably more roles than ever for Indian actors in mainstream popular media, and Indian images are everywhere in our culture. But these roles are inevitably subordinate and either rooted in the past or in a conception of Indians as "traditional." Most important, as I have endeavored to show, the representations we do see are structured in predictable, gendered ways. Women are faceless, rather sexless Squaws in minor roles, such as in *Legends of the Fall,* or sexy exotic Princesses or Maidens who desire white men. Men are either handsome young Warriors, who desire white women, or safely sexless Wise Elders, who dispense ancient wisdom. Nowhere in this iconography do the male and female images meet—the world where Indian men and women love, laugh, and couple *together* lurks far away in the shadows. These days, representations of Indians tend to be much more "authentic" in terms of costume, cultural detail, and so on than in, say, the 1950s, when white actors darkened their skins to play Indians. But as far as media presenting an authentic, subjective Indian experience, there has been little progress.

The objectification of the male and female Indian is embedded in a complex set of cultural attitudes to both race and gender. One of the most common ways to deny other races subjectivity is to either deny their sexuality or to define it as somehow inferior or more animalistic than white sexuality. From early times, descriptions of Indian cultures have presented them as emotionally "unnatural"—they did not care for their children or their spouses; they had sex "like dogs in the dirt," as Ward Churchill puts it, and could only be stirred to more honorable feelings of love by white partners.[89] The degraded Squaw, for example, is rejected every time by decent Indian men in favor of virginal white women. This sexualization of dominated races was and is an important component of colonial domination.[90] By labeling others as sexual savages, whites "reassured themselves that their own race was indeed the civilized one it aspired to be. Distancing themselves from the sexuality of other races served instrumental, as well as symbolic, purposes. By characterizing other races as, at best, remote sexual pagans and, at worst, sexual monsters in pursuit of white women, whites could manipulate the sexual fears of their own culture in order to justify the conquest of Indians, Mexicans, and blacks."[91]

People of other races become sexually available to the dominant culture; in some sense, the dominant culture is perceived as actually elevating the oppressed by coupling with them. Thus, the gendered stereotyping of other racial groups serves to maintain white male definitions of self. The early demonizing of both Indian males and so-called squaws served to emphasize the central importance of purity among white women, allowing white men to destroy rapacious Indian men while using Indian women as conveniences, and thus helping them maintain their own racial and gender superiority. The more erotic presentation of Indian men, in times when they were not a threat, also defined the essential power of white men, in that Indian men could be displayed, naked and powerless, in a way unthinkable for their white counterparts.

The rarity with which white culture acknowledges Indian affection and sexuality is emphasized in two unrelated vignettes. Sherry Smith describes Captain John Gregory Bourke's account of his visit to Santa Domingo Pueblo in New Mexico in 1881, where, unnoticed, he watched two lovers: "The Indian man approached the woman, Bourke wrote, and 'was received with a disdain tempered with so much sweetness and affection that he wilted at once, and instead of boldly asserting himself, dared do nothing but timidly touch her hand.' Finally, she took his grasp and 'he, with earnest warmth was purring into her ears words whose purport it was not difficult to conjecture.' "[92] Bourke continued, "So much stuff and nonsense have been written about the entire absence of affection from the Indian character, especially in relations between the sexes, that it affords me great pleasure to note this little incident, in which the parties acted with perfect freedom from the restraint the known presence of strangers imposes."[93]

A century later, one of the most striking scenes in the television movie *Lakota Woman* was a moment when Mary, as a young girl, dances with and kisses her young Indian boyfriend. It was the kind of scene that would be totally unremarkable in any white movie, yet it stood out as something we simply do not see—Indian people laughing, cuddling, and exploring their own sexuality, without regard to whites. Tantoo Cardinal, the Canadian Metis actor who has had more than her share of thinly drawn roles in movies and television, has appealed, "We have to get to a place where our Native women have a sexuality, a sensuality, an intelligence."[94] But the stereotypes of Indians, male and female, will be hard to shatter—their role as the exotic, fascinating Other is so entrenched and so naturalized. As Gayatri Spivak comments, "The person who *knows* has all of the problems of selfhood. The person who is *known* seems not to have a problematic self."[95] That has been the issue with the representation of American Indians for centuries: White culture has "known" them, gazed on them, and objectified them, appropriating their sexual and personal identities for its own purposes. The 1990s' lovely Princess and Indian Stud may be more benign images than the Squaw or the Crazed Savage, but they are equally unreal and, ultimately, equally dehumanizing.

Notes

This chapter is an expanded version of the article "Gendered Construction of the American Indian in Popular Media," *Journal of Communication* 49, no. 4 (1999): 61–83.

1. See Berkhofer; Bird, "Not My Fantasy"; Churchill; and Francis.
2. See Derounian-Stodola and Levernier; Namias; and Strong.
3. See Griffiths.
4. Dippie, 236.
5. Deloria, 81.
6. Biolsi, 136.
7. Whiteley, 188.
8. Rosaldo, 15.
9. Greer, "Imagining," 144.
10. Ibid., 144.
11. Bird, "Not My Fantasy," 253.
12. Ibid., 253.
13. Ibid., 256.
14. Ibid., 254.
15. Morgan, 322.
16. Berkhofer, especially 72–85.
17. Namias, 88.
18. Hanson, 147.

19. See, for example, Ramsey.

20. Quoted in Kasson, 76.

21. Seaver, 52.

22. Ibid., 112.

23. Drake, 334.

24. Edgerton, 1.

25. Ibid., 6.

26. Berkhofer, 138.

27. Van Lent, 217.

28. Quoted in Billington, 110.

29. Gerdts, 129.

30. Berkhofer, 94.

31. Namias, 107.

32. Quoted in Dippie, 216.

33. Van Lent, 214.

34. Quoted in Barker and Sabin, 68.

35. See Van Lent.

36. Camp, 184.

37. As of 1997, Edwards had written seventeen books in the "Savage Series." Quotes are taken from a publicity insert (pages unnumbered) for the series included in her latest book, *Savage Longings*.

38. Kirkham and Thumim, 25.

39. Kitzmiller has written several Indian romances, including *Fires of Heaven* and *Embrace the Wind*. She kindly shared with me her account of her on-line survey summarizing "The Allure of the Indian Romance."

40. Camp, 2.

41. Ibid., 245.

42. Fabio, 54.

43. The historical facts of the case are hazy. Namias gives Morgan's name as Anna Brewster Morgan, captured by Sioux, whereas Derounian-Stodala and Levernier call her Anna Belle Morgan, taken by Cheyennes, which points to the slippery nature of these narratives.

44. Namias, 102.

45. Derounian-Stodola and Levernier, 158.

46. See Brand.

47. Francis, 139.

48. Carlos Castaneda sold millions of copies of his books, *The Teachings of Don Juan* and its sequels, but his work is now widely accepted as fabricated. See DeMille, *Castaneda's Journey* and *The Don Juan Papers*.

49. See Russell.

50. See Green, "The Tribe."

51. For a discussion of the recent appropriations of Native cultures, see Whitt. Andy Smith takes issue especially with white feminists who appropriate Indian spirituality, whereas Churchill targets the Men's Movement.

52. I am uncertain when this episode was filmed; it aired in syndication in my hometown on 22 November 1997.

53. Green, "The Pocahontas," 703.

54. Fischer, 104.

55. Tilton, 55.

56. Green, "The Indian," 593.

57. Francis, 111–21.

58. Quoted in Namias, 45.

59. Ibid., 104.

60. Green, "The Pocahontas," 702.

61. Quoted in Berkhofer, 9.

62. Quoted in Washburn, *The Indian,* 47, 46.

63. Quoted in Derounian-Stodola and Levernier, 68.

64. See Green, "The Indian." Having lived in Minnesota for eight years, teaching folklore classes in which students frequently collect jokes in field projects, I have heard many offensive jokes about Indians of both sexes. They tend to play on stereotypes of laziness, lechery, and drunkenness. I prefer not to detail any specific examples here.

65. D'Emilio and Freedman, 86.

66. McKenney and Hall, 199.

67. For a discussion of traditional roles for women in several Native cultures, see Tsosie; Lewis; and Medicine. Foster describes how strong female roles have been erased from the historical literature on the Iroquois.

68. Green, "The Pocahontas," 713.

69. Tompkins, 8.

70. See Marsden and Nachbar.

71. Indian actor Lois Red Elk remarked in 1980 that of the many minor characters she had played in her career, none was given a name (see Leuthold).

72. Churchill, 128.

73. See Bird, "Not My Fantasy."

74. See Dow.

75. Greer, "Tantoo," 153.

76. Tilton, 90.

77. See DeCaro.

78. Edwards, 25.

79. Ibid., 99.

80. Ibid., 68.

81. Advertisement for "Native Harmony" limited-edition collector plate,

produced by Bradford Exchange of Niles, Illinois, priced at $29.95, appearing in several, undated issues of the *St. Petersburg Times* Sunday newspaper advertising supplement, June 1997.

82. Babcock, 44.

83. See Weatherford.

84. Leuthold, 155.

85. *Smoke Signals,* directed by Eyre from a story by Alexie, premiered at the Sundance Film Festival. It was shown at the Taos Talking Picture Festival in April 1998. Rick Romancito, a reviewer for the *Taos News,* wrote that the film helps "to define an American Indian genre in film . . . that neither relies on or even feels a need to acknowledge the dominant cinematic culture."

86. See Prins.

87. Merritt, 90.

88. Shiveley, 733.

89. Churchill, 128.

90. See Hall.

91. D'Emilio and Freedman, 107.

92. S. Smith, 63.

93. Ibid., 63.

94. Greer, "Tantoo," 153.

95. Gunew, 202.

Works Cited

Albers, Patricia C., and William R. James. "Illusion and Illumination: Visual Images of American Indian Women in the West." Pp. 35–52 in *The Women's West,* edited by S. Armitage and E. Jameson. Norman: University of Oklahoma Press, 1987.

Babcock, Barbara. "Pueblo Cultural Bodies." *Journal of American Folklore* 107 (1994): 40–54.

Baird, Robert. "Going Indian: Discovery, Adoption, and Renaming Toward a 'True American,' from *Deerslayer* to *Dances with Wolves.*" Pp. 195–210 in *Dressing in Feathers,* ed. S. Elizabeth Bird. Boulder, Colo.: Westview Press, 1996.

Barker, Martin, and Roger Sabin. *The Lasting of the Mohicans: History of American Myth.* Jackson: University Press of Mississippi, 1995.

Bataille, Gretchen M., and Kathleen M. Sands. *American Indian Women: Telling Their Lives.* Lincoln: University of Nebraska Press, 1984.

Berkhofer, Robert F. *The White Man's Indian.* New York: Vintage Books, 1979.

Billington, Ray A. *Land of Savagery, Land of Promise.* Norman: University of Oklahoma Press, 1981.

Biolsi, Thomas. "The Anthropological Construction of 'Indians': Haviland Scudder Mekeel and the Search for the Primitive in Lakota Country." Pp. 133–59 in *Indians and Anthropologists: Vine Deloria Jr. and the Critique of Anthropology*, ed. T. Biolsi and L. J. Zimmerman. Tucson: University of Arizona Press, 1997.

Bird, S. Elizabeth. "Not My Fantasy: The Persistence of Indian Imagery in *Dr. Quinn, Medicine Woman.*" Pp. 245–62 in *Dressing in Feathers*, ed. S. Elizabeth Bird. Boulder, Colo.: Westview Press, 1996.

Brand, Stewart. "Indians and the Counterculture, 1960s–1970s." Pp. 570–72 in *Handbook of North American Indians*, Vol. 4, ed. Wilcomb E. Washburn. Washington, D.C.: Smithsonian Institution Press, 1988.

Camp, Deborah. *Too Tough to Tame*. New York: Avon, 1996.

Churchill, Ward. *Indians Are Us: Culture and Genocide in Native North America*. Monroe, Maine: Common Courage Press, 1994.

DeCaro, Francis. "Vanishing the Red Man: Cultural Guilt and Legend Formation." *International Folklore Review* 4 (1986): 74–80.

Deloria, Vine Jr. *Custer Died for Your Sins: An Indian Manifesto*. Norman: University of Oklahoma Press, 1988.

D'Emilio, John, and Estelle Freedman. *Intimate Matters: A History of Sexuality in America*. New York: Harper and Row, 1988.

DeMille, Richard. *Castaneda's Journey*. Santa Barbara, Calif.: Capra, 1976.

——, ed. *The Don Juan Papers: Further Castaneda Controversies*. Belmont, Calif.: Wadsworth, 1990.

Derounian-Stodola, Kathryn Z., and James A. Levernier. *The Indian Captivity Narrative, 1550–1900*. New York: Twayne, 1993.

Dippie, Brian W. *The Vanishing American: White Attitudes and U.S. Indian Policy*. Lawrence: University Press of Kansas, 1982.

Dow, Bonnie. *Prime Time Feminism: Television, Media Culture, and the Women's Movement since 1970*. Philadelphia: University of Pennsylvania Press, 1996.

Drake, Samuel G. "Narrative of the Captivity of Frederick Manheim." Pp. 123–39 in *Tragedies of the Wilderness, or True and Authentic Narratives of Captives*, ed. S. G. Drake. Boston: Antiquarian Bookstore, 1844.

Edgerton, Gary. "'A Breed Apart': Hollywood, Racial Stereotyping, and the Promise of Revisionism in *The Last of the Mohicans.*" *Journal of American Culture* 17 (1994): 1–19.

Edwards, Cassie. *Savage Longings*. New York: Leisure Books, 1997.

Fabio. *Comanche*. New York: Avon, 1995.

Fischer, Roger A. *Them Damned Pictures: Explorations in American Political Cartoon Art*. North Haven, Conn.: Archon, 1996.

Foster, Martha H. "Lost Women of the Matriarchy: Iroquois Women in the Historical Literature." *American Indian Culture and Research Journal* 19 (1995): 121–40.

Francis, Daniel. *The Imaginary Indian: The Image of the Indian in Canadian Culture.* Vancouver, B.C.: Arsenal Pulp Press, 1992.

Gerdts, William H. *American Neo-Classical Sculpture: The Marble Resurrection.* New York: Viking, 1973.

Green, Rayna A. "The Indian in Popular American Culture." Pp. 587–606 in *Handbook of North American Indians,* Vol. 4, ed. Wilcomb E. Washburn. Washington, D.C.: Smithsonian Institution Press, 1988.

———. "The Pocahontas Perplex: The Image of the Indian Woman in American Culture." *Massachusetts Review* 16 (1975): 698–714.

———. "The Tribe Called Wannabee: Playing Indian in America and Europe." *Folklore* 99 (1988): 30–55.

Greer, Sandy. "Imagining Indians: Native People Voice Their Concerns, Beliefs, and Action Plans at Arizona Film Festival." *Winds of Change* 9 (1994): 142–44.

———. "Tantoo Cardinal: A Part of All Nations." *Winds of Change* 9 (1994): 150–53.

Griffiths, Alison. "Science and Spectacle: Native American Representation in Early Cinema." Pp. 79–96 in *Dressing in Feathers,* ed. S. Elizabeth Bird. Boulder, Colo.: Westview Press, 1996.

Gunew, Sneja. "Questions of Multiculturalism: Interview with Gayatri Chakravorty Spivak." Pp. 193–202 in *The Cultural Studies Reader,* ed. Simon During. London: Routledge, 1993.

Hall, Stuart. "The Whites of Their Eyes: Racist Ideologies and the Media." Pp. 18–22 in *Gender, Race and Class in the Media: A Text-Reader,* ed. G. Dines and J. M. Humez. Thousand Oaks, Calif.: Sage, 1995.

Hanson, Elizabeth. "An Account of the Captivity of Elizabeth Hanson, Now or Late of Kachecky, in New England." Pp. 130–50 in *Held Captive by Indians: Selected Narratives, 1642–1836,* ed. R. Van Der Beets. Knoxville: University of Tennessee Press, 1973.

Kasson, Joy. *Marble Queens and Captives: Women in Nineteenth Century Sculpture.* New Haven, Conn.: Yale University Press, 1990.

Kirkham, Pat, and Janet Thumim, eds. *Me Jane: Masculinity, Movies, and Women.* New York: St. Martin's Press, 1995.

Leuthold, Steven M. "Native American Responses to the Western." *American Indian Culture and Research Journal* 19 (1995): 153–89.

Lewis, Oscar. "Manly Hearted Women among the South Peigan." *American Anthropologist* 43 (1941): 173–87.

Marsden, Michael T., and Jack Nachbar. "The Indian in the Movies." Pp. 607–16 in *Handbook of North American Indians,* Vol. 4, ed. Wilcomb E. Washburn. Washington, D.C.: Smithsonian Institution Press, 1988.

McKenney, Thomas L., and James Hall. *The Indian Tribes of North America.* 1844. Reprint, Edinburgh: John Grant, 1933.

Medicine, Beatrice. "Warrior Women: Sex Role Alternatives for Plains Indian

Women." Pp. 267–75 in *Hidden Half: Studies of Plains Indian Women,* ed. P. Albers and B. Medicine. Lanham, Md.: University Press of America, 1983.

Merritt, Judy. "*Lakota Woman:* Authentic Culture on Film or Exploitation?" *Winds of Change* 8 (1994): 90–93.

Morgan, Lewis Henry. *The League of the Iroquois.* 1851. Reprint, New York: Corinth, 1962.

Namias, June. *White Captives: Gender and Ethnicity on the American Frontier.* Chapel Hill: University of North Carolina Press, 1993.

Prins, Harold. "American Indians and the Ethnocinematic Complex: From Native Participation to Production Control." *Visual Sociology* 4 (1989): 85–89.

Ramsey, Colin. "Cannibalism and Infant Killing: A System of Demonizing Motifs in Indian Captivity Narratives." *Clio* 24 (1994): 53–63.

Romancito, Rick. "*Smoke Signals* Defines the Modern Indian Film," *Taos News,* 16 April 1998, C22.

Rosaldo, Renato. *Culture and Truth: The Remaking of Social Analysis.* Boston: Beacon Press, 1989.

Russell, Ron. "Make Believe Indian." *New Times Los Angeles,* 8–14 April 1999.

Scherer, Joanna C. "You Can't Believe Your Eyes: Inaccuracies in Photographs of North American Indians." *Studies in the Anthropology of Visual Communication* 2 (1975): 67–79.

Seaver, James E., ed. *A Narrative of the Life of Mrs. Mary Jemison.* 1824. Reprint, New York: Corinth, 1961.

Shiveley, JoEllen. "Cowboys and Indians: Perceptions of Western Films among American Indians and Anglos." *American Sociological Review* 57 (1992): 725–34.

Smith, Andy. "For All Those Who Were Indian in a Former Life." *Ms.* 2 (1991): 44–45.

Smith, Sherry L. "Beyond Princess or Squaw: Army Officers' Perceptions of Indian Women." Pp. 53–75 in *The Women's West,* ed. S. Armitage and E. Jameson. Norman: University of Oklahoma Press, 1987.

Strong, Pauline T. "Animated Indians: Critique and Contradiction in Commodified Children's Culture." *Cultural Anthropology* 11 (1996): 405–24.

Tilton, Robert. *Pocahontas: The Evolution of an American Narrative.* Cambridge, U.K.: Cambridge University Press, 1994.

Tompkins, Jane. *West of Everything.* New York: Oxford University Press, 1992.

Tsosie, Rebecca. "Changing Women: The Cross Currents of American Indian Feminine Identity." *American Indian Culture and Research Journal* 12 (1988): 1–38.

Van Lent, Peter. "Her Beautiful Savage: Current Sexual Images of the Native American Male." Pp. 211–28 in *Dressing in Feathers,* ed. S. Elizabeth Bird. Boulder, Colo.: Westview Press, 1996.

Washburn, Wilcomb E., ed. *The Indian and the White Man.* Documents in American Civilization Series. New York: Anchor Books, 1964.

Weatherford, Elizabeth. "Starting Fire with Gunpowder." *Film Comment* 28 (1992): 64–67.

Whiteley, Peter. "The End of Anthropology (at Hopi)?" Pp. 177–208 in *Indians and Anthropologists: Vine Deloria Jr. and the Critique of Anthropology,* ed. T. Biolsi and L. J. Zimmerman. Tucson: University of Arizona Press, 1997.

Whitt, Laurie A. "Cultural Imperialism and the Marketing of Native America." *American Indian Culture and Research Journal* 19 (1995): 1–32.

4

"Beyond Feathers and Beads"

Interlocking Narratives in the Music and Dance of Tokeya Inajin (Kevin Locke)

PAULINE TUTTLE

> Oh God, my God! Make of me a hollow reed
> from which the pith of self hath been blown,
> that I may be a clear channel
> through which Thy love may flow to others. . .
> —KEVIN LOCKE

THIS IS ONE OF THE PRAYERS Tokeya Inajin utters as he takes the stage. He embarks on this journey with certitude, exuberance, and a sense of humility, engaging and moving his audiences beyond the inscribed boundaries in which their lives and worlds unfold.[1] Be it on the grounds of a community gathering, in the center of a powwow circle, in an auditorium, or on a concert-hall stage, Kevin Locke carries the audience in and out of an interactive performative space with ease. He weaves his song, dance, and stories into an intricate polyphony highlighted by his warm sense of humor and an ongoing dialogue with those who have gathered to share this space with him.

As Kevin reenacts the Lakota music, stories, and dances that have been shared with him, he stands at the confluence of past, present, and future as an embodiment of "what can be remembered and what is imaginable."[2] This integration of physical, spiritual, conceptual, and temporal is reflected in his performances, which give voice to notions of complementarity and unity through movement, texture, color, symbol, and sound. As Kevin explains, this confluence unfolds in a detemporalized space created and transformed as he integrates the dreams and visions of his ancestors with those of his own: As soon as I play those songs I can just feel the presence of the ancestors there. It puts me in a kind of timeless place, you know. It's just like the boundary between the present and the past is dissolved and the boundary between the present and the future is evaporated and the boundary between this world and the next world is all conjoined, it all comes together. . . . I feel that way when I'm dancing too. It's really powerful. You can just feel the focus . . . and the people can feel it out there too. The many narratives and interconnecting facets of knowledge that are given form as Tokeya Inajin's performance unfolds are the focus of this chapter.

Interactive Roles of Ethnographer, Performer, and Band Historian

Scholarship on American Indian dance and music has been slow to move beyond descriptive modes and bring us closer to an understanding of both "sacred space" and "intersubjective time," which are integral to much American Indian dance, music, and ceremony.[3] Rather than being seen as a vital component of worldview and spiritual belief, scholarship has too often served as an inscriptional tool for perpetuating the age-old myth of the "noble savage."[4] The difficulties that inform Fabian's call for deeper analyses of "intersubjective time" have also generated numerous discussions about what could be termed "intersubjective space," that is, the shared space in which the interactions of performer, audience, and ethnographer take place. Here, the complementarity of their roles shapes the reinterpretation and reinscription of how song, dance, story, and performance space give form to cultural knowledge, social processes, and individual agency.

In my attempts to move beyond static theoretical and methodological parameters rooted in locale and anachronistic notions of tradition, studies of the performing arts in Africa have proven helpful. Fabian's "performative ethnography" of the emergence and actualization of the Mufwankolo theatre troupe's performances in Lubumbashi, Zaire and Erlmann's groundbreaking study of the integration of "what can be remembered and what is imaginable" in South African *isacathamiya* (nightsong) provide insightful models for both the conceptualization of my ethnographic role and my approach to this chapter. These studies are rooted in Fabian's methodology of performative ethnography, an approach that strives to enter the creative process at the heart of the performance; to determine how it gives form to cultural knowledge and social processes; and to discern the relationship between the performance, its underlying text, and the tradition in which it is embedded.[5] Thus, the focus is on process rather than product, performance as communication rather than commodity or artifact. In looking beneath the surface of a given performance, beyond what can be readily seen by either the public eye or that of the trained "observer," the interconnected strands of knowledge woven into each movement and narrative can be discerned. Entering the heart of Kevin's performance practice also gave me a keener sense of the commonalities between my role as ethnographer, his role as performative interpreter, and the role of the Lakota band historian from centuries past.

As Sandoz notes, the work of the band historian was taken extremely seriously. He was responsible for capturing up to 300 years of historical events in ledger paintings during the winter counts: "The picture is the rope that ties memory solidly to the stake of truth," was the saying of the old band historians. This task is as reminiscent of what many of us strive to achieve through our ethnographic work as it is of Kevin Locke's role as a communicator of Lakota cultural knowledge through the vehicles of song and dance. The band historian had two primary requirements. As Sandoz notes, the first was "objectivity, the ability to be in a fight or a ceremonial or hunt and yet view it beyond the purely personal involvement, observe what happened all around, see it with the eye of the people as well as an individual." To translate his observations into a meaningful form, the band historian also required artistic ability. He was expected "to portray the event or the incident so others could grasp the action and the meaning, with something beyond the factual content, something broader, . . . a meaning more elevated, more profound." Finally, after withstanding any challenges from those involved, a formal band history had to be sanctioned by the "headman" to stand as an accurate historical representation.[6]

The above criteria capture the essence of what many scholars struggle to achieve: accountability for what we write and for whom; integration of the "objective" or informative with the "subjective" or performative—to see with both "the eye of the people as well as an individual"; and translation of our experiences into a language that allows the reader to go beyond description, to grasp not only the external action and meaning of the event but also the inner meaning and its broader implications. The challenge herein is to balance the voices and conceptualization of ethnographer and performer in both description and interpretation.

Just as "the picture is the rope that ties memory solidly to the stake of truth" for the band historian, Tokeya Inajin's performances can be interpreted as a link between the traditions and dreams of the past, the truths of the present, and the potential actualization of those visions in the future. As his performances unfold, he calls his audience to serve as witness and to be accountable for their role in this process.[7] The inner meaning of this link between past, present, and future unfolds through the many narratives of

Kevin's dances and songs in a way that takes us beyond "factual content" to a "more elevated, more profound" understanding of their contemporary significance. By giving textual form to this process, I hope to contribute to the development of a performative language that acknowledges the complementarity of tradition and modernity, physical and spiritual, global and local in contemporary performance practice and speaks to ethnographer, performer, and audience alike.

To bridge the distance between ethnographer and consultant, to give visual credence to the fluidity of Kevin's performance practice, and to reflect our complementary roles in the inscription of this text, I have built on the work of Marcus in choosing to set our voices side by side rather than in the offsetting fashion of most academic writing. Throughout the chapter, Tokeya Inajin's voice is articulated using a different font, which is more reflective of his creative performance style than of my own attempt to give textual form to that style, thus eliminating the need for quotation marks.[8]

Kevin's voice is drawn primarily from recordings made between 1997 and 2000. These were made during my fieldwork with him in Canada, Germany, and the United States, including the Muckleshoot, Makah, Standing Rock, Cowichan, Round Valley, and Sto:lō Nations, as well as the cities and towns of Portland, Oregon; Bettendorf, Iowa; Boston, Massachusetts; Lake Cowichan, British Columbia; and several other communities in Germany and the states of California, South Dakota, and Washington. I have also drawn on secondary sources such as recorded talks, published articles, releases of commercial audio and video recordings, liner notes, websites, and transcriptions of his radio and television appearances in Canada, the United States, and Japan. I take this approach to unravel how Appadurai's notion of the "warp of . . . stabilities," as seen in Kevin Locke's Lakota experiences, intersects with what Appadurai refers to as the "woof of human motion."[9] Thus, the translocal inner dialogue embedded in Kevin Locke's performance practices is given emphasis in this chapter. First, though, we look briefly at the life-path that informs the voice of Tokeya Inajin and the contemporary milieu in which both his work and this chapter is received, particularly with regard to the representation and commercialization of the "Plains flute."

The Life-Path of Tokeya Inajin (Stands First)

Tokeya Inajin has been a pivotal force in the revitalization of Lakota *wiikjo* (courting flute) repertoire and the *cangleška wacipi* (Hoop Dance).[10] While striving to move the conceptual boundaries of performance beyond the rigidity of what we have come to think of as "tradition," Kevin remains rooted in and dedicated to his traditional Lakota cultural Teachings. He is a fluent speaker of three Lakotan dialects, performs an almost exclusively traditional flute and vocal repertoire, is an avid grass dancer, and is immersed in the life of his reservation through ongoing, albeit intermittent, residence. His commitment to the preservation and development of Lakota lifeways is also reflected in the hundreds of educational and environmental workshops he offers in local reservation schools throughout the year, the joy he takes in sharing his arts and knowledge with American Indian students, and his ongoing participation in and respect for Lakota ceremonial life.

Kevin's link to tradition goes deeper yet, for he carries the name of his great-grandmother's uncle Tokaheya Inajin (First to Arise), a member of Sitting Bull's Hunkpapa band during the mid to late nineteenth century, who in turn is said to have carried the name of Tokahe—the first human to emerge from the underworld in some Lakota creation stories.[11] Tokeya Inajin (Stands First), Kevin Locke, is a Hunkpapa Lakota member and lives with his *tiošpaye* (extended family) at the juncture of the Missouri and Grand Rivers in Wakpala, Standing Rock Nation (northeastern South Dakota), where he has been immersed in his traditional music, dance, and Teachings for much of his life. As Jacqueline Left Hand Bull (Sicangu Lakota) points out, it is fitting for Kevin to live at the confluence of the Missouri and Grand Rivers: "The Missouri is the river of our people— vitally alive—changing in each moment yet always the same river. Its head- waters are in Montana, as is some of Kevin's lineage, while the Grand collects from Hunkpapa lands, his home; a little further downriver the Cheyenne flows into the Missouri bringing with it the flecks of life and scents of the Black Hills." From the bluffs that border his family's home, she notes, he can stand in one spot and turn full circle, seeing a distant horizon extending far beyond his family and community in all directions; "each horizon becomes part of another circle or hoop as one travels in any direction, a hoop of many hoops of life—be it the lives of family and community, flora and fauna, winds that bring and take, near-blinding light at midday, and at midnight an incredible star-life. It is in fact a metaphor for the circle of life, a hoop of life itself."[12]

Reflecting on his youth, Kevin recalls that while most teenagers around him grew up listening to the Beatles, his music of choice were early field recordings issued by the Library of Congress, American Indian Soundchief, and Canyon Records in the 1940s and 1950s. On returning home after spending his high school years at New Mexico's Institute of the American Indian Arts, Kevin renewed a commitment he had made earlier to seek out his elder's linguistic, spiritual, and musical knowledge—a process he continued while teaching school and completing his master's degree in the 1970s. By 1975, Kevin began to take his dancing very seriously. Two years later he learned to play his mother's flute, which had been sitting around collecting dust until then. In 1977, he played this flute at an international exposition in Stuttgart during his first overseas performance tour.

Although he gleaned much from his home community, where his maternal grandfather and uncle sang to him as a child, the key individuals who influenced Kevin's vocal style and repertoire choices in his early years were his uncle Abraham End of Horn and, during his early flute years, his adopted Mesquakie uncle Everett Kapayou. To this day, his most treasured flute is the one he received from Bernice Senache, who had ceremonially adopted Kevin to take the place of her son when he left this world. This flute, which Kevin has carried around the world, had belonged to Bernice Sanache's grandfather, Poweshiek. The highly expressive style in which Tokeya Inajin translates vocal songs into flute melodies, coupled with his keen ability to achieve the rich and resonant overtones so characteristic of the ideal Plains flute timbrel aesthetic—referred to by the Lakota as *gnagnaŋs'e* (flutter / vibrato)—was influenced by the styles and readily identifiable sound of early Lakota flute players such as Richard Fool Bull and John Coloff, as well as Omaha flute player John Turner. Kevin's unique use of ornamentation and vibrato resulted from his own embellishment and interpretation of the traditional style of these players. Although Kevin met Comanche flute player Doc Tate Nevaquayah in 1981 when they shared a performance bill at the Kennedy Center, he was already well-established as a flute player by then.

During the 1970s, Kevin also completed all predissertation requirements for his doctorate and began to pursue a degree in law.[13] After three days of law school, however, he decided that academia was not where his heart was. Switching tracks completely, he immersed himself in his traditional heritage, his music and dance, and the Teachings of Ptehincala Ska Win (White Buffalo Calf Maiden) who, many Lakota believe, came to share the sacred Teachings of the Creator with them.[14] While Kevin's vocal repertoire quickly grew to include hundreds of songs, he reserves the vast majority of these for personal and ceremonial use. To expand his traditional flute repertoire for public presentation, he began actively searching out and methodically collecting *wiilowan* (courtship songs) from known songkeepers who were in their later years. Whereas Ben Black Bear Sr., from Rosebud, had the greatest impact on the development of Kevin's vocal style and repertoire, Charles Kills Enemy, Joe Flying By, Charles Wise Spirit, Joe Rock Boy, Madonna Beard, Vine Deloria Sr., William Horn Cloud, Bill Black Lance, Dave Marks, and the families of John Coloff and Sitting Bull also shared many songs with him. These singers, most of whom have now left this world, shared in Kevin's vision of the importance of preserving and transmitting traditional Lakota wiilowan and readily offered their songs and those of their ancestors for Kevin's public use.

In the late 1970s, Kevin Locke also began to learn about the Bahá'í Faith, a worldwide religion with more than 5 million adherents in 235 countries and dependent territories, represented by 2,112 tribes and ethnic groups in 127,683 locales around the world.[15] The Bahá'í Faith originated in Persia in the mid-nineteenth century and was brought to the United States shortly after the close of the late-nineteenth-century Ghost Dance era.[16] Although records do not confirm when the first American Indian became a Bahá'í, Choctaw filmmaker Phil Lucas asserts that today 75 percent of the Bahá'ís in the Americas are indigenous peoples—the vast majority being from South America. Whereas Van den Hoonard notes that in 1989 20 percent of Canada's Bahá'í population were First Nations members, in the United States the ratio is much lower and, as Stockman notes, "no comprehensive ethnic survey of the American Bahá'í community has ever been undertaken."[17] Stockman further states that in 1995 there were "several thousand Indian and Eskimo Bahá'ís, especially in rural Alaska and on the Navajo and Sioux reservations."[18] The previous figures, however, are only estimates because only in recent years have local communities made serious efforts to maintain Bahá'í statistics, and this is not a global practice by any means. In 1989, Counselor Jacqueline Left Hand Bull, who has worked extensively with indigenous Bahá'ís throughout the Americas and in Siberia since 1988 as a member of the Continental Board of Counselors for the Bahá'í Faith in the Americas, noted:

There are probably over 200,000 Indian Bahá'ís in the Americas. The vast majority are in South America, where there are very large populations of Indians, many who don't even speak Spanish. But Central America also has quite a few thousand especially among the Mayan Indians. . . . In Central and South America the pressure to give up Indian ways has been going on somewhat longer than in North America. But millions of Indians have hung on to their language and their ways. Those are the places where there are now the most Indian Bahá'ís. In other places, the Indians had nearly lost the language and the arts—music, dance, special clothing, but among the Indian Bahá'ís in those places there is an active effort to protect what is left and to nurture it back to full blossom again. It's the only place where I've observed that actually happening.[19]

This focus on the protection and nurturing of indigenous languages, music, dance, and culture is a direct result of putting the Bahá'í Teachings into action on a community level.

Expressed through the essential requisite of "unity in diversity," the Bahá'í Faith is embedded in the principle of the "oneness of humanity." From Kevin Locke's perspective, this Teaching readily relates to the Lakota worldview that all nations, peoples, and "hoops of life" are part of, and play a vital role in, "the hoop of many hoops."[20] Although the Bahá'ís are spread across the globe, they see themselves as part of one worldwide religious community that is closely linked at local, regional, national, and international levels and has remained intact since its 1844 inception—that is, it has not split into sects as have many other world religions. Thus, the principle of "unity in diversity" requires a global perspective that goes beyond appearances and is deeper than regalia or song.

From a Bahá'í perspective, "unity in diversity" does not derive its meaning from the catchy slogans that have become part and parcel of today's multicultural/pluralistic notion of popular culture or the rhetoric of nation building, although these factors have led some individual Bahá'ís, American Indian and otherwise, to tap into this sociopolitical hype and reshape their identities accordingly—but no more so than in American popular culture at large. As Jacqueline Left Hand Bull notes, however, those Native American Bahá'ís who turn to spiritual huckstering for personal gain are often self-identified Indians who have come to the culture as adults.[21] Kevin Locke further points out that Bahá'ís who become immersed in the New Age scene tend to disassociate themselves from the Bahá'í Faith fairly quickly because the motivations at the heart of the two do not mesh: I've seen a lot of people do that and the first thing that they'll do is *not* to mention the Bahá'í Faith. . . . They've either resigned from the Faith or they quickly deemphasize or somehow distance themselves from the Bahá'í Faith. Yeah, they completely sublimate that because they know that the Bahá'í Faith is sacred and they can't mess around with it. . . . The two can't mix, it's just like oil and water.[22] For many, the difficulty seems to lie in the placement of the self rather than the sacred at the center of the hoop.

As Kevin notes, the Bahá'í conceptualization of "unity in diversity" is derived from the 1873 text, the *Kitáb-I-Íqán* (Book of Certitude), written by the founder of the Bahá'í Faith, Bahá'u'lláh, while he was imprisoned in Akká in the Ottoman Empire.[23] His great-grandson, Shoghi Effendi, appointed by his grandfather Ábdu'l-Bahá as the only authoritative interpreter of the Writings of Bahá'u'lláh and Ábdu'l-Bahá after Their passing, explains this principle as follows:

> Far from aiming at the subversion of the existing foundations of society, it seeks to broaden its basis, to remold its institutions in a manner consonant with the needs of an ever-changing world. It can conflict with no legitimate allegiances, nor can it undermine essential loyalties. Its purpose is neither to stifle the flame of a sane and intelligent patriotism in men's hearts nor to abolish the system of national autonomy so essential if the evils of excessive centralization are to be avoided. It does not ignore, nor does it attempt to suppress, the diversity of ethnical origins, of climate, of history, of language and tradition, of thought and habit, that differentiate the peoples and nations of the world. It calls for a wider loyalty, for a larger aspiration than any that has animated the human race. It insists upon the subordination of national impulses and interests to the imperative claims of a unified world. It repudiates excessive centralization on one hand, and disclaims all attempts at uniformity on the other. Its watchword is unity in diversity such as Ábdu'l-Bahá Himself has explained.[24]

Putting this principle into action in a way that speaks to the complexities discussed by Shoghi Effendi has been a slow and often painful process in the Bahá'í community, particularly at the local level. Although "unity in diversity" has sometimes been illustrated through what could be perceived as stereotypical "feathers and beads" representation of peoples of various cultures, Tokeya Inajin was quick to look deeper and distinguish between the actions of individuals and the spiritual principles that lay at the heart of the Bahá'í Teachings. For him, it was no different than drawing a distinction between the actions of "spiritual hucksters and plastic medicine men" and the sanctity of the knowledge and practices that he had learned from his Lakota Elders.[25]

This, coupled with what Kevin describes as the fulfillment of the prophetic elements implicit within Lakota spiritual traditions prompted Kevin to become a Bahá'í in 1979.[26] In the early 1980s, his interactions with Quechua, Mapuché, Aymara, and Guaymi Bahá'ís who had come to Standing Rock to meet and consult with their northern relatives inspired Kevin to begin dedicating his work to giving form to the integration of Lakota and Bahá'í Teachings through his music and dance.[27] Shortly after Kevin became a Bahá'í, he was taught the basic moves of the Hoop Dance by Arlo Good Bear, a Mandan Hidatsa dancer from Shell Creek, North Dakota. Within a short time, Kevin traveled to Senegal, where he performed the Hoop Dance for the first time using just twelve hoops. This tour took him to several African countries under the auspices of the U.S. State Department Arts America program. Since then, Kevin has become a renowned international artist with close to twenty recordings to his credit.[28] The National Endowment of the Arts appointed him a National Heritage Fellow in 1990 and he has shared his songs and dances with audiences in seventy-nine countries as an active agent in the fulfillment of Black Elk's vision of the "hoop of many hoops."

Kevin writes: With my music and dancing I try to celebrate and create an awareness of the oneness of humankind. I dedicate everything to that theme. We are in the process of building a sustainable, unified, global civilization that will cherish the nobility of the human spirit and take care of the environment. I believe these are the hopes and dreams that all people are longing for. This means creating a circle of unity worldwide that everyone is invited to be a part of. He points to the importance of the Lakota contribution to this "hoop of many hoops": I see that the Lakota people have many gifts to bring to the world. . . . The people are desperate for these gifts. We know that humankind is in a crisis. Now we need to draw from all of these wellsprings of knowledge that are within the treasuries of the hearts of the peoples of the world.[29] Although Kevin is quick to point out that he is representative of only himself, many of the elders I have spoken with from the Northwest Coast to the Plains not only feel that Kevin brings honor to the Lakota and to the American Indian Nation as a whole by sharing these gifts with audiences around the world, but they have high expectations regarding his responsibility to undertake this work with integrity, serve as a cultural ambassador, and show through his actions that the Lakota have a rich and valued voice that is as worthy of recognition and respect as any other. This integration of tradition and modernity, local and global, spiritual and physical goes beyond notions of the market so prevalent in contemporary studies on the globalization and transculturation of indigenous musics. It urges a fuller discussion of the place of Kevin's life-work in today's "Native American flute" scene.[30]

Representation and Notions of Commercialization

The public perception of Kevin Locke's music and dance is informed and shaped by the exoticized strains of the "Native American flute" and the rhythms and vocalizations of powwow drummers that punctuate virtually every contemporary film about American Indians. As Leuthold points out, "Nakai's solitary flute, combined with sweeping pans or flyover shots of landscapes, instantly signifies Indianness in recent documentaries."[31] Perhaps one of the most subtle and pervasive misrepresentations of American Indian cultures is found in this pan-Indian approach to the aural representation of a people. Yet, contemporary scholarship on the representation of American Indians has primarily focussed on visual and literal depictions of First Nations peoples through the heritage industry, literature, advertising, film, sports, and art, which all but ignore the living traditions lying at the heart of community life.

Countless examples come to mind where the improvisatory strains of the Native American flute serve as a decontextualized aural backdrop for nostalgic photographs of American Indian historical leaders, newspaper clippings, and even genocidal battle scenes.[32] To some, this decontextualization of the flute differs from the use of Indian team mascots in degree, not in kind. In juxtaposing images of the past with creations of popular culture, both contribute to the reinscription of what Fabian has called "a history without Time of peoples 'without history.' "[33] Although music is not visible, it is certainly not voiceless or timeless. A soundtrack or a film score is as powerful a form of representation as is a photograph, a museum exhibit, an advertisement, or an ethnographic description.[34]

If a flute is to provide the soundscape for photographs of historical figures such as Hunkpapa Lakota leader Sitting Bull, could those images not be juxtaposed with aural markers of his day and his culture? Accessibility issues notwithstanding, Sitting Bull was a prolific singer and historical and contemporary recordings of his songs are readily available. Contrary to popular thought, these songs are not just another lost artifact of a people "with no history," songs that do not speak to the contemporary struggles of this day. Not only are these songs found in the transcriptions of Natalie Curtis and Francis Densmore and on the early wax cylinder and 78-rpm recordings of Walker, Densmore, Radin, and Rhodes, but these are some of the very songs performers such as Doc Tate Nevaquaya (Comanche), Tom Mauchahty-Ware (Kiowa/Comanche), Robert Tree Cody (Dakota/ Maricopa), Fernando Cellicion (Zuni), Ben Peas (Crow), and Kevin Locke (Lakota) have painstakingly revitalized as a living tradition. These perform-ers are rarely heard in contemporary films and are mentioned only in passing in scholarship that speaks to "Native American flute" performance.[35]

Kevin Locke, whose repertoire includes a number of Sitting Bull songs, speaks to the need to honor those who struggled to maintain and share their song traditions: The social context for the flute dwindled after the reservation period but there were those individuals who just kept it alive— Dan Red Buffalo; Lakota Richard Fool Bull; a Dakota elder from Sisseton—David Marks; an Omaha from Macy, Nebraska—John Turner. Kevin also speaks to the struggles they went through to retain their traditional songs and pass them on to future generations: I just was thinking about the context where I learned those from—from my uncles and them who really sacrificed to hold on to those things. It was so hard because they faced overwhelming negativity or forces that were compelling them to invalidate all those things and give it up—but they knew the value and they kept those things and they passed them on. They freely shared their music and they're gone now—they're all deceased. These are not songs that belong to this generation, so I like to honor them. The songs Kevin speaks of remain a vital part of contemporary community life, although held intact by tenuous threads in years past. It is with a sense of loss, then, that traditional flute players acknowledge the abrupt temporal disjuncture of locale, image, and sound in most contemporary films featuring Native American flute scores.

Perhaps the melancholy timbre of the "Native flute," the breath of life, resonates with the nostalgia of lost homelands, speaking as easily to those whose aesthetics are attuned to the strains of the Japanese *shakuhachi* as to those whose memories are embedded in the echoes of the Galicean pipes— an aural marker for the equally romanticized Celtic music market. How-ever, it is not the shakuhachi or the Irish pipes, but "Native American flutes" that are sold at curio stores across the United States, in high-end Native art shops, New Age stores, at powwows and folk festivals, work-shops, conferences, and even on the Internet. As Navajo singer and flute player Arlie Neskahi points out, "You can come to some stores these days and even get a flute assembly kit complete with an instructional video on how to play! Something is lost when this begins to happen. There is no Root . . . no connection to a Source."[36]

Today, collectors can purchase veritable objets d'art carved from every exotic wood imaginable, many of which are all but unplayable. This, some say, is the epitome of commercialization in the world of music—the sale of an instrument as an unplayable artifact with profit, rather than artistry, as the primary aim. Of what use is a flute to the flute player or the listener if it cannot be played? Others, however, would say that the reinvention of traditional instruments to meet the tastes of popular culture and the demands of the mass market is a more legible marker of commercialization. Andrew Means minces no words in his analysis of the Native American flute market: "The instrument has even become the basis for natural, culturally correct therapy in some New Age spheres. . . . The results sometimes display more enthusiasm than taste, and resonate louder at the cash register than in the heart."[37]

Adorned in all manner of feathers and beads, contemporary "Native American flute" players have all but saturated the market.[38] Many of these musicians have not grown up in areas where the Plains flute was traditionally played and many do not have American Indian ancestry. Of those who do, few had traditional teachers; even fewer play traditional music; almost none play in traditional solo style; and the vast majority do not perform on traditionally tuned instruments, but on flutes tuned to the Western tempered scale, thus enabling them to play with instruments such as the piano, keyboard, or guitar. From an American Indian perspective, this is inconsequential as long as musicians make their identity and intentions clear in public presentations. It is when artists do not identify their ancestry while promoting themselves in a way that misleads the consumer that difficulties arise.[39] For these artists, favored performance venues are often urban recording studios where they can portray themselves in whatever way they choose. As Neskahi laments,

> One of the sad things I have seen is many New Agers have attached themselves to the music of persons who have copied our traditional flute playing styles and put out albums directed at this market. Many of the persons who buy this music do not know that the persons playing are not of North American Indigenous ancestry and are being fooled by these tapes and CD's [sic]. As a musician myself, I believe that persons can learn other people's music, but I draw the line if musicians make money by posing as a Native artist.[40]

In this highly commercialized and romanticized market, there is little room for traditional artisans or musicians, who are often represented as

anachronisms. When asked about his views on the contemporary proliferation of the "Native American flute," Kevin Locke focuses on form, pitch,
and song type: It's really deviated a long ways from the original intent of it. . . .
Structurally it's a very distinctive genre of music. Here was this tradition that
developed over many generations, the whole category of love songs. . . . And
then suddenly somebody just changes it and makes it into this whole New Age
thing which is totally unrelated and they say this is Indian flute music. . . . To me,
the frustrating thing is that the instruments they're playing are all symphonically
tuned, they have nothing to do with the traditional intervals.

Although style, form, and repertoire are crucial identifying markers,
the crux of the polemic between "traditional" and "contemporary" flute
practices is found in the tuning of the instrument. As Conlon's survey of
ninety-seven American Indian museum flutes tells us, none of the playable
flutes she analyzed were tuned to the tempered scale and no two pitch
systems had the same intervalic structure.[41]

Conversely, most Native flute websites advertise flutes in a variety of
Western scales, an essential factor for the growing number of flute players
involved in New Age "flute circles" across the country.[42] The two instruments, the traditional and the contemporary, are virtually incompatible, as
was made vividly apparent in Round Valley when Kevin Locke and Mary
Young Blood (Aleut/Seminhole; fig. 4.1), attempted to share songs with
each other during one of my field trips.[43] The two flutes merged into an
eerie but somewhat captivating dissonance that would likely appeal to
those attuned to the avant-garde. Although they had a great time sharing
songs, the only song their musical paths meshed on was the Zuni Sunrise
Song—only because Kevin finally pulled out a flute he had been given in
Michigan that was tuned to the tempered scale.[44]

I do not raise the previous issues as a caveat to the "authenticity"
debate, but simply to clarify the point that the contemporary Native American flute and its repertoire are different from that of the traditional Plains
flute. Why, then, is the Native American flute so often glossed as the
"Plains flute" by flute players, their audiences, and their record companies?
Perhaps the answer lies more in issues of identity and the market-based
exotica of American Indianness than it does in the organological concerns
of traditional flute players or ethnomusicologists.[45] It is my hope that future
research will offer a much deeper analysis of the impact of identity issues on
the American Indian music scene than can be provided in these pages.

Kevin Locke's concerns regarding the style and tuning of Plains flutes
are expanded on by Hunkpapa elder Patricia Locke, who explains that the

FIGURE 4.1. Kevin Locke and Mary Young Blood sharing songs in Round Valley, California. (Photograph by Pauline Tuttle)

music of the Lakota courting flute was not only structurally and stylistically distinct, it was also a socially distinctive genre of music. She further notes that contemporary composers and musicians generally ignore the original social purpose of courting flute composition and performance practice; consequently, "many traditionalists count on Kevin to preserve the integrity of Lakota music and songs."[46] While reflecting on the proliferation of the Native American flute, Kevin laughs, sits back, and regains the posture of the band historian as he carefully considers both sides of the issue: I try to look at it from both sides. Myself, I'm supposed to be Mr. Purist, Mr. Preservationist, so from that angle I can say it's a big travesty. But from another angle I can say it's probably good in the long run, you know. Who am I? I can't judge, I can't say. Ultimately, Kevin summarizes the positive aspects of the phenomenon: People are kind of awakening and freeing themselves from the straightjacket of this rigid culture. . . . I guess it's all over the world, the rigidity, especially in North America. I think it's a good thing that people are kind of waking up—trying to search.

Yet, Kevin is careful to point out the difficulties he sees and how he deals with it in his own work: I think there's also a dangerous side to it all. . . . They begin to open their eyes and they see all these beautiful things and they just kind of pick out whatever suits them. Whatever appeals to your ego you can just pick that out and just put that up on your little display and then this becomes the New Age. This approach contradicts Kevin's experience as both a Lakota and a Bahá'í, which has taught him that it is essential to strive to sublimate the ego, to put the sacred at the center rather than the self. Thus, Tokeya Inajin focuses on maintaining his own integrity and upholding the responsibility that has been passed down to him by his elders. To him, this means the stories, songs, and dances he has learned must be perpetuated in a good way and presented in a manner that will be encouraging and nurturing to people and will really convey the dignity, in the true sense, of what the people who were the carriers of those traditions wanted. Kevin also aims to give these songkeepers a voice, to enable them to make a contribution in this wonderful time when all the peoples are coming together. Most importantly, he states: I just try and do the best I can to uphold that trust that I have with them and convey it in a good way . . . all I can do is just do the best I can you know, when I render a song and if I try to interpret it or try to portray it in a certain way, is for me just to have my integrity.

One could ask how he manages to keep his integrity and humility intact amid the global recognition and, at times, even idolization of his public presence. Completing his previous thoughts, he answers my unspoken question: The way I try and keep my integrity is I pray every day—I try to have a strong sense of humor—and I try as best I can to have love in my heart wherever I go. His approach is returned full circle whenever he sees his elders at a powwow or a community gathering. Kevin quietly confides, They always tell me "whenever I see you it really makes me happy." Whenever I see any of the older people then they always just talk to me like that in Lakota, so this is real good.

This is not to suggest that Kevin has no detractors. In my experience, those who have had difficulty with his work seem to come from one of three camps: fundamentalist Christians who are opposed to the fact that he is Bahá'í, particularly in areas where religion and state are intertwined; nationalists, especially in countries and tribal areas where exclusivity is the political modus operandi; and select American Indian academics with tentative tribal links and protectionist agendas or non-Indian scholars who remain attached to static notions of "tradition" and stoic understandings of the "sacred." One academic in the latter camp, for example, once questioned his right (via me) to teach the Hoop Dance to young girls as well as young boys, when it had traditionally been a dance for men only. From my perspective as an ethnomusicologist, it is not my prerogative to criticize performers for the performance decisions they make, but rather to try to understand the cultural and spiritual Teachings that inform those choices and the ramifications they have on musical and cultural lifeways.

With respect to the criticisms of academics with rigidly defined notions regarding the sharing of Indian culture, Cree scholar Danielle Locke had the following to say:

> My father's upbringing from my grandfather embodied prayer at every step. They would wake in the morning first before anything was prayer, they would leave to check the rabbit snares, they would pray, then when they would reach the snares, they would pray, if they went to visit someone, they would pray, when they would leave, my grandfather would say a prayer for them, everything involved prayer. I would say to these Indian academics, before you begin your day, do you pray, before you sit down to your computer and start your work do you pray? Before you enter your classroom to teach do you pray?

From her perspective, it is not enough for scholars to attend ceremonies and gatherings, their life-work must be embedded in prayer: "ceremonies are there to assist us to lead a spiritual life, not as essential elements of a spiritual life."[47]

For Danielle Locke, to follow the Indian ways means that she must do her utmost to refrain from criticism and avoid offending any heart, and she must never interject or correct someone's beliefs or thinking, judge anyone, or measure another person's authenticity by her own standards: "To do so is contrary to the internalized spiritual discipline that governed Indian peoples' whole existence in this world," she writes.[48] These statements have rung true in my work with Kevin. As an academic, it is not always possible or even advisable to avoid all contentious issues. Yet, whenever I have broached potentially confrontational topics with him, my queries have generally been met with thoughtful silence, caution, a quiet chuckle, or a simple reflection: I really can't say. I just observe and wonder what it all means, and I am left to ponder the implications of my asking such a question in the first place.

Among Kevin Locke's detractors are also those who see him as an entertainer, someone making a profit as a showman through the display of his Lakota culture. As Kevin points out, however, while his personal Lakota spiritual practices give him strength, inspiration, and sustenance during his travels at home and abroad, he does not incorporate them into his stage presentations or sell them to anyone. If he did, Kevin would surely be on one of the "huckster hit lists" mentioned by authors such as Whitt.[49] As Jacqueline Left Hand Bull notes, "His is such a fundamentally different presentation than most, because it is both deep and lofty, and speaks to universal truths rather than describing, explaining or promoting isolated cultural spiritual viewpoints, with himself as the expert." She goes on to note that in his performances she does not "recall his ever mentioning what happened when he sundanced, or fasted and sang for guidance, or any of the intimate spiritual practices" but only that he "honors others and thus brings honor to the Lakota people."[50]

The notion of Kevin as an entertainer or a showman is incongruent with his own perspective of his role and purpose in the performance world. In typically Lakota fashion, he notes, I don't really think of myself as a musician. I think of myself more as somebody who's trying to communicate. He asserts that those who criticize performers for earning an income through the arts operate from a conceptual framework that says anything that is done in public or on stage or uses the arts is in the category of entertainment. . . . In so-called Western culture, the arts have been profaned. . . . People use music as entertainment, just as a diversion to kind of distract them and take their minds off of everyday life. But I think that most traditional cultures throughout the world use the arts, especially in North America, to connect us to reality, to connect us to that which is true, that which is good, that which has a foundation, to that which is real. . . . So you have these two paradigms coming together and they haven't really meshed very well yet.

This conceptual dilemma is further frustrated by the prevalence of Western definitions of what work is and is not—the whole Protestant work ethic that led to the "gift" being defined as a profit-making investment.[51] As Kevin Locke notes, I think people have the assumption that work is something that is profane and mundane and the sacredness has been taken out of it. That's strictly an old world notion that we have to try and free ourselves from, it's hard. The Bahá'í Teachings on this topic are very much in harmony with Kevin's traditional understanding: You see, in the Bahá'í Faith Bahá'u'lláh has elevated work to the station of worship when done in the spirit of service to humankind. This concept, coupled with the Teaching that music is prayer, allow Kevin to embed his work and his life in the sacred without exploiting it.

Tokeya Inajin is quick to assert his right and even familial obligation to earn a livelihood: I can derive a livelihood from that and that's good, that's a blessing. Everybody needs to make a livelihood in this world. . . . I have my family to feed and provide for so I have to do that. However, the discussion does not end here. People always say that "money's the root of all evil" but it's really not and it doesn't have to be—because we have an opportunity to utilize our wealth, to channel that wealth, and to enable it to be a source of good for humanity. One of the ways in which he accomplishes this is by donating portions of all compact disc and tape sales to organizations such as the Sitting Bull College Scholarship Fund, the Comprehensive Chemical Prevention and Drug Treatment Program at Standing Rock, the South Dakota Arts Council (earmarked for Lakota youth), the InterTribal Sinkyone Wilderness Park, the Environmental Protection Information Center, and similar organizations.

In Kevin's view, monetary benefits arising from his performances are a potential means of purification, a marker for the complementarity of work and worship and of service and prayer. During our interviews, Kevin used the ecology of the Great Lakes as a metaphor of profit-oriented versus service-oriented approaches to the accruement of capital: Some of the lakes are so clear and crystalline and some of the lakes are putrid, they're dead—why? His analogy lies in the contamination of the lakes, which jeopardizes their connection to the rivers and the ocean, limiting their ability to support organic life. For Kevin, the ocean is a metaphor for the guidance of the Creator whose Teachings have been shared through sacred Personages—the rivers that carry the lake waters to and from the ocean—such as White Buffalo Calf Maiden and the mid-nineteenth-century founder of the Bahá'í Faith, Bahá'u'lláh. The lake, in turn, represents the performer or those involved in the promotion of American Indian music. In Kevin's view, if we earn our living and use our funds in the spirit of service to humanity, we have an opportunity to connect ourselves through our wealth, through our resources, to this ocean of bounty, ocean of grace. It's not like this thing that taints you and is dirty—no, it can be like a source of purification. Again, the band historian's ability to see both sides is revealed in Kevin's interpretation of the impact of commercialization on his individual, family, and community life.

Breaking the Stereotypes through Performative Interaction

The lessons shared in the metaphor of the ocean carry over into Kevin's performance practice in that his songs are often embedded in stories and Teachings that are designed to offer guidance, to empower listeners to search out answers to their questions. Through his music and dance, Kevin seeks to express the process of searching, reflecting, internalizing, and putting into action the lessons learned. Donning the traditional regalia of his Hunkpapa Lakota ancestry, he is quick to take his audience beyond what many may see as simply a collection of feathers and beads in motion—beautiful, but void of meaning if not coupled with a deeper understanding of their cultural and spiritual significance and their historical and contemporary representation.

As a prelude to a dance performance at a 1987 youth conference, Kevin Locke called the youth to look beyond the feathers and beads of his dance regalia: I would like for you all just to kind of ignore that I have this part of my outfit on here because you know what I really hate to do is to reinforce stereotypes. Everybody seems to have the American Indian encapsulated in some little container. They've got him stuck back a hundred-fifty years in the past—caught in a time warp. In reality the American Indians are the victim of what they call objectification. You see them in the alphabet—A is for apple and B is for baseball, on down; and I is for Indian and E is for Eskimo, right? It's really subtle—we don't realize it but in our minds we begin to think of these people as not really people but as objects. It's very, very dangerous. It's one of the many facets of prejudice, one of the many barriers that we have to overcome.[52]

Tokeya Inajin explains how he came to address these stereotypes through performance, particularly in light of the responsibility he carries when performing for audiences around the world: "What am I going to say to them?" I wonder. "What am I going to say to all of you wonderful people here, to create some kind of a lasting impression?" "What can I do?" I think to myself, wonder to myself—because of all the major races of humankind, the Native people of this hemisphere have suffered the greatest loss in number, the greatest population decline, have never attained seating or stature on any type of international forum, have never had a voice heard. And now is the time! So this is why, I thought: "I will try and do whatever I can to make some kind of an impression—maybe I can use this beautiful gift of music, gift of dance"—because after all, as human beings we are communicators.[53]

The stereotypical feathers and beads imagery of contemporary American Indian musicians and dancers that Kevin simultaneously dispels and honors is a legacy that has been kept alive both through the traditional Teachings, practices, and sufferings of countless ancestral generations and through the confluence of the ethnographic imaginations of centuries of travellers, collectors, scholars, "spiritual hucksters," and "plastic medicine men," often driven by the insatiable hunger of those searching for a life-style to call their own. It is the notions perpetuated by the latter group that Kevin seeks to move his audiences beyond—notions that, today, embody the dreams and aspirations of the disenfranchised "seekers" of the world—"wanna-be Indians" shadow-dancing with the "noble savage of the New Age."[54] Although conceptually debunked, the myth of the "noble savage" remains a stereotypical construct in popular culture that lies at the heart of much of the objectification of "the American Indian" for purposes of marketing and entertainment—no less than does the image of the Plains Indian.[55] Even renowned contemporary Navajo/Ute flute player R. Carlos Nakai, who Means notes "at one time vehemently condemned pan-Indianism," dons Plains regalia in his public persona and attests that "while the Navajo did not possess the Plains-style flute, it seems that related linguistic and cultural groups might have."[56] Recalling stays with "traditional Cheyenne and Kiowa families" during his U.S. Navy service in the 1970s, Nakai asserts that "wearing Plains-style dress honors those tribal cultures."[57] With regard to the New Age label, Nakai emphatically states: "I get a lot of this talk about being a New Age musician, bringing the Indian out of the past. I say, write what you will. I don't care. I just play the music."[58] Adding to the nonchalant approach to the topic, Kevin Locke simply says: I'm not New Age, I'm Old Age.[59] Whether "New Age," "Old Age," or, as Kevin Locke recently joked, "middle-aged," their instrument of choice is the "Plains flute."

When speaking of traditional American Indian flutes, the commonly used term "Plains flute" is a misnomer. As has been documented in accounts of flute performance in the eighteenth and nineteenth centuries, pictographs and ledger drawings, transcriptions, early recordings of flute songs, and catalogues and studies of flutes housed in museums, these instruments were traditionally found in the Plains, Plateau, Great Basin, Woodlands, and Algonquin areas, as well as isolated pockets of the Southwest, Southeast, and even the Northwest Coast.[60] When talking about the Plains-style flute, we are not speaking of the most frequently appropriated and hotly contested musical icon of contemporary Native American popular culture—the flute of the sacred Hopi Kokopelli, whose image, Means notes, "has now become a subject for cultural pop art, appearing on everything from T-shirts and coffee mugs to business logos."[61] I would add to Means's list car air fresheners, cigarette lighters, record jackets, and more. The International Native Flute Association website even offers "Kokopelli bucks" in return for subscriptions, listing nineteen retailers who will trade the bucks for discounts.[62]

When we speak of the "Plains flute," we are referring to a whistle-type flute with an internal split air chamber and an external block. Although the block is often carved into a shape that is symbolic for either flute player or flute maker, its function goes beyond aesthetics in that the block is essential for the instrument's sound production. The Plains-style flute generally has five or six holes, with many songs giving voice to seven notes. These seven notes represent the seven generations, the seven points on the Evening Star, the seven rites brought by the White Buffalo Calf Maiden, and the seven "council fires" or divisions of the Oceti Sakowin (Dakotas).[63] Tokeya Inajin also draws a link between the seven notes and the seven directions: east, south, west, north, above (the world beyond), below (the earth), and inside (the heart and spirit, the center of the sacred circle, a place of renewal). As he explains, the seventh direction is a holy place. It is in the pure soil of the heart that we find the garden of understanding, wisdom and love. Without a profound awareness of this seventh direction, the Lakota cannot survive as a people. For this awareness is the pivot round which the Lakota understanding of the world revolves. Without it, education of the child or adult is incomplete, without a center, without orientation and purpose. Without it, our songs and dances and social rules would soon become forms without function—how often has one friend walked into this territory, this holy place, planting seeds of wisdom and understanding, making a place for "Tunkansila" and renewing the pledge to await the signs foretold by the White Buffalo-calf Woman.[64]

As Kevin walks with the listener into this territory of the seventh direction, he hopes to bridge the isolation and prejudice characterizing the 500-year history of the American Indian–European relationship. He does not have to travel far to encounter this prejudice, which is manifest in the exaltation of difference and exoticism—even in his own backyard: If you look at the travel stuff put out by South Dakota, North Dakota, they always feature the *exotic* Indian people as being something which is attractive and this appeals to the intended consumer market. Their view is that these people are extrinsic to them, they're something that's interesting to them and they don't see themselves as a world citizen. It's *themselves* and *others,* and these others, you know, they might have something quaint or interesting, certainly not *vital* but interesting, which we may be interested in sampling, you know—it's the whole consumer mentality.

For Kevin Locke, the flute is clearly a means for bridging diversity on both local and global levels: As a Bahá'í I know that all the peoples of the world have something very beautiful and meaningful and valid and *vital* to offer the world. The whole thing that I am trying to convey is that as world citizens we should really be engaged in the process of seeing how all the beautiful things that we have from our various respective heritages are part of this emerging global civilization of which we are all legitimate heirs. And so we have to begin the process of seeing different people as not foreign or extrinsic or alien to ourselves but as being part of our identity, who we are, part of our global heritage. In other words to see them as intrinsic to ourselves. Bringing the concept to a personal level in which the past and the present coexist, Kevin clarifies his point: Just like myself, you know—a year ago this time I was in Yakutsk in the Sakha Republic, so every day, every hour practically, I have these real *strong* images and feelings of being right in Northeastern Siberia and I can just hear the people speaking Sakha language, I can hear the songs that they sing this time of year. Its very, very fresh in my mind right now, all the imagery. So you see it's really part of me and when the people were doing their songs and dances I didn't feel it was foreign to me but I could really involve myself in the feeling that they had and in the way they were trying to create unity through their music and dance and it just felt so natural, to me, to be there. So my whole point is to create this feeling of familiarity and universality and not to perpetuate this we/them type of a thing you know. I don't talk to people that way, I try to involve everyone.

For Tokeya Inajin the flute is the perfect vehicle to accomplish this task: The flute is really nice because it's a universal instrument, it represents the wind—the breath of life—and all cultures use it. It's kind of like opening a doorway and looking at a different way of life, a different culture. Even if you can't appreciate the Oriental people's music, if you just listen to the shakuhachi you can't help but fall in love with it and it'll just open that up. Then we use these different holes [in the flute]—like you can't just play a song with one note. That's what they're trying to do in the world today, always trying to be exclusive and trying to just keep to themselves. It's just like trying to play a song with only one note on an instrument. You can't really do it. You have to have all these notes, you have to have all of them. Kevin's efforts to give voice and form to these concepts, to connect the many hoops or nations of the world in a way that is true to his cultural heritage and his personal belief system, are most readily grasped through his rendition of the Hoop Dance.

The Hoop of Many Hoops: Interlocking Narratives

The first recording of a Hoop Dance song that I am aware of was made during Fewkes's 1924 Hopi fieldwork, a recording that was followed with songs from the Plateau (Umatilla), Southwest (Hopi, Navajo, Jemez, and

Taos Pueblo), Eastern Woodlands (Seneca, Oneida, Chippewa, Winnebago), and Plains (Kiowa, Sarcee, Lakota). The bulk of these songs are Navajo renditions dating from 1950. This proliferation of Hoop Dance songs, though, has not been reflected in ethnomusicological studies to date.

Although several writers touch on the Hoop Dance in Charlotte Heth's richly illustrated compilation *Native American Dance,* we glean nothing of its symbology, history, or cultural function. Heth simply notes: "The Hoop Dance, a 'show dance' of many tribes, is one of the most individual— it features a dancer's manipulation of a dozen or more hoops over and around his torso, legs and arms to form a variety of geometric shapes."[65] Kavanagh defines it as a "performative dance . . . in which an agile dancer weaves his way through a series of hoop figures."[66] Huenemann notes that the Hoop Dance is one of the "few specialized dances . . . that require years of practice" and is "usually used as [a] special program entertainment dance."[67] Finally, Jones notes that the highlight of the repertoire of the American Indian Dance Theatre—a highly polished dance troupe established in 1987—"is a spectacular triple-speed Hoop Dance that culminates in the weaving and holding aloft of a globe, or 'earth' sphere, fashioned with twenty or so hoops."[68] In summary, we are told that the dancer must be agile and practice for many years; the dancer forms hoops into geometric shapes and figures; and the dance is a dramatic and entertaining solo showpiece—a notion that is, again, incongruent with Kevin Locke's understanding of its significance.

Tokeya Inajin was taught the basic Hoop Dance moves by Arlo Good Bear, a Mandan Hidatsa dancer from Shell Creek, North Dakota. Arlo promised to give Kevin four lessons. The first lasted all of fifteen minutes and took place in the New York hotel room they were sharing during a performance tour. Kevin says he was less than enthusiastic when Good Bear told him: "I'll give you one now and I'll give you three later. It'll be great. You'll do good. It'll take you a long ways and be a real good blessing for you."[69] Arlo left this world a few days later and Kevin was taught the remaining lessons through dreams. As Wilson notes,

> Not once, not twice, but again and again, he met his friend in his dreams. And there were others too, people from across the generations, people from around the globe, from many other tribes, Europeans, Asians, Africans. In the dream, Good Bear danced designs—designs of nature, of birds and flowers and rainbows. Locke saw that his brother had kept his promise. The lessons were

continuing, and with them, a clearer definition of Kevin's role. He saw that he must carry this thing forward, create patterns of beauty that would unite peoples around the Earth.[70]

Kevin reflects, I took those dreams as a catalyst to personally get me going on that. I thought to myself, "He did his part." I had a reciprocal obligation.[71] These dreams resurface as Kevin introduces his dance: I want you guys to watch closely—it's not a show, it's not entertainment. It's what you call a Vision Dance.

In discussing Kevin's rendition of the Hoop Dance, I draw on Fabian's criteria for performative ethnography: "ethnography is essentially, not incidentally, communicative or dialogical."[72] Recall that Kevin sees his role in the performance industry as a communicator rather than an entertainer. Thus, we must use a performative approach to his work if we are to gain an understanding of the cultural knowledge and social processes communicated through his dance. During my field research for this chapter, it became clear that two primary narratives lie at the heart of Kevin's Vision Dance and serve as catalysts for the many narratives that unfold during his performances.

First, Tokeya Inajin speaks of Ptehincala Ska Win, whose Teachings and inspiration are ingrained in his identity, his music, his dance: The area where I live, the kindred there are the Lakota people. When you analyze what it is that constitutes their identity as Lakota then you see that really the essence of it are all these spiritual verities which were communicated to the people by this Messenger—in this case, a Woman. She was the one who enabled the people to have a sense of identity, a sense of history, but most importantly a sense of destiny, a sense of purpose. And this sense, this identity, this purposefulness, all of these things—since there's not a written tradition, the body of this inspiration is contained in the music and the dances, you see.

White Buffalo Calf Maiden was a divine Personage who brought the sacred Calf Pipe to the Lakota, teaching them its use in seven sacred rites.[73] Citing Išna'la-wica' (Lone Man), Densmore notes that Ptehincala Ska Win offered the Pipe to Buffalo Stands Upward, prior to addressing those gathered: "You are to receive this pipe in the name of all the common people. Take it, and use it according to my directions." She asked that it be used as a tool for healing, for personal prayer, as a means of fostering peaceful relations between individuals, families, tribes, nations, and circles of life, and that it stand as a symbol of the binding agreement enjoined upon those present.[74] These Teachings and their implications are embedded in the music and dance Kevin Locke performs.

The second, but no less important, narrative running through Kevin Locke's Vision Dance is the Bahá'í concept of "progressive revelation," the belief that the Creator has always provided divine guidance to the peoples of all nations through the Teachings of "a myriad Messengers," who have been sent "unto the cities of all nations."[75] During their respective lives, these Wakaŋ, or Holy Souls, were charged with imparting an ever-widening understanding of the unity and interconnection of the vastly diverse elements of creation and, in so doing, providing guidance regarding the individual's relationship to these Messengers and Their Teachings—concepts that Bahá'ís refer to as the "Greater" and "Lesser" Covenants.[76] From a Bahá'í perspective, the spiritual Lessons of these sacred Personages are eternal and fundamentally one and the same—lessons that have been brought forth at approximately 1,000-year intervals through spiritual and social guidelines designed to meet the needs and capacities of the ages and cultures in which they were revealed.[77] Thus, the "Revelation of Bahá'u'lláh" speaks specifically to the interrelationship of the whole human race and all that lies within and beyond its borders.

For the Lakota, this belief is encapsulated in the expression *mitakuye oyas'in*, transliterated as "all my relations," a term that refers to the totality of creation, the Concourse on High, the mineral kingdom, the plant, the animal, this physical world, the spiritual world, everything. It invokes the Covenant that the White Buffalo Calf Woman came to establish, Her main Teachings—how the people are to treat each other. She's given the instructions to the people, and the Covenant that they have is to understand the relationship which they are to establish with God, to create unity, to understand the relatedness of all things and to mirror this in their lives.

Kevin's understanding of the "Greater Covenant" has been an essential component in the development of his personal interpretation of sacred Lakota lifeways. If he were to somehow segregate his performances from the Teachings of Bahá'u'lláh or Ptehincala Ska Win, who he sees as one and the same at the deepest level, the music wouldn't mean anything, the dances wouldn't mean anything, it would be totally meaningless. It would be nothing more than a show, sheer entertainment, a total waste of time! If an informative approach were taken to this work, with the analysis of form rather than content taking precedence, Kevin's identity as a Bahá'í would be ignored altogether; such an approach would contribute little to our understanding of his conceptualization of his performance practice. Given the seemingly wide gulf between Persian and Lakota spiritual practices and sacred Teachings, it is important to ask how Tokeya Inajin's Vision Dance can simultaneously embody the inspiration and Teachings brought by White Buffalo Calf Maiden, which constitute the very identity of the Lakota, and at the same time give form to the Teachings of Bahá'u'lláh.

The key to understanding the connections Tokeya Inajin draws between the Knowledge imparted by Ptehincala Ska Win and Bahá'u'lláh, in my view, is found in his articulation of the confluence of past, present, and future; motion and time; and the conflation of this world and the next that he spoke of when describing the spatial and temporal aspects of his performance in the opening pages of this chapter. It is also seen in Kevin's interpretation of the visions and dreams of his ancestors, which he reenacts through his dance and music, and in the ancestral knowledge he has gleaned during the course of his traditional learning. As Black Elk stated, "we too were taught that this White Buffalo Calf Woman who brought our sacred pipe will appear again."[78] Black Elk's words are echoed and expanded on by Jacqueline Left Hand Bull: "The White Buffalo Calf Woman said we'd go through tests and difficulties, and that she would return in the dawn of a new day. . . . When she said she'd return, it was a promise. Some of us believe that the promise has been fulfilled."[79] For Kevin Locke, Bahá'u'lláh is the fulfillment of that promise. He is the embodiment of the spirit of Ptehincala Ska Win, the fulfillment of her prophecies and those of Hunkpapa and Oglala visionaries such as Sitting Bull, Black Elk, and Crazy Horse. This is why Kevin is a Bahá'í, and this understanding lies at the core of what is being expressed in his Vision Dance.

The outward symbol of the inner connections that Kevin Locke sees between traditional Lakota Teachings and the Bahá'í Faith is found in the beadwork designs of his regalia, which feature intricate eight-pointed Morning Stars and the nine-pointed stars seen in figure 4.2. Kevin narrates his perception of the relationship between Ptehincala Ska Win and Bahá'u'lláh, as well as the significance of the Morning Star, while imparting visual imagery through the expressive use of American Indian sign language: Many hundreds of years ago, in the oral traditions of the Lakota, they speak of a Woman who was sent by God—Wankaŋ Taŋka, the Most Great Spirit—down to the earth to give them a gift and to establish a relationship and to tell the people of the sacredness of life. And so She gave the people spiritual laws and Teachings and She also gave them signs or prophecies to recognize the conditions that would be consonant with the return or the renewal of the Spirit—and there's many things that She indicated. One of them was that the new Spirit or Messenger would come in the form of the Morning Star.

Referring to his regalia, Kevin notes: Of course, you see on my outfit that

FIGURE 4.2. Kevin Locke playing his Richard Fool Bull flute. Note the beaded nine-pointed stars on his regalia. (Photograph by Paul Slaughter)

I wear, I have a lot of Morning Stars—that's the eight-pointed star—and this is a very prominent design in many tribes, including the Lakota tribe. The promi-nence of the Morning Star is carried over into the designs Kevin has painted on his flute cases and the beadwork on his moccasins (figs. 4.3 and 4.4). Initially, Kevin Locke was attracted to the Bahá'í Faith by an image of the Morning Star, which he saw while watching aerial slides of the Shrine

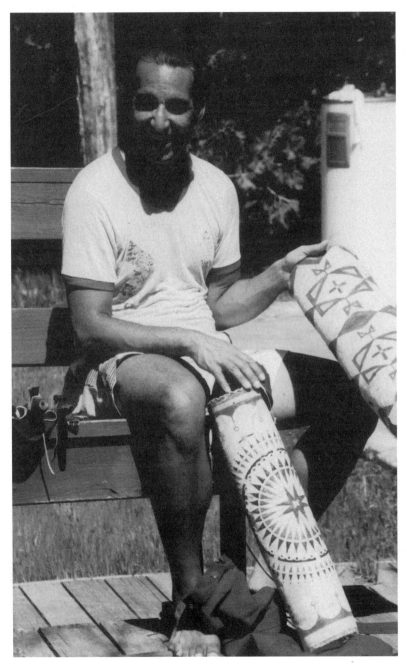

FIGURE 4.3. Kevin Locke showing the Morning Star design he painted on his flute case. (Photograph by Pauline Tuttle)

FIGURE 4.4. Eight-pointed Morning Star beadwork on one of Kevin Locke's moccasins. (Photograph by Suzanne Haldane)

of The Báb, the precursor of Bahá'u'lláh, at a friend's home in Standing Rock. The Báb, which means the door or the gate in Arabic, which of course is what the Morning Star represents—that's the door, that's the gate by which the new day will be ushered in. I looked at that aerial photograph and I could see that the upper part of the Shrine, this beautiful building in which the remains of The Báb are entombed, is an eight-sided building. Then quite prominently displayed around the Shrine of The Báb are these beautiful gardens in which there's some large eight-pointed stars around there and this was what really caught my attention. It really struck me, you know, the prominence of that design, that eight-pointed star, and of course the meaning of it.[80]

In addition to the image of the Morning Star, Kevin was also struck by the way in which Bahá'u'lláh received his Revelation: Of course, another thing is that this Woman, this Maiden who brought the law, who instilled the sense of the sacredness of life among the Lakota, said that She would return too. And when Bahá'u'lláh was imprisoned in the Síyáh Chál [black pit], which was a prison in Tehran—what's now Iran and then known as Persia—it was a woman who appeared to Him as an apparition and intimated His Revelation, who announced to Him His ministry. So this also to me was a fulfillment when I discovered that.[81] Patricia Locke explains that the Maiden who revealed Herself to Bahá'u'lláh in the Síyáh Chál was dressed in white; she sees "her dressed in white buckskin."[82] She believes this factor further impacted Kevin's interpretation of the connection between Bahá'u'lláh and White Buffalo Calf Maiden. As Shoghi Effendi explains, frequently citing Bahá'u'lláh:

In that year [1853], while the Blessed Beauty lay in chains and fetters, in that dark and pestilential pit, "the breezes of the All-Glorious," as He Himself described it, "were wafted" over Him. There, whilst His neck was weighted down by the Qará-Guhar, His feet in stocks, breathing the fetid air of the Síyáh-Chál, He dreamed His dream and heard, "on every side," "exalted words," and His tongue recited words that "no man could bear to hear" . . . under the impact of this dream, He experienced the onrushing force of His newly revealed Mission, that "flowed" even as "a mighty torrent" from His "head" to His "breast," whereupon "every limb" of His body "would be set afire." There, in a vision, the "Most Great Spirit," as He Himself has again testified, appeared to Him, in the guise of a "Maiden" "calling" with "a most wondrous, a most sweet voice" above His Head.[83]

As Shoghi Effendi notes, Bahá'u'lláh wrote that this "Luminous Maid" was "clad in white" when she appeared to him in the Síyáh Chál.[84]

As Jacqueline Left Hand Bull noted earlier, "When she [Ptehincala Ska Win] said she'd return, it was a promise. Some of us believe that the promise has been fulfilled." She clarifies her meaning: "The same Creator that sent Moses and Jesus also sent the White Buffalo Calf Woman and Baha'u'llah—the prophet founder of the Bahá'í Faith. So it's not difficult for me to reconcile the teachings of the White Buffalo Calf Woman and Bahá'u'lláh." For those who take issue with these beliefs, I refer them to Left Hand Bull's counsel: "One thing about Lakota ways that I'm really proud of is the respect for another's vision, for their spiritual understanding. No need to condemn. It seems to me that to argue about spiritual belief would be most disrespectful of each other and of the Creator."[85]

For Kevin Locke, the narratives embedded in his Vision Dance articulate the unifying points of the two belief systems that lie closest to his heart and that offer him empowerment in his daily life. These are things that are very meaningful to me so every time I do the Hoop Dance, even though it looks really repetitive and everything like that, its very empowering to me because I just can reconnect with that which is really meaningful and significant to me. So the more I do that, you know, the more I feel grounded, the more I feel connected. Whereas Arlo Good Bear's Hoop Dance told the story of sites encountered during a physical journey, Kevin Locke's Hoop Dance tells the story of the struggles and celebrations encountered on a spiritual journey—the journey of transformation—beginning with the metanarrative of "progressive revelation" and incorporating individual change and empowerment, collective societal transformation, the emergence of new spheres of knowledge, the cycles of the body and the seasons, the realization that the actions of one impact the body of the whole, the importance of song and dance as a mediator between this world and the world beyond, and the fulfillment of the prophecies and the dreams of the ancestors.

Black Elk's oft-cited vision saw the unification of all nations and all peoples in a "hoop of many hoops" through the nurturing of the "herb of understanding." In his vision, the herb grew into a sacred flower with four petals of different colors—blue/black, white, yellow, and red—emblematic of the concept of unity in diversity that Kevin Locke gives form to through the moves of his Vision Dance (see fig. 4.5).[86] Kevin notes that, although Black Elk did not live to see the fruition of his vision, he, along with those in the spirit world, the Concourse on High, are no doubt in a state of celebration: Now is the day, now is the time, when really all of the Concourse on High

FIGURE 4.5. Kevin Locke making a multicolored, four-petaled flower formation during his Hoop Dance. (Photograph by Suzanne Haldane)

are in a state of celebration because we have the opportunity here on this earth to fulfill, to answer all of their prayers. You see, when they were on this earth they prayed and they had visions and they had great longings and dreams and today we're living in a time when that's possible. It wasn't possible in the past but today we can do it—we can fulfill all those things. We can bring their dreams to fruition and to attain fulfillment—yeah, fulfillment. And so this is great, this is great. And so these dreams and these things are really contained also in these musical traditions.

The above narratives unfold through the moves in Kevin's Vision

Dance as they are enacted to the rhythm of the drum—the heart beat of the people and the nation—and the sound of the voice, which the Lakota see as the link between the physical and spiritual worlds, the breath of life. The symbology embedded in the telling of these stories, however, runs much deeper. Each figure created through the constant manipulation of the hoops and movement of the body is a microcosm of all of the narratives comprising the whole, as is each hoop itself.

Kevin uses twenty-eight hoops in his Hoop Dance, seven each of four colors: black, white, red and yellow. All three numbers hold within them a world of esoteric knowledge. The number twenty-eight, for example, is indicative of the twenty-eight days in the lunar cycle, the twenty-eight poles that Ptehincala Ska Win directed the Lakota to build Her welcoming lodge out of, the twenty-eight rafters in a Sun Dance lodge, the twenty-eight poles in a prayer lodge, and much more.

The number four is understood in terms of the four directions, the four ages, the four major ethnic groupings, the four seasons, the four worlds of creation (mineral, vegetable, animal, human), the four powers in creation (air, water, earth, fire), and the four human capacities (intellectual, physical, emotional, and spiritual). Each hoop can be understood as an aspect of creation, or as an individual, a nation, the world, the universe. Thus, the Lakota phrase "hoop of many hoops" is all-encompassing, indicative of the interconnectedness within an individual, of individuals within a family, a community, tribe, band, nation, or the world, and between any or all of these groupings and every component of creation in the universe.

The number seven represents the *wicioicage icišakowiŋ* (seventh generation) prophecy, which has been attributed through oral tradition to the contemporaries of Crazy Horse and Sitting Bull. It has been said that in approximately seven generations there would be a reawakening—a time in which the American Indians would regain their voice and come to understand and act on the inner meaning of the many American Indian prophetic movements that have swept across the continent over the centuries. As Kevin notes: This time is now, and this is the generation of fulfillment.[87] Also, the number seven represents the seven rites brought by White Buffalo Calf Maiden, the seven points on the Evening Star, the seven divisions or "council fires" of the Oceti Sakowin. It also speaks of the seven notes given voice through the songs of the flute and the seven directions. It is on the level of the seventh direction, the inner city of the heart, that Kevin seeks to communicate through his Vision Dance.

Closing the Circle: The Enactment of Tokeya Inajin's Vision Dance

Although Kevin Locke's primary audiences are American Indians, particularly on-reservation school children, he never practices exclusivity when urging audience participation—whether in his Standing Rock home or across the world. For example, if an emcee at a gathering does not call the girls out onto the powwow grounds when Kevin is going to teach the dance, as occurs at some very traditional powwows, Kevin gently reminds the emcee that the lesson is for all young people, both boys and girls.[88] This represents a major shift in transmission process, because the Hoop Dance was traditionally only performed by American Indian adult males and was taught either on a one-to-one basis or simply through observation. Yet, Kevin finds that an experiential approach is the most effective means of reaching the audience on the level of the seventh direction. Many times, I have heard Tokeya Inajin call those between nine and ninety-nine to the floor, where he gives them their own hoops and walks and talks them through the first few moves of his Hoop Dance—all the while calling on the audience to translate these lessons into action in their own lives. Once again, Kevin notes, If I didn't try to explain anything to the people then I would just be appealing to the audience's conceptual framework of entertainment and gratifying that.

The following composite summarizes some of the lessons Tokeya Inajin conveys through his Vision Dance. It is drawn from transcriptions of numerous performances that I videotaped between 1997 and 2000 and is intended as an interlocking performative narrative rather than a move-by-move, word-for-word prescriptive analysis of the dance. I aim to give the reader an understanding of how the previous narratives are given form in his dance. During the performances I have taped, Kevin has stopped the dance midway to offer an instant replay, to "give expression to expression."[89] During this process, Kevin repeats the key moves of the dance in a slower mode while he narrates the transformational journey at the heart of the dance—a story that is given form and voice through his explanation of the symbology embedded in the separate moves. In effect, several stories are told at once while he walks the audience through the dance, a process further amplified when he brings audience members to the floor and teaches them select hoop formations.

Tokeya Inajin's Vision Dance moves at about 186 beats per minute for more than ten minutes—even faster and lasting longer when he is accompanied by a live drum, which allows him to do four complete rotations with each formation. If the dance changes speed at all, it is to gain momentum rather than to slow down. He begins the dance holding half of the twenty-eight hoops in each hand as he twirls, moving his feet in rhythm to the drum, in nine clockwise circles. As he gains speed, the hoops fan out on either side, like the sun and the moon as they compete for space in the sky during daybreak and twilight. Kevin swoops to the ground and back up, drops about half of the hoops in a pile in front of him, spins around, and makes three more piles as he turns, leaving him with one hoop spinning around each of his hands. The two hoops, one yellow and one white, represent the sun and the moon—one whirls through the air in a clockwise direction while the other spins counter-clockwise, signifying the tension between chaos and order, marking the breaking point between night and day or the change of the seasons, and speaking to the struggle of individual transformation.

As Kevin teaches the dance to the children, he tells them: This is about our life. Think about our role in this new life before us. It's a new day we're living in, so these designs represent the sun and the moon. As he brings the hoops forward, the one in his right hand continues spinning while the other is brought down to the ground as he slides one foot through the hoop, then the other, continuing to alternate as he walks forward through the hoop without missing a step. As Kevin walks, he narrates: The sun and the moon and the light cast before us—every day we have here a chance to walk this road of life, this beautiful road of life. As he speaks, he brings the right hoop down and begins to walk through it, joining the two on his journey and as we walk—walk on our journey, accelerating . . . With one hoop, he bounces another off of the pile and incorporates it into the dance, stepping through the small space in which the two overlap with his right leg, quickly filling the vacant space of the new hoop with his left foot and solidifying its place in the dance by wisping the free hoop down and stepping through it with his left leg, all the while circling on one foot in four clockwise sweeps.

The outer hoops glide over his head as his right arm and then left arm reach through the hoops as they interlock and are brought down the length of his body until he is able to step backward out of the formation—accelerating, coming out of our shells, plants emerging in the spring-time. He spins counter-clockwise, still at 186 beats per minute, marked by the rhythm of the drum, while the terraced vocals of the singers synchronize with the larger movements of the hoops. Kevin lets the left hoop go, flipping a new hoop up with his right foot and then the other, reversing his spin as one hoop interlocks with another, stretching in an arc from ground to sky, creating the image of a plant reaching up to the sun: emerging, reaching up to new horizons. The design collapses and is recast as a flower, transforming into the wings of one bird after another, to hills, thunder, valleys. The flower is transformed into clouds, stars, and butterflies as Kevin adds hoops to the dance, culminating in the emergence of a twenty-eight-hoop eagle (fig. 4.6): The eagle, soaring, inspiring new patterns of unity. Who is the eagle? You are the eagles, he tells the children. The hoops reform and are drawn up, over, and around his body, as we grow together, we will reach up and spread out in the new day. The eagle is transformed into a globe of twenty interlocking, multicolored hoops. In a hoop, in a circle, there are no corners; there are no dark places; there's no balcony, no third row; there's not even a second row—only first row seats!

Kevin spins the globe above his head, as we celebrate the inclusion of all the kindred in the circle of life, the hoop of many hoops, drawing him back to the circles upon circles that surround and intersect his Standing Rock Nation home and back again. He places the interlocking globe gently on the ground. If we can't be together now, then we will end up—with the removal of just one hoop—just like this: the hoops scatter to the ground haphazardly, graphically illustrating the impact of one on the integrity of the whole. Leaving the hoops where they fell, Kevin picks up the remaining pile and forms an interlocking, open-ended pattern that slices through the air as he swings them in a far-flung arc above his head, signifying the accelerating speed with which the global civilization is emerging and the pressing need to fulfill the visions and dreams of the ancestors. As Kevin tosses the hoops toward the sky, they form a bridge—we need to cross the bridge that will carry us beyond the obstacles of racism, prejudice, intolerance, inflexibility. The bridge becomes a ladder reaching toward the sky, empowering ourselves to climb the ladder of life. Finally, a rainbow is formed, with the proverbial pot of gold to be discovered only after intense searching, reflection, and striving: We are all part of the rainbow and we all need to find that pot of gold—dig deep, for the gold is here in each of our hearts. The closing shapes continue as beautiful visions unfold before us and Kevin brings the dance to a close with a prayer in Lakota and English, which appears at the close of this chapter.

Amid the energetic applause as he closes the dance, Kevin responds: Don't applaud me! But please do applaud—applaud our singers, applaud your communities and yourselves, all the kindreds of the hoop of life. Don't applaud me but applaud yourselves. You guys with me? Do you understand enough? Do

FIGURE 4.6. Kevin Locke making an eagle formation during his Hoop Dance at Standing Rock Nation. (Photograph by Bruce Wendt)

you guys really understand? Everybody say: Hoop—there it is! The voices of the audience ring out in response: "Hoop—there it is!"[90] This interactive finale brings us full circle, back to Kevin's sacred performative space where temporal distancing dissolves into a sense of shared vision, where past, present, and future are palpably linked, with the audience being as integral to the sacredness of the space as are the dancer, the drum, and the singers.

As is true of both the ledger paintings of the old Lakota band historian and Tokeya Inajin's contemporary reenactment of the events and dreams that inspired those paintings, this chapter leaves much unsaid. Only faint glimmerings of the complexity and richness at the heart of Kevin Locke's approach to performance can be captured with the written word. As such, this text is but a dimly lit reflection of the many pockets of knowledge embedded in his song and dance—knowledge that can, in my view, be gleaned more fully in an experiential setting. Kevin's articulation of the sacred space he creates during his performance, along with his eloquent descriptions of the narratives and beliefs at the core of his art forms, bring a deeper meaning to Fabian's keen observation: "Performance may inform while information may require performances to be realized."[91] Clearly, there is much to learn by integrating performative and informative approaches to ethnography. Kiowa/Delaware playwright, director, and producer Hanay Geiogamah notes, with regard to the spiritual dimension underlying the interrelationship of performer, script, and audience in American Indian theatre: "You get taken into their world. It's not just something that's on the page. It's something that you experience. It's something that you share. And all the Indians have known it before and experienced it before, but it is recreated there for the community, as an experience to study, to learn from."[92]

Kevin brings his audience into his performative world by encouraging them to watch closely, to celebrate their individual and collective role in the hoop of life in this critical time, and to join him in learning the moves—enhancing the internalization of his message through a running dialogue that encapsulates the many narratives to which the dance gives form. So many narratives unfold at once in this dance that it is hard to imagine being disassociated from the experience. Regardless of the individual's level of knowledge, each audience member is called on to walk with Kevin through his Vision Dance and to carry its lessons into the wider world. He also draws the audience into the performative experience by teaching them to sing some of the songs, while ensuring that they understand what the Lakota words mean through aural repetition and by teaching them the hand signs that signify the words. Perhaps most importantly, though, Kevin encourages the audience to applaud themselves and their common nobility, to celebrate the things that they have in common, the diverse gifts they bring from the past, and to recognize and act on the teaching that each individual has a vital contribution to make toward the emerging global civilization.

Challenging the audience to move beyond notions of entertainment, Kevin notes that the dance, music, and stories help us to better understand who we are and how we are interconnected. Speaking to the children, he says, Well, that's what I want you guys to think about—all the opportunities you'll have to grow and develop just like a beautiful spring-time, everything unfolding before you. And in sharing his motivations for integrating moral lessons into his children's programs, he tells the adults: It's better to build children than fix adults. We all have to move on this road—to progress on this great accelerated learning curve, this great movement that's occurring throughout the world. When you use the arts in this way—you can really move a population further. You can move 'em—just pick 'em up and move 'em further. That's what I feel a lot of times—if I do my part, then all these people out there can create this energy that will enable them to get thinking, to move closer in this direction. That's what I feel.

To accomplish these goals, Kevin integrates all of the narratives and art forms at his disposal: I find through music you can just connect with the people and weave stories in there and build this theme and just build it and build it. He fully realizes the impact of his performances on the audience and feels a great responsibility to move them closer to understanding and acting on the knowledge that we all need to contribute to the unfolding of Black Elk's vision of the hoop of many hoops: The only way we can make that contribution is through unity and the only way we can unite is through seeing our spiritual connectedness. In encouraging people to identify with this sense of mitakuye oyas'in, with that which is real, he is also dispelling the stereotypical romanticization and objectification of the American Indian so prevalent in today's market. Kevin chooses to give voice to this struggle, which he sees as an educational process, not through militancy, resistance, and harsh words, but through service, song, story, and dance. He approaches his task with a warm sense of humor, thus breaking down notions of the stoic so often coupled with representations of American Indian performance practice, emphatically telling his audience: If I didn't do that dance, I'd be absolutely hopeless!

In closing, the spirit of both this chapter and Tokeya Inajin's performance practice is captured in the prayer he shares with his audience as his Vision Dance draws to a close:

Mitakuyepi—le oíhaŋke ki haŋ iyuha enanakiya
iyotaŋ caŋte wašteya nape ciyuzapi nahaŋ anamiyeciguptapi
ca wopila taŋka eciciyapelo!
My relatives—in conclusion, to each and all I extend the
warmest heart-felt handshake. And a big thank you for giving me
your attention!
Ohini waŋkata tuŋkaŋšila kaŋyela awaŋniciglakapikte
nahaŋ niyawaštepikta na napogna oniyuspapikte.
May our Heavenly Grandfather above, God, eternally watch over you
and bless you and keep you in the palm of His hand.
Nahaŋ caŋku wašte na luta na wakaŋ na owotaŋla ohini
paŋgeya na bliheic'iya tokata omayanipikte na waniyetu
koktopawiŋge nuŋpa ecetkiya ecelahci wowašte na wowakaŋ
iyeyakiyapikte!

And may you always with confidence and strength travel the good,
red, sacred, straight path leading to the millennium and beyond
and may you experience goodness and blessings there!
Mitakuye oyas'in—all my relations.[93]

Notes

I am deeply grateful to Kevin Locke, whose English and Lakota names are used interchangeably throughout, for reading and rereading this chapter as editorial changes from diverse sources were incorporated. Without his unfailing assistance and that of his producer and manager, Jim Deerhawk (Lakota Performing Arts/ Hawksong Productions), this work would not have moved beyond the realm of idle fancy. They have been integral parts of the textualization of Kevin's performance practice from the inception of the idea to its appearance in print. I also gratefully acknowledge financial support from a Social Sciences and Humanities Research Council of Canada Doctoral Fellowship and several scholarships and fellowships from the University of Washington School of Music, Ethnomusicology Division.

Finally, I must express my immense gratitude to Counselor Jacqueline Left Hand Bull for the painstaking and invaluable guidance she offered for all final revisions made to this chapter; to Patricia Locke for her insightful editorial comments, her dedicated guidance on protocol and Lakota lifeways, and for welcoming me into her home and heart; to Danielle Locke for her frank analysis of the issues at hand and her loyal dedication to Kevin's life-work; to Ter Ellingson for his unfailing guidance; to Cynthia Schmidt for her many insightful comments; and to the Canadian National Bahá'í Centre's archivist, Ailsa Hedley, and the Director of the United States Bahá'í National Center's Research Department, Robert Stockman, for prompt assistance in locating obscure citations.

1. This chapter's opening prayer has often been incorrectly attributed to Ábdu'l-Bahá (1844–1921), the eldest son of Bahá'u'lláh (1817–1892), the Persian Prophet-founder of the Bahá'í Faith. In response to a query regarding this prayer's origin, the Bahá'í World Centre's Research Department in Haifa, Israel, wrote: "The Research Department has tried unsuccessfully to locate the original text of this statement, which is attributed to Ábdu'l-Bahá. We are, therefore, unable to verify its authenticity." Although the prayer's author cannot be confirmed, as a postlude to the previous note Robert Stockman pointed out: "Rumi, the great Persian Sufi poet, who lived in the 1200s, often used the reed and the reed bed as images in his poems in exactly the fashion Ábdu'l-Bahá is said to have used it. . . . It was a very common image in Islamic mystical poetry and Ábdu'l-Bahá was no doubt using it with this background in mind" (e-mail correspondence, 24 November 1997).

2. Erlmann, xix.

3. The work of Geiogamah and Darby, Champagne, Allen, Leuthold, and others are certainly recent exceptions to this.

4. The term "noble savage" did not arise from the writings of Rousseau, but from Lescarbot's 1606 travels to Acadia. Ellingson points out that when Lescarbot encountered the Mi'kmaq and saw that they were hunters, he determined that "we must say of them that they are truly noble" (Lescarbot, 276). Lescarbot's legalese mindset led him to conclude that they must be "noble," because only the nobility were legally permitted to hunt in France. Ellingson's *Myth of the Noble Savage* offers a comprehensive and far-reaching analysis of the impact of this term on the ethnographic imagination and how it came to be ascribed to Rousseau.

5. See the introductions to Fabian's *Power* and Erlmann's *Nightsong*. Ultimately this task is only possible for those who are steeped in traditions of the performance practice in question. With regard to the Lakota, Jacqueline Left Hand Bull noted, "It would take many, many years of quiet observance to begin to understand that depth . . . if it is possible at all, if it did not come with mother's milk and in the cradle, by nuances only learning children pick up" (e-mail communication, 26 June 2000). Because I come to this work from the life-experience of a woman with Mi'kmaq, West African, and British Isles ancestry who was raised in an Irish Catholic family on the West Coast of Canada, rather than that of a Lakota woman, I cannot offer the level of experiential depth to which Left Hand Bull refers. By rooting my methodology in consultation, however, and drawing on the framework of performative ethnography, I can offer a deeper understanding of Kevin Locke's performance practices than would be possible were I to adopt a strictly descriptive approach.

6. Quoted in Bad Heart Bull, xx, xx–xxi, xx–xxi.

7. My understanding of the role of the witness is rooted in my experiences on the Northwest Coast, where witnesses play an essential role in the retention and sharing of history among their communities—akin in some ways to the duty of the band historian. Here, when individuals are called on to witness an event it is a binding duty, with the witnesses being responsible for remembering what has transpired during the course of the event, publicly commenting on the significance of what they have seen and heard, and sharing this knowledge with those who are not present.

8. Any editorial alterations in Kevin Locke's quotations were done at either his request or that of his mother Patricia Locke, with all final decisions being made by Kevin Locke. Pauses in speech are indicated with a dash, whereas an ellipsis indicates a shift from one interview excerpt to another.

9. Appadurai, 192.

10. In the Teton dialect, the courting flute is also referred to as the *šiyotaŋka* (big prairie chicken), a term that also refers to eagle-bone whistles and dance whistles.

11. Powers, *Oglala*, 79–81. Jim Deerhawk explains that the name Tokeya Inajin is a contemporary contraction of the name Kevin received from his maternal grandmother's aunt, Alice Mahot, in 1973—Tokaheya Inajin. The two names actually differ in meaning: Tokeya means "first" and Tokaheya means "moving from one place to the first place." Tokaheya Inajin, "first to arise," also refers to a "scout who had a special position and responsibilities" and further suggests "standing first, and praying first" (personal correspondence, winter 1998).

12. E-mail correspondence, 4 June 2000. See also Left Hand Bull and Haldane, 7.

13. Kevin received his B.S. in 1976 (University of North Dakota, Grand Forks), his M.A. in 1977 (University of South Dakota, Vermillion), and his Ed.D. candidacy in 1981.

14. Ptehincala Ska Win's Lakota name will be used interchangeably with its English translation, White Buffalo Calf Maiden (or Woman), throughout this chapter. In respect of both Lakota and Bahá'í protocol, I have followed Patricia Locke's suggestion to capitalize all pronouns when referring to Personages who are at the center of their respective spiritual practices. For the Lakota, this includes all references to White Buffalo Calf Maiden and Her sacred Calf Pipe; and for the Bahá'ís, this includes all references to The Báb, Bahá'u'lláh, and Ábdu'l-Bahá (see Hornby, 105–106). Also included are the Teachings and, where applicable, the Sacred Texts or Writings of these Individuals.

15. Universal House of Justice, *The Bahá'í World,* 317. Given that this large-scale growth has occurred over the course of a comparatively short time, it is important to note that proselytizing is forbidden as a means of fostering expansion (Shoghi Effendi, *Advent,* 55). It is also important to point out some common misconceptions about this religion. In my experience, I have encountered those who are very knowledgeable and have high regard for the work of the Bahá'ís on local and international levels; those who have an absolute lack of knowledge or even interest in the religion; those whose knowledge is based on unfounded assumptions gleaned through the eyes and ears of others rather than through serious research and analysis; those who misconstrue it as an offshoot of Islam comprised of an invisible body of persecuted Persian adherents; and, more recently, those who have the erroneous idea that it is some sort of New Age cult. While this is not the place to evaluate these perceptions, for further information on this religion I refer the reader to the bibliographic resources cited by Braun or Stockman and Winters.

16. The first Bahá'í to come to North America was Antún Haddád, from Áyn Zhaltá, who arrived in Chicago in 1892 for the 1893 World's Columbian Exposition (Stockman, *Origins,* 26–30). By 1899, the Bahá'í community in the United States numbered close to 2,000 (Stockman, *Early Expansion,* 7–9, 383). By 1995, it had grown to more than 120,000 (Stockman, "American Bahá'í," 1.)

17. Jacqueline Left Hand Bull notes that the first American Indian to become a Bahá'í may have been Marian Steffes, an Oneida woman from Wisconsin (e-mail

correspondence, 5 July 2000). The first Canadian Indian Bahá'í was Melba Whetung Loft, an Ojibwa woman from Curve Lake Reservation (Ontario) who became a Bahá'í in Detroit in 1938 and moved to her husband's Mohawk home on Tyendinaga Reservation when he also joined the Bahá'í Faith in 1948 (see Watts and Jardine, "Alfred," "Melba"). The figure of 75 percent was suggested by Phil Lucas during an American Indian Studies guest lecture he gave at the University of Washington, Seattle (Spring 1998). See also Smith and Momen. For Canadian statistics, see van den Hoonard, 23.

18. Stockman, "American Bahá'í," 6 n. 1.

19. Quoted in P. Locke.

20. Neihardt, 42–43.

21. E-mail correspondence, 25 June 2000.

22. For a fuller discussion of the incongruence of Bahá'í Teachings and the New Age movement, see Dodenhoff, Lundberg. See Spangler for a history of the New Age movement.

23. Bahá'u'lláh, *Kitáb-I-Íqán,* 160.

24. Shoghi Effendi, *The World,* 41–42; see also 38–45. Shoghi Effendi's role as authorized interpreter of the Bahá'í Sacred Texts (the Writings of Ábdu'l-Bahá, Bahá'u'lláh, and The Báb—Bahá'u'lláh's precursor) was codified in Ábdu'l-Bahá's *Will and Testament* and is further discussed in Hofman.

25. See Churchill, "Spiritual"; and Kehoe.

26. Cited on the "The Bahá'í Faith" page of Kevin Locke's website: www .kevinlocke.com.

27. In the 1980s, First Nations and North American Indian Bahá'ís began to organize international interchanges with South American indigenous Bahá'í performers from numerous tribal areas. Jacqueline Left Hand Bull clarifies that First Nations Bahá'ís traveled from as far away as northern Alaska for a week of preparation in Navajoland before leaving on the first journey to South America in 1982. The journey was reversed in 1983, focused in Central America in 1985, traveled again from North to South America in 1988, and from South to North America in 1992. These journeys, known as the Trail of Light, were inspired by Ábdu'l-Bahá's *Tablets of the Divine Plan* and were preceded by a 4,000-mile journey through the Amazon River Basin and the Andean highlands undertaken by Canadian Bahá'í Madame Rúhíyyíh Rabbáni, who spent most of her life in Haifa, Israel, fulfilling her weighty duties as the wife and widow of Shoghi Effendi. See *The Green Light Expedition* for video documentation of her journey.

28. See the discography that follows the bibliography.

29. Locke recording, *Open Circle.*

30. For studies on the interaction of local and global in the world music industry, see Wallis and Malm; Keil and Feld; Gronow; and Racy.

31. Leuthold, 180.

32. Two examples include *In Whose Honor?* and *500 Nations.* Both feature the music of contemporary flute player Douglas Spotted Eagle, who has adopted a Native American identity in his public persona.

33. Fabian, *Time,* 18.

34. For references on the representation of American Indians, see Mignolo (cartography); Greenblatt (historicity); Harrison, Bohlman (ethnomusicology); Stedman, Churchill, "Literature" (literature); Steele, Pearlstone (advertising); Hedlund, Ames (museum exhibits); Trennert, Francis (heritage industry); Churchill, "Lawrence," Morris (film); Bird, "Not My Fantasy," *Dressing in Feathers;* A. Taylor (television); Hauptman, Churchill, *Indians* (sports); Moffitt and Sebastian (art); and Slemens, Dippie (photography).

35. See Locke recordings *Dream Catcher* and *The First Flute* for contemporary flute renditions of two of Sitting Bull's songs. Kevin Locke's flute and vocal works will be featured in two upcoming films, *The Peace Pilgrim* by Wakan Films and *To Dance the Vision* by Jim Deerhawk and Phil Lucas. See *Songkeepers* for a documentary on flute players Kevin Locke, R. Carlos Nakai, Sonny Nevaquaya, Richard Payne, Tom Mauchahty-Ware, and Hawk Littlejohn. For Native flute scholarship see Buss, Conlon, Galpin, Reimer, and Wapp. For articles on contemporary flute performance practice, primarily limited to Nakai's viewpoint, see Nakai and De-Mars; McAllester; Means; and Tayac. For an overview of Lakota song texts, including love songs, see Young Bear.

36. Neskahi, 7. How-to authors include Crawford; Price; Nakai and De-Mars; *Instructional Flute Video;* and *How to Craft.*

37. Means, 43.

38. In a cursory survey of Native American/American Indian flute recordings, I came across nearly 300 post-1985 releases.

39. Churchill summarizes some of the implications of the 1990 Indian Arts and Crafts Act in "The Crucible," 55. See also Sheffield.

40. Neskahi, 4.

41. The flutes Conlon documented were acquired between 1853 and 1982 by various museums. The twenty-five flutes on which she based her tuning analysis included: two Algonkian (Delaware, Saux/Fox); twelve Iroquoian (Huron, Cayuga, Oneida, Onondaga, Seneca, Iroquois); one Southeast (Muskokee/Creek); seven Plains (Cree, Kiowa, "Sioux"); one Plateau (Nez Perce); and two Basin (Paiute, Ute). Conlon, 52.

42. Worldflutes, the International Native American Flute Association's (INAFA) website, which ironically has no international affiliates, lists forty registered flute circles in twenty-six states across the country, as well as twenty-six flute instructors in twenty states. These statistics were last updated 8 November 2000.

43. Multicategory Native American Music Award nominee Mary Young-blood *(The Offering)* was the first American Indian woman to issue a full-length

compact disc of Native flute music. She and Kevin spent 14 April 1999 trying to work out some songs in preparation to play together during a concert at Round Valley High School in California.

44. This is the only flute I have seen Kevin refer to by the name of the locale in which he received it rather than by the name of the maker; he calls it his "Michigan flute." One myth perpetuated by some makers of "Native American flutes" is that a flute can be made in the traditional manner (using the width of the maker's fingers to determine the distance between holes) and still come out tuned to the tempered scale. This misconception gives those flute makers who allege to use those methods an edge of "authenticity" on the New Age market. Most flute makers, however, use more conventional measuring standards.

45. Although the controversial issue of American Indian and First Nations identity is seen by many as a divisive invention of the dominant culture's "divide-and-rule" mindset, as is discussed by Churchill, "The Crucible," and Mihesuah, that is not to say that it should be ignored.

46. Personal correspondence, spring 1998. Patricia Locke's input has been invaluable; she is not only Kevin Locke's mother, but is a strong protector of Lakota culture with a formidable list of accomplishments in the American Indian world and abroad, including serving as a MacArthur Fellow (1991–1996).

47. E-mail correspondence, 4 July 2000.

48. E-mail correspondence, 4 July 2000.

49. Whitt, 186, n. 10.

50. E-mail correspondence, 4 July 2000.

51. This definition arose out of Boas's research on the Northwest Coast potlatch and was promulgated by him in the hope of convincing the government that the potlatch, rather than signifying a "wanton waste of wealth," was simply an economic system and should therefore not be legally banned (341, 353). Unfortunately, his argument was to no avail and this theme became an ingrained rationale for the anthropological misrepresentation of the give-away that is perpetuated to this day.

52. Locke recording, *Prophecies of Peace*.

53. Ibid.

54. For the development of North American "would-be Indian" movements, see Kealiinohomoku; Powers, "The Indian." For similar movements in Europe, see C. Taylor; *Rockin' Warriors*. In Siberia, see *Seeking the Spirit*. For contemporary "wanna-be" trends, see Rose; Kehoe; Churchill, "Spiritual." Insightful references on the objectification of American Indians include Dorris; Berkhofer; and Steele. For discussion of the emergence of the term "New Age," see Heelas; Spangler; and Melton and Lewis. The term's centuries-old use has been reinscribed by a myriad of urban and Internet subcultures, as is attested by the 152,596 websites that came up on a capricious "exact text" search for "New Age" early in 1998.

55. Contemporary marketing of this myth is perhaps most visible today in the

use of sports mascots, team names, compact-disc jackets, and the packaging of food products such as Land 'O Lakes butter, Kraft's Calumet baking powder, and Best Foods Argo corn starch.

56. Quoted in Means, 43–44.

57. Quoted in Means, 44.

58. Quoted in Tayac, 38–41.

59. See K. Locke website.

60. See Sachs; Roberts; Reimer; Conlon; Gombert; Keeling; and Lee. The first recordings of love songs of which I am aware are found in Paul Radin's Winnebago collection (1908).

61. Means, 43.

62. Worldflutes.

63. This is not meant to imply that only seven pitches can be rendered on the flute, for many feature full chromatic ranges of up to a major tenth. It simply indicates that many traditional flute songs use seven pitches, including grace notes. For a discussion of the seven Dakota divisions, see Feraca and Howard.

64. Liner notes of the Locke recording *The Seventh Direction*.

65. Heth, *Native American Dance*, 10–12.

66. Kavanagh, 107.

67. Huenemann, 146.

68. Jones, 174. What is meant by "triple speed" is unknown. Kevin Locke's Hoop Dance footwork moves comfortably at a speed of 186 beats per minute. While not inordinately fast for a powwow or show dance, it is difficult to imagine a hoop dancer moving any faster and maintaining the fluidity of the dance. Regarding the globe formation, Kevin has used this move in his dance since Arlo Good Bear taught it to him in 1980.

69. Gannett News Service.

70. Wilson, 14.

71. Gannett News Service.

72. Fabian, *Power*, 4.

73. Imparted to a handful of individuals over the years through dreams, in recent years these rites have been exploited for profit in many New Age circles, resulting in what was referred to earlier as "huckster lists," which are occasionally circulated throughout Indian Country to alert people to transgressors. Although these rites are discussed by numerous scholars, Brown is the most commonly cited.

74. Densmore, 65, 63–67. Earlier accounts include Dorsey; E. S. Curtis.

75. Bahá'u'lláh, *Gleanings*, 62, 145.

76. The "Greater Covenant" guides the relationship between the Creator and the created, whereas the "Lesser Covenant" guides that of the Creator's Messengers and Their respective adherents. For a fuller discussion of this core Bahá'í concept, see Taherzadeh.

77. Bahá'u'lláh, *Gleanings*, 62. Bahá'u'lláh wrote: "Once in about a thousand

years shall this City be renewed and readorned. . . . That City is none other than the Word of God revealed in every age and dispensation" (*Gleanings*, 169–70).

78. Brown, xx.

79. Quoted in P. Locke.

80. *Morning Stars*. Located at the Bahá'í World Centre in Haifa, Israel, Bahá'u'lláh chose this site for the Shrine of The Báb in 1890 and Ábdu'l-Bahá completed the first stage of its construction in 1909 after his release from prison in Akká (Universal House of Justice, *Bahá'í Holy*, 42, 46). During the early 1920s, Shoghi Effendi began to design and lay out the gardens with large eight- and nine-pointed stars being prominent features throughout the landscape of both this sacred site and that of the Shrine of Bahá'u'lláh, across the bay in Bahji—an immense, ongoing project.

81. *Morning Stars*. Bahá'u'lláh describes this event in Marks (65–70).

82. Personal communication, 14 July 2000.

83. Shoghi Effendi, *Citadel*, 101. Bahá'u'lláh wrote about this experience in the Lawh-i-Ru'yá (Tablet of the Vision), revealed 1 March 1873 in Ákká (Marks, 283). The Qará-Guhar was the name of the heaviest of "one of two chains [that] was placed around Bahá'u'lláh's neck at all times" in the Síyáh Chál. This particular chain weighed 112 pounds and had to be supported with a special wooden fork (Marks, 61 n. 3).

84. Bahá'u'lláh, "Tablet of the Vision," cited by Shoghi Effendi, *God*, 221. This Tablet has not been published in English to date.

85. Quoted in P. Locke.

86. For further discussion, see *Vision of the Hoop;* Neihardt, 20–47. For a more in-depth discussion of Neihardt's *Black Elk Speaks,* see DeMallie.

87. Liner notes of the Locke recording *Open Circle.*

88. Quoted in Bahá'í International Community, 1.

89. Fabian, *Power*, 8–10.

90. For a photographic overview of Kevin Locke's Hoop Dance, see Swenson. For beautifully illustrated children's books on the Hoop Dance, see Haven-Finley; Left Hand Bull and Haldane. Although Left Hand Bull and Haldane have used a similar approach in describing the Hoop Dance, I first encountered their book a year after I finished writing this essay.

91. Fabian, *Power*, 9.

92. Quoted in Darby, 203.

93. Personal communication from Kevin Locke, 18 May 1998.

Works Cited

Ábdu'l-Bahá. *Tablets of the Divine Plan, 1916–17.* 7th ed. Trans. Shoghi Effendi. Reprint, Wilmette, Ill: Bahá'í Publishing Trust, 1993.

——. *The Will and Testament of Ábdu'l-Bahá, 1908–10.* 2d ed. Trans. Shoghi Effendi. 1944. Reprint, Wilmette, Ill: Bahá'í Publishing Trust, 1971.

Allen, Paula Gunn. "The Ceremonial Motion of Indian Time: Long Ago, So Far." Pp. 69–75 in *American Indian Theatre in Performance,* ed. Hanay Geiogamah and Jaye T. Darby. Los Angeles: UCLA American Indian Studies Center, 2000.

Ames, Michael. "The Politics of Difference: Other Voices in a Not Yet Post-Colonial World." *Museum Anthropology* 18, no. 3 (1994): 9–17.

Appadurai, Arjun. "Global Ethnoscapes: Notes and Queries for a Transnational Anthropology." Pp. 191–213 in *Recapturing Anthropology: Working in the Present,* ed. Richard Fox. Sante Fe: School of American Research, 1991.

Bad Heart Bull, Amos. *A Pictographic History of the Oglala Sioux* [1890–1913]. Lincoln: University of Nebraska Press, 1967.

Bahá'í International Community. *One Country: The Bahá'í International Community* 8, no. 2 (1996): 1–7.

Bahá'u'lláh. *Gleanings from the Writings of Bahá'u'lláh, 1853–92.* 2d ed. Trans. Shoghi Effendi. 1939. Reprint, Wilmette, Ill: Bahá'í Publishing Trust, 1976.

——. *The Kitáb-I-Íqán (the Book of Certitude).* 1873. 2d ed. Trans. Shoghi Effendi. Reprint, Wilmette, Ill: Bahá'í Publishing Trust, 1989.

Berkhofer, Robert. *The White Man's Indian.* New York: Alfred A. Knopf, 1978.

Bird, S. Elizabeth. "Not My Fantasy: The Persistence of Indian Imagery in *Dr. Quinn, Medicine Woman.*" Pp. 245–61 in *Dressing in Feathers,* ed. S. Elizabeth Bird. Boulder, Colo.: Westview Press, 1996.

——, ed. *Dressing in Feathers.* Boulder, Colo.: Westview Press, 1996.

Boas, Franz. "The Social Organization and the Secret Societies of the Kwakiutl Indians." Report of the U.S. National Museum for 1895. Washington, D.C.: Government Printing Office, 1897.

Bohlman, Philip V. "Representation and Cultural Critique in the History of Ethnomusicology." Pp. 131–51 in *Comparative Musicology and Anthropology of Music: Essays on the History of Ethnomusicology,* ed. Bruno Nettle and Philip V. Bohlman. Chicago: The University of Chicago Press, 1991.

Braun, Eunice. *A Reader's Guide: The Development of Bahá'í Literature in English.* Oxford, U.K.: George Ronald, 1986.

Brown, Joseph Epes, ed. *The Sacred Pipe: Black Elk's Account of the Seven Rites of the Oglala Sioux.* The Civilization of the American Indian Series. 1953. Reprint, Norman: University of Oklahoma Press, 1989.

Buss, Judy Epstein. "The Flute and Flute Music of the North American Indians." M.M. thesis, University of Illinois, 1972.

Champagne, Duane, ed. *Contemporary Native American Cultural Issues.* London: AltaMira Press, 1999.

Churchill, Ward. "The Crucible of American Indian Identity: Native Tradition versus Colonial Imposition in Postconquest North America." Pp. 39–67 in

Contemporary Native American Issues, ed. Duane Champagne. London: Alta-Mira Press, 1999.

——. *Indians Are Us?* Monroe, Maine: Common Courage Press, 1994.

——. "Lawrence of South Dakota." Pp. 243–47 in *Fantasies of the Master Race: Literature, Cinema, and Colonization of American Indians,* ed. Annette Jaimes. Monroe, Maine: Common Courage Press, 1992.

——. "Literature as a Weapon in the Colonization of the American Indian." Pp. 17–41 in *Fantasies of the Master Race: Literature, Cinema, and Colonization of American Indians,* ed. Annette Jaimes. Monroe, Maine: Common Courage Press, 1992.

——. "Spiritual Hucksterism: The Rise of the Plastic Medicine Men." Pp. 215–28 in *Fantasies of the Master Race: Literature, Cinema, and Colonization of American Indians,* ed. Annette Jaimes. Monroe, Maine: Common Courage Press, 1992.

Conlon, Paula. "The Flute of the Canadian Amerindian: An Analysis of the Vertical Whistle Flute with External Block and its Music." M.A. thesis, Carleton University, 1983.

Crawford, Tim R., with Kathleen Joyce. *Flute Magic: An Introduction to the Native American Flute.* Canal Fulton, Ohio: RainDance Publications, 1998.

Curtis, Edward S. *The North American Indian.* Vol. 3. 1908. Reprint, New York: Johnson Reprint Corporation, 1970.

Curtis, Natalie. *The Indians' Book.* 1907. Reprint, New York: Harper and Brothers, 1968.

Darby, Jay T. " 'Come to the Ceremonial Circle': Ceremony and Renewal in Hanay Geiogamah's 49." Pp. 195–227 in *American Indian Theatre in Performance,* ed. Hanay Geiogamah and Jaye T. Darby. Los Angeles: UCLA American Indian Studies Center, 2000.

DeMallie, Raymond J. *The Sixth Grandfather: Black Elk's Teachings Given to John G. Neihardt.* Lincoln: University of Nebraska Press, 1984.

Densmore, Francis. *Teton Sioux Music.* Smithsonian Institution Bureau of American Ethnology Bulletin, no. 61. 1918. Reprint, Lincoln: University of Nebraska Press, 1992.

Dippie, Brian. "Representing the Other: The North American Indian." Pp. 132–36 in *Anthropology and Photography,* ed. Elizabeth Edwards. New Haven, Conn.: Yale University Press, 1992.

Dodenhoff, Paul. " 'Buddy, Can You Spare a Paradigm?': The Bahá'í Faith and the New Age Movement." Paper presented at the Fifteenth Irfan Colloquium, 8–10 August 1997. Bahá'í National Center, Wilmette, Ill. Posted on website managed by Jonah Winters: http://bahai-library.org/conferences/new.age .html.

Dorris, Michael. " 'I' is Not for Indian." Pp. 27–28 in *Through Indian Eyes,* ed. Beverly Slapin and Doris Seale. Philadelphia: New Society Publishers, 1992.

Dorsey, George A. "Legend of the Teton Sioux Medicine Pipe." *Journal of American Folk-Lore* 19 (1906): 626–29.

Ellingson, Ter. *The Myth of the Noble Savage.* Berkeley: University of California Press, 2001.

Erlmann, Veit. *Nightsong: Performance, Power, and Practice in South Africa.* Chicago: University of Chicago Press, 1996.

Fabian, Johannes. *Power and Performance: Ethnographic Explorations through Proverbial Wisdom and Theatre in Shaba, Zaire.* Madison: University of Wisconsin Press, 1990.

——. *Time and the Other: How Anthropology Makes Its Object.* New York: Columbia University Press, 1983.

Feraca, Stephen E., and James H. Howard. "The Identity and Demography of the Dakota or Sioux Tribe." *Plains Anthropologist* 8 (1963): 80–84.

Fewkes, Jesse Walter, collector. *Hopi Katcina Songs and Six Other Hopi Chanters.* 1924. Reprint, Smithsonian Folkways no. 04394, 1960.

500 Nations. Film. Produced by Jack Leutisig. TIG Productions in association with RCS Film and TV, Majestic Films, and Television International, 1994.

Francis, Daniel. *The Imaginary: The Image of the Indian in Canadian Culture.* Vancouver, B.C.: Arsenal Pulp Press, 1992.

Galpin, Frances W. "The Whistles and Reed Instruments of the American Indians of the Northwest Coast." *Proceedings of the Musical Association* 29 (1902/1903): 115–38.

Gannett News Service. "Curious Prophecy Preserves Hoop Dance: Performer Steps into Window of Opportunity." *The Bellingham Herald,* 4 November 1997, C1, 3.

Geiogamah, Hanay, and Jaye T. Darby, eds. *American Indian Theatre in Performance: A Reader.* Los Angeles: UCLA American Indian Studies Center, 2000.

Gombert, Greg. *A Guide to Native American Music Recordings.* Summertown, Tenn.: Book Publishing Co., 1994.

Greenblatt, Stephen. *Marvelous Possessions: The Wonder of the New World.* Chicago: University of Chicago Press, 1991.

The Green Light Expedition: An Unforgettable Journey Through South America. NTSC/ PAL/SECAM/VHS videocassette. Produced by Madame Rúhíyyíh Rabbáni. 'Amatu'l-Bahá Rúhíyyíh *Khanum* Production V-29FR, V-30EN, V-31SP, 1975.

Gronow, Pekka. "Ethnic Music and Soviet Record Industry." *World of Music* 19, no. 1 (1975): 91–99.

——. "The Record Industry Comes to the Orient." *Ethnomusicology* 25, no. 2 (1981): 251–84.

Harrison, Frank. *Time, Place, and Music: An Anthology of Ethnomusicological Observation c. 1550 to c. 1800.* Amsterdam, the Netherlands: Frits Knuf, 1973.

Hauptman, Laurence. *Tribes and Tribulations: Misconceptions about American Indians and Their Histories.* Albuquerque: University of New Mexico Press, 1995.

Haven-Finley, Jan. *The Hoop of Peace.* Happy Camp, Calif.: Naturegraph Publishers, 1994.

Hedlund, Ann. "Speaking *For* or *About* Others? Evolving Ethnological Perspectives." *Museum Anthropology* 18, no. 3 (1994): 9–17.

Heelas, Paul. *The New Age Movement.* Cambridge, U.K.: Blackwell Publishers, 1996.

Heth, Charlotte. "American Indian Dance: A Celebration of Survival and Adaptation." Pp. 1–32 in *Native American Dance: Ceremonies and Social Transitions,* ed. Charlotte Heth. Washington, D.C.: National Museum of the American Indian, 1992.

——, ed. *Native American Dance: Ceremonies and Social Traditions.* Washington, D.C.: National Museum of the American Indian, 1992.

Hofman, David. *A Commentary on the Will and Testament of Ábdu'l-Bahá.* 4th ed. 1982. Reprint, Oxford, U.K.: George Ronald, 1989.

Hornby, Helen, compiler. *Lights of Guidance: A Bahá'í Reference File.* 2d ed. New Delhi: Bahá'í Publishing Trust, 1988.

How to Craft Your Own Native American Flute. Videocassette. Produced by Lee La Croix. Echoes Past, n.d.

Huenemann, Lynn F. "Northern Plains Dance." Pp. 125–47 in *Native American Dance: Ceremonies and Social Transitions,* ed. Charlotte Heth. Washington, D.C.: National Museum of the American Indian, 1992.

Instructional Flute Video. Videocassette. Produced by Lakota George. Estes Productions, 1994.

In Whose Honor? Videocassette. Produced by Jay Rosenstein. POV Film, 1996.

Jaimes, Annette, ed. *Fantasies of the Master Race: Literature, Cinema, and Colonization of American Indians.* Monroe, Maine: Common Courage Press, 1992.

Jones, Rosalie M. "Modern Native Dance: Beyond Tribe and Tradition." Pp. 169–83 in *Native American Dance: Ceremonies and Social Transitions,* ed. Charlotte Heth. Washington, D.C.: National Museum of the American Indian, 1992.

Kavanagh, Thomas W. "Southern Plains Dance: Tradition and Dynamism." Pp. 105–24 in *Native American Dance: Ceremonies and Social Transitions,* ed. Charlotte Heth. Washington, D.C.: National Museum of the American Indian, 1992.

Kealiinohomoku, Joann W. "The Would-Be Indian." Pp. 111–26 in *Explorations in Ethnomusicology: Essays in Honor of David P. McAllester,* ed. Charlotte J. Frisbie. Detroit: Information Coordinators, 1986.

Keeling, Richard. *North American Indian Music: A Guide to Published Sources and Selected Recordings.* New York: Garland, 1997.

Kehoe, Alice. "Primal Gaia: Primitivists and Plastic Medicine Men." Pp. 193–209 in *The Invented Indian: Cultural Fictions and Government Policies,* ed. James A. Clifton. New Brunswick, N.J.: Transaction Publishers, 1990.

Keil, Charles, and Steven Feld. *Music Grooves.* Chicago: University of Chicago Press, 1994.

Lee, Dorothy Sarah. *Native North American Music and Oral Data: A Catalogue of Sound Recordings, 1893–1976.* Bloomington: Indiana University Press, 1979.

Left Hand Bull, Jacqueline, and Suzanne Haldane. *Lakota Hoop Dancer.* New York: Dutton Children's Books, 1999.

Lescarbot, Marc. *Nova Francia: A Description of Acadia.* 1606. Trans. P. Erondelle. Reprint, London: Routledge, 1928.

Leuthold, Steven. *Indigenous Aesthetics: Native Art, Media, and Identity.* Austin: University of Texas Press, 1998.

Locke, Kevin. "Kevin Locke (Tokeya Inajin)." Website managed by Jim Deerhawk: www.kevinlocke.com.

Locke, Patricia. "The Return of the 'White Buffalo Calf Woman': Prophecy of the Lakota—Interview with Jacqueline Left Hand Bull." 1989. Available via http://bci.org/prophecy-fulfilled/wbcalf.htm.

Lundberg, Zaid. "The New Age Movement and the Bahá'í Faith." Paper presented at the Fourteenth Irfan Colloquium, 4–6 July 1997, Manchester Bahá'í Centre, Manchester, U.K; posted on website managed by Jonah Winters: http://bahai-library.org/conferences/newage.lundberg.html.

Marcus, George E., ed. *Perilous States: Conversations on Culture, Politics, and Nation.* Late Editions Cultural Studies for the End of the Century, vol. 1. Chicago: University of Chicago Press, 1993.

Marks, Geoffry W., compiler. *Call to Remembrance: Connecting the Heart to Bahá'u'lláh.* Wilmette, Ill: Bahá'í Publishing Trust, 1992.

McAllester, David P. "The Music of R. Carlos Nakai." Pp. 189–210 in *To the Four Corners: A Festschrift in Honor of Rose Brandel,* ed. Ellen C. Leichtman. Warren, Mich.: Harmonie Park Press, 1994.

——. "North America/Native America." Pp. 17–70 in *Worlds of Music: An Introduction to the Music of the World's Peoples,* ed. Jeff Todd Titon. New York: Schirmer Books, 1996.

Means, Andrew. "Tools of the Trade: The Native American Flute." *Songlines: Journeys in World Music* (Spring/Summer 2000): 42–49.

Melton, J. Gordon, and James R. Lewis, eds. *Perspectives on the New Age.* Albany: State University of New York Press, 1992.

Mignolo, Walter. "Misunderstanding and Colonization: The Reconfiguration of Memory and Space." *The South Atlantic Quarterly* 92, no. 2 (1993): 209–60.

Mihesuah, Devon A. "American Indian Identities: Issues of Individual Choice and Development." Pp. 13–38 in *Contemporary Native American Issues,* ed. Duane Champagne. London: AltaMira Press, 1999.

Moffitt, John, and Santiago Sebastian. *O Brave New People: The European Invention of the American Indian.* Albuquerque: University of New Mexico Press, 1996.

Morning Stars: A Profile of Kevin Locke. VHS videocassette. Coproduced by David Andrews and Shar Lenz. Stay Focused Productions, 1990.

Morris, Rosalind C. *New Worlds from Fragments: Film, Ethnography, and the Representation of Northwest Coast Cultures.* Studies in the Ethnographic Imagination Series. Boulder, Colo.: Westview Press, 1994.

Nakai, R. Carlos, and James DeMars. *The Art of the Native American Flute* (with additional material by David P. McAllester and Ken Light). Phoenix: Canyon Records Productions, 1996.

Neihardt, John G. *Black Elk Speaks: Being the Life Story of a Holy Man of the Oglala Sioux as Told through John G. Neihardt (Flaming Rainbow).* 1932. Reprint, Lincoln: University of Nebraska Press, 1989.

Neskahi, Arlie. "Flute and Whistle Traditions." Posted 5 August 1997 on Flute Traditions page, *Rainbow Walker Productions:* www.rainbowwalker.com.

Pearlstone, Zean. "Native American Images in Advertising." *American Indian Art Magazine* 20, no. 3 (1995): 36–43.

Powers, William K. "The Indian Hobbyist Movement in North America." Pp. 557–61 in *Handbook of North American Indians.* Vol. 4, *A History of Indian-White Relations,* ed. Wilcomb Washburn. Washington, D.C.: Smithsonian Institution Press, 1988.

——. *Oglala Religion.* Lincoln: University of Nebraska Press, 1977.

Price, Lew Paxton. *Creating and Using the Native American Love Flute.* Garden Valley, Calif.: Lew Paxton Price, 1994.

——. *Creating and Using Smaller Native American Flutes.* Garden Valley, Calif.: Lew Paxton Price, 1995.

Racy, Ali Jihan. "Arabian Music and the Effects of Commercial Recording." *World of Music* 20, no. 1 (1978): 47–55.

Radin, Paul, collector. *United States, Nebraska, Winnebago Indians.* 1908. Fifty-six cylinders, including love songs, housed in Indiana University Archives of Traditional Music, Bloomington.

Reimer, Mary F. "Instrumental and Vocal Love Songs of the North American Indians." M.A. thesis, Wesleyan University, 1978.

Rhodes, Willard, collector. *United States, South Dakota, Pine Ridge and Ft. Thompson, Teton Sioux Indians.* 1939. 104 78-rpm discs, including flute and love songs, housed in the Indiana University Archives of Traditional Music, Bloomington.

Roberts, Helen H. *Musical Areas in Aboriginal North America.* Yale University Publications in Anthropology, no. 12. New Haven: Yale University Press, 1936.

Rockin' Warriors. Beta SP, VHS videocassette. Coproduced by Phil Lucas and Larue Hall. Lynx Productions, 1997.

Rose, Wendy. "The Great Pretenders: Further Reflections on White Shamanism."

Pp. 403–22 in *Fantasies of the Master Race: Literature, Cinema, and Colonization of American Indians,* ed. Annette Jaimes. Monroe, Maine: Common Courage Press, 1992.

Rousseau, Jean-Jacques. *A Discourse on Inequality.* 1755. Trans. Maurice Cranston. Reprint, London: Penguin, 1984.

Sachs, Curt. *Geist und Werden der Musikinstruments.* Berlin: Dietrich Reimer, 1929.

Seeking the Spirit: Plains Indians in Russia. VHS videocassette. Produced by Bea Medicine. Warrior Women, Inc., 1997.

Sheffield, Gail K. *The Arbitrary Indian: The Indian Arts and Crafts Act of 1990.* Norman: University of Oklahoma Press, 1997.

Shoghi Effendi. *Advent of Divine Justice: Letter to the Bahá'ís of the United States and Canada, December 25, 1938.* New Delhi: Bahá'í Publishing Trust, 1968.

——. *Citadel of Faith: Message to America, 1947–1957.* Comp. National Spiritual Assembly of the Bahá'ís of the United States. 1965. Reprint, Wilmette, Ill.: Bahá'í Publishing Trust, 1995.

——. *God Passes By.* 1944. 2d ed., reprint, Wilmette, Ill.: Bahá'í Publishing Trust, 1995.

——. *The World Order of Bahá'u'lláh: Selected Letters, 1929–1936.* 1938. Reprint, Wilmette, Ill: Bahá'í Publishing Trust, 1991.

Slemens, Rod. *Shadowy Evidence: The Photography of Edward S. Curtis and His Contemporaries.* Seattle: Seattle Art Museum, 1989.

Smith, Peter, and Moojan Momen. "The Bahá'í Faith 1957–1988: A Survey of Contemporary Developments." *Religion* 19 (1989): 63–91.

Songkeepers: A Saga of Five Native Americans Told through the Sound of the Flute. Beta SP, 35-mm film, VHS videocassette. Produced by Dan King. America's Flute Productions, 1999.

Spangler, David. "The Movement toward the Divine." In *New Age Spirituality,* ed. Duncan S. Ferguson. Louisville, Ky.: Westminster/John Knox Press, 1993.

Stedman, Raymond. *Shadows of the Indian: Stereotypes in American Culture.* Norman: University of Oklahoma Press, 1982.

Steele, Jeffrey. "Reduced to Images: American Indians in Nineteenth-Century Advertising." Pp. 45–64 in *Dressing in Feathers,* ed. S. Elizabeth Bird. Boulder, Colo.: Westview Press, 1996.

Stockman, Robert H. "The American Bahá'í Community in the Nineties." In *America's Alternative Religions,* ed. Timothy Miller. Albany: State University of New York Press, 1995. Posted on website managed by Jonah Winters: http://bahai-library.org/articles/american.community/html.

——. *The Bahá'í Faith in America.* Vol. 1, *Origins, 1892–1900.* Wilmette, Ill.: Bahá'í Publishing Trust, 1985.

——. *The Bahá'í Faith in America.* Vol. 2, *Early Expansion, 1902–1912.* Oxford, U.K.: George Ronald, 1995.

Stockman, Robert H., and Jonah Winters. *A Research Guide for the Scholarly Study of* the *Bahá'í Faith*. Wilmette, Ill.: Research Office of the Bahá'í National Center, 1997.

Swenson, David. "Makoché Records." Available via: www.makoche.com.

Taherzadeh, Adib. *The Covenant of Bahá'u'lláh.* 1992. Reprint, Oxford, U.K.: George Ronald, 1995.

Tayac, Gabrielle. "Interview: Living in Two Worlds—R. Carlos Nakai, Ute/Navajo Flutist." *Southeast Indian Quarterly* (Fall 1989): 38–41.

Taylor, Annette. "Cultural Heritage in *Northern Exposure.*" Pp. 229–44 in *Dressing in Feathers,* ed. S. Elizabeth Bird. Boulder, Colo.: Westview Press, 1996.

Taylor, Colin. "The Indian Hobbyist Movement in Europe." Pp. 562–69 in *Handbook of North American Indians.* Vol. 4, *A History of Indian-White Relations,* ed. Wilcomb Washburn. Washington, D.C.: Smithsonian Institution Press, 1988.

Trennert, Robert. "Fairs, Expositions, and the Changing Image of Southwestern Indians, 1867–1904." *New Mexico Historical Review* 62, no. 2 (1987): 127–50.

The Universal House of Justice. *Bahá'í Holy Places at the World Centre.* Haifa, Israel: Bahá'í World Centre, 1968.

——. *The Bahá'í World 1998–99, 155 of the Bahá'í Era: An International Record.* Haifa, Israel: Bahá'í World Centre, 2000.

van den Hoonaard, Will C. "Socio-demographic Characteristics of the Canadian Bahá'í Community." Paper presented at the Annual Meetings of the Canadian Sociology and Anthropology Association, Laval University, Québec, 3 June 1989. Revised 1991. Posted on website managed by Jonah Winters: http://bahai-library.org/conferences/canada.demographics.html.

Vision of the Hoop. VHS videocassette; excerpts from footage shot at the Second Bahá'í World Congress in New York, November 1992. Produced by the National Spiritual Assembly of the Bahá'ís of the United States. Bahá'í Distribution Service, 1993.

Wallis, Roger, and Krister Malm. *Big Sounds from Small Peoples: The Music Industry in Small Countries.* Sociology of Music Series, no. 2. New York: Pendragon Press, 1984.

Wapp, Edward R. "The American Indian Courting Flute: Revitalization and Change." Pp. 49–60 in *Sharing a Heritage: American Indian Arts.* Contemporary American Indian Issues Series, no. 5. Los Angeles: UCLA American Indian Studies Center, 1984. Reprinted on Kevin Locke's website under the name Edward Wapp Wahpeconiah: www.kevinlocke.com.

——. "Sioux Courting Flute: Its Tradition, Construction, and Music." M.A. thesis, University of Washington, 1984.

Washburn, Wilcomb, ed. *Handbook of North American Indians.* Vol. 4, *A History of Indian-White Relations.* Washington, D.C.: Smithsonian Institution Press, 1988.

Watts, Evelyn Loft, and Charles Jardine. "Alfred James Loft." *Bahá'í World* 16: 514–16.

———. "Melba Whetung Loft." *Bahá'í World* 19: 696–99.

Whitt, Laurie Ann. "Cultural Imperialism and the Marketing of Native America." Pp. 169–92 in *Contemporary Native American Issues,* ed. Duane Champagne. London: AltaMira Press, 1999.

Wilson, Jerry. "Dancing in the Sacred Hoop." *South Dakota Magazine* 15, no. 5 (2000): 8–15.

Worldflutes: International Native Flute Association. Website managed by Fr. Ka: www.worldflutes.org.

Young Bear, Severt, and R. D. Theisz. *Standing in the Light: A Lakota Way of Seeing.* Lincoln: University of Nebraska Press, 1994.

Youngblood, Mary. *The Offering.* No. SD917, Silver Wave Records, Inc., 1998.

Chronological Discography of Published Audio Recordings by Kevin Locke (Tokeya Inajin)

North American Native Cultural Presentation. Images International audiocassette, n.d.

Love Songs of the Lakota. Produced by Tony Issacs. Indian House audiocassette IH4315, 1983.

Lakota Wiikijo Olowan: Lakota Flute Music Vol. 2. Featherstone audiocassette FS4004-C, 1983.

Arts and Education: The Cultural Context. University Lecture Series: Symposium on the American Indian. Iowa State University audiocassette, 1984.

Prophecies of Peace. Presentation given at Bahá'í International Youth Conference, London, Ontario. Bahá'í Distribution Canada audiocassette CYL103, 1987.

Traditional Native American Creation and Teaching Stories. Marcie Telander, with flute performed by Kevin Locke. West of the Moon Productions audiocassette, 1987.

Lakota Love Songs and Stories. Produced by Kevin Locke. Meyer Creative audiocassette MC0101, 1990.

Make Me a Hollow Reed. Produced by Kevin Locke. Meyer Creative audiocassette MC0102C, 1990.

The Seventh Direction. Produced by Kevin Locke. Meyer Creative audiocassette MC0103C, 1990.

The Destiny of Native Americans. University Lecture Series: Symposium on the American Indian. Iowa State University audiocassette, 1991.

Dream Catcher. Produced by Tom Bee and Kevin Locke. EarthBeat! Records compact disc EB42538, 1993.

Wopila, a Giveaway: Lakota Stories Retold by Dovie Thomason with Flute by Kevin Locke. Produced by Robert Smyth. Yellow Bird Press audiocassette, 1993.

The Flash of the Mirror: Traditional American Indian Flute. Produced by Kevin Locke and David Swenson. Program notes by Kevin Locke and Jacqueline Delahunt. Makoché Records compact disc MC0104, 1994.

Keepers of the Dream: Vol. 2 of the Dream Catcher Series. Produced by Jim Deerhawk and David Swenson. Program notes by Jim Deerhawk and Kevin Locke. EarthBeat! Records compact disc EB2968, 1994.

Lullaby: A Collection. Produced by Leib Ostrow. Includes one flute piece played by Kevin Locke (produced by Jim Deerhawk). Music for Little People compact disc 42565, 1994.

Tribal Winds: Music from Native American Flutes. Includes flute pieces played by Kevin Locke, Tom Mauchahty-Ware, R. Carlos Nakai, et al. Produced by David Swenson. Earthbeat! Records compact disc 35260, 1995.

Lunar Drive: Here at Black Mesa, Arizona. Includes three flute pieces (two with vocals) played/sung by Kevin Locke. Produced by Count Dubulah and Sandy Hoover. Nation Records (England) audio cassette NR1076MC, 1996.

Open Circle. Produced by Jim Deerhawk with David Swenson. Program notes by Kevin Locke and Jim Deerhawk. Makoché Records compact disc MM0135D, 1996.

Proud Heritage: A Celebration of Traditional American Indian Music. Includes flute performances by Kevin Locke and Tom Mauchahty-Ware. Indian House compact disc IH9601, 1996.

Tribal Voices: Songs from Native Americans, an Intertribal Collection. Includes flute pieces performed by Kevin Locke, Joseph Fire Crow, Robert Tree Cody, and Andrew Vasquez. Produced by David Swenson, Agnes Patak, and Leib Ostrow. EarthBeat! Records compact disc R272538, 1996.

Tiwahe. Sissy Goodhouse, flute accompaniment performed by Kevin Locke. Makoché Records compact disc MM140, 1997.

The First Flute. Produced by David Swenson. Makoché Records compact disc MM0147D, 1999.

PART II

Marketing the Indian

5

"The Idea of Help"

White Women Reformers and the Commercialization of Native American Women's Arts

ERIK TRUMP

> Angela Lachapa, mother of our good Petria made this basket for La Constancia whom she loves very much. She told me her story as she sat warming her frail old hands. She was a girl when the chimes at Santa Ysabel rang, silver chimes calling a thousand Indians to prayer. We laughed at her account of her girlish pranks, and tears came when she showed the brown welts made by the lash to punish her for not *praying* correctly. She laughed until the tears came when she told of marrying a man of ninety years and blind in order to have the freedom accorded to married women.
>
> —MARY B. WATKINS, Indian Workers and Record [1905?][1]

CONSTANCE GODDARD DU BOIS, executive committee member of the Indian Industries League and president of the Waterbury Indian Association (Connecticut), received this note from Mary B. Watkins, her friend and contact among the Indians living at Mesa Grande, California. The note reveals dimensions of the early-twentieth-century Indian art trade not readily apparent in the texts and images crafted by commercial dealers for mass audiences of the time. Most apparently, whereas the majority of objects were sold to either the curio or the art market, Du Bois represented a third market: the philanthropist, the white woman who bought Indian arts from the conviction that doing so gave economic support to individual Indians. Other details in Watkins's note point to additional differences between these markets. The Indian artist, although not famous, is named. The complex power relations involved in the exchange are revealed: A single Indian woman living in apparent poverty makes a basket for a white patron whom she may or may not have really loved, but whose economic beneficence made her important. Moreover, the value of this particular basket appears to have been increased by the stories of population decline, poverty, and violent oppression that accompanied it, stories that were erased from commercially available baskets. Finally, the unmistakable sense of a shared, cross-cultural gendered experience, a common language of freedom, is intriguing. This was a basket made by a woman, for a woman, and its exchange produced tears on both sides.

Beginning at the end of the nineteenth century, American Indian baskets and other arts were widely sold and promoted, distributed by large department stores, offered through Indian traders' catalogues, recommended in arts and crafts publications, and sold directly to tourists who visited Indian country. Each of these realms played a visible and well-studied role in the commercialization of Native American arts, developing an image of the Indian artist that romanticized and, many would argue, further exploited Indians by packaging their culture for white, middle-class consumption. The resulting images—of Pueblo women carrying pots on their heads, Navajo women weaving blankets in front of hogans, Pomo women making baskets in front of brush huts that echoed the art's material—reinforced the idea that Indians were from another time, exotic, peaceful, and doomed to extinction in the face of modernity. At the same time, the Indian arts appealed to white Americans' concerns about labor, modernity, and lost values: Modern America's ills might be cured by contemplating lessons from the primitive past. Such images erased historical conflict and ignored present political realities, selling art objects that could be consumed without guilt.[2]

Among the many groups involved in the commercialization of Indian arts, however, one has received little attention from scholars: Indian reform organizations that seized on Indian arts and crafts as a means of developing economic self-sufficiency for Indian women and promoting philanthropic enthusiasm among white women. These organizations published comparatively little for a mass audience, but in their pamphlets, letters, meetings, parlor talks, and unpublished manuscripts, one can find a discourse that emphasized the female artist's independence, creativity, individuality, and close ties with the spheres of nature, family, and tradition. Unlike their commercial counterparts, these organizations blended aesthetic and philanthropic appeals, insisted on a kind of gender loyalty, and recognized the individual artist. I argue that the reform market created an image of Indian arts that paralleled that of the commercial market in many respects, but differed in its insistent attention to the gendered nature of the production and consumption of Indian arts. For the reformer, each purchase of Indian arts signified not just the female consumer's good taste, but also her desire to protect a feminine art and its makers, who were under attack from many quarters. If white female consumers constructed their identities through their purchases, Indian baskets suggested the independence and creativity widely ascribed to female Indian artists.[3]

At the 1892 annual meeting of the Women's National Indian Association (WNIA), Frances Sparhawk proposed the establishment of an Indian Industries League, which she imagined "would open individual opportunities to individual Indians and concomitantly encourage self-supporting industries in Indian communities."[4] By supporting the development of "civilized" industries, the league hoped to assimilate Indians into the national life and break up the tribes. Committed to a vision of evolutionary social progress, the Indian Industries League firmly believed that Indians could be integrated into American society only after they received an education and mastered a proficiency in civilized industries such as carpentry, dress making, harness making, blacksmithing, and farming. Indian women, who were perceived as the key to reforming their communities, would have to learn proper housekeeping and wage-labor skills. In the development of these industries, the league planned to be a spur, supporting individual efforts where it could and drawing public interest to such efforts as a way to modify white Americans' view of Indians as racially incapable of equality with whites. The proposal complemented efforts by the WNIA, which since 1879 had labored under the belief that women (white and Indian) played a central role in the civilizing process. Sparhawk's plan was well received by many New England members of the WNIA, and in late 1893, under her guidance, the Indian Industries League formed at a meeting in Boston.[5]

Underlying the motivations of white women in the Indian reform movement was a key perception that Indian women were degraded and abused by the conditions of tribal life. In the reformers' minds, Indian men and women did not conform to white gender roles. The men were lazy, interested only in leisure activities such as hunting, and the women did too much men's work; moreover, sexual morals were too loose, as evidenced by polygamy and easy divorce. The image of overworked and sexually exploited "squaw drudges" suffering at the hands of their husbands was widespread in nineteenth-century America. As a double insult, the squaw drudge was also imagined as prone to drunkenness, violence, and cruelty. Equally troubling were the stories of Indian girls "civilized" at places such as the Carlisle Indian Industrial School and returned to horrible reservation conditions where their new skills were scorned by traditional Indians. League member Sibyl Carter, who ran a lace industry for Indian women in Minnesota, claimed "that the time to get the girls was before they returned to the reservations for that when there the mothers would not let them go again."[6] These images rallied women to the civilizing cause and figured prominently in Sparhawk's writing during the 1880s and 1890s.

Ironically, at the very moment the Indian Industries League was preparing to civilize Indian women by reshaping their tribal communities, other white women were beginning to find much to admire in primitive women's lives. The harbingers of change can be seen in exhibits and speeches from the 1893 World's Columbian Exposition in Chicago, in popular articles about American Indian women, and in the rhetoric of the arts and crafts movement. Together, these voices challenged the squaw drudge image by suggesting that Indian women exhibited numerous domestic virtues on which civilization rested, demonstrated superior aesthetic sensibilities, and enjoyed social and political rights unequaled by most white women. Thus, the Indian Industries League had been born into a period when many of the concepts that undergirded Indian reformers' work were being overturned by several overlapping and somewhat contradictory ideas: degraded squaw drudges were being reimagined as independent craftswomen, the womanly ideal of the domestic helpmate was giving way to the new woman, and the supposed virtues of civilized industries were being attacked on several fronts. Its foundational terrain shifting underfoot, the league reshaped its ideas and activities to fit the new landscape.

In Chicago at the 1893 World's Columbian Exposition, primitive women, Indians included, were being held up by some as exemplars of feminine artistry, domesticity, and independence. The Woman's Building, erected as a dedication "to elevated womanhood," was on the border between the genteelly inspirational official White City and the basely exotic Midway Plaisance. Thus, women and savages, their mental abilities often linked by leading anthropometrists of the day, were geographic neighbors at the White City.[7] Inside the Woman's Building were exhibits of primitive handicrafts and even a female Navajo weaver with her loom. Taken together with speeches given during the Congress of Women, these exhibits suggested that the distance between the primitive woman and the modern civilized woman was a small one and that the primitive woman—far from an object of derision, pity, or curiosity—was a figure of respect.

The Woman's Building stood as a *history* of woman's work, as a testi-

mony to the fact that women "were the originators of most of the industrial arts, and that it was not until these became lucrative that they were
appropriated by men, and women pushed aside." To reveal this past, the
managers of the Woman's Building enlisted the aid of the Smithsonian
Institution in creating a "primitive feminine industrial exhibit," which
showed that women had been the "firsts" in many industries: pottery,
weaving, basket making, architecture, decorative arts, and so on. Mary
Lockwood, a feminist whose interest in history earned her the job of designing historical exhibits for the Patents Office and the Smithsonian, enthusiastically championed the concept. Her own investigations had turned
up convincing evidence of women's role "as inventors from the industrial
age to the present," and she pointed out that an impressive exhibit of
women's work, especially pottery and basketry, could be culled from the
Smithsonian's collections.[8] The resulting eighty-case exhibition, "Woman's Work in Savagery," was installed in the Woman's Building in June, after
the fair had opened. This installation was joined throughout the building
by other exhibits of primitive women's work. American Indian handicrafts
from many states and territories were "scattered around the building," and a
Navajo woman was on hand to demonstrate her weaving skills. Moreover,
many of the displayed objects from other countries, even European ones,
were actually pre-industrial handicrafts.[9]

The object lesson that visitors took away from the Woman's Building
was that primitive woman's work was worthy of exhibition next to modern
woman's fine arts. Indeed, many reviewers found more to admire, artistically, in the primitive work than in the modern. A contemporary potter,
Mary Louise McLaughlin, argued that in the decoration of ceramics, "we
fall behind our aboriginal models, who in their simplicity never lost sight of
the fitness of things, and whose work consequently ranks high in true
artistic beauty." Candace Wheeler pointed out the admirable quality of the
primitive applied arts, reminding visitors that "we are considering a new
birth, a revival of ancient handcrafts." The growing popularity of Southwestern Indian pottery confirmed these opinions, as did the Rookwood
Pottery Company's wares decorated with images of Indian potters, weavers, and basket makers; other pottery companies went as far as copying
Indian ceramic forms and designs. No one suggested that women's decorative arts had been improved by modern civilization. Instead, many women
articulated variations of the theme that women's productive labor, and even
their social purpose, had been stolen from them by industrialization.[10]

The squaw drudge stereotype was challenged in several speeches given in the Woman's Building. Juliet Corson, an advocate of domestic science, found unexpected moral lessons in the exposition's anthropological exhibits. For evidence of the ancient, noble history of motherhood, Corson urged the mothers in her audience to visit the Anthropological Building, where they could gaze on the "relics" of long dead American Indian mothers, "poor shreds and patches of humanity, and yet so eloquent of mother-love, for who but a mother would have swathed those small bodies in softest feather cloth, and placed in the little hands food for that last long spirit-journey." Eulogizing these vanished Indian mothers, Corson chided those observers who insisted on separating modern women from the "*so-called* uncivilized races" (emphasis added).[11] For Corson, any culture with loving mothers was civilized.

Where Corson found womanly domesticity, other speakers discovered female power. Kirstine Fredericsen, a Dane, recast women's demands for equality as a return to an earlier division of labor: "the Woman's Rights movement . . . means going back to a more simple arrangement of the relations between the sexes." Primitive women's work was physical, not restricted to the home, and of equal value to the men's. Such division of labor was still practiced among "Indians and Greenlanders," and Fredericsen rejected the idea that these women needed to be liberated: "Now these women are by no means subjugated. On the contrary, they are very independent, really much more so than their sisters in the city." She referred to Alice Fletcher, an American anthropologist, for confirmation that American Indian women were better off than their white sisters. Another American, Clara McDiarmid, described the lives of native Alaskan women and quoted approvingly from a historian who noted that " 'The woman's rights and her sphere and influence have reached a development among the Sitkans that would astonish the suffrage leaders of Wyoming and Washington Territories.' "[12]

Throughout the 1890s, other white women continued to challenge the idea that Indian women lived degraded and abused lives. Elaine Goodale (who in 1891 married the Sioux physician and author Charles A. Eastman) wrote that after several years of assimilation work among American Indians, she had "been unwillingly impressed by the fact that barbarism offers several points of evident superiority to our civilization." For example, Indian clothing was more hygienic and practical, particularly women's dress, which boasted "ease and freedom, mental and moral," by its "fixed standard." A visitor to a Hopi village noted that labor was divided equally between Hopi men and women, with men doing some "feminine" tasks such as weaving and child care, and women doing some "masculine" tasks such as house building. In addition, the women enjoyed the equivalent of " 'suffrage' or 'rights.' "[13] Alice Fletcher's articles and lectures impelled some white women to write of their "free sisters in savage life." In 1889, Fletcher reported that in many cases Indian women "carried the clan," "held the household property as their own," and even "held public office."[14] At the 1893 Columbian Exposition she hoped that her lecture on "Love Songs among the Omaha Indians" would belie the image of the Indian woman abused by her husband. These images not only challenged the old "squaw drudge" stereotypes, but also raised the possibility that the nineteenth-century domestic ideal would be a step backward for Indian women.[15]

The most visible sign of the "new" Indian woman was her art. Large city newspapers included frequent articles about Indian craft arts, women's magazines offered advice about how to decorate with such arts, and books provided guides to collecting and identifying. In all of these texts the arts and crafts movement offered a theoretical defense of the value of primitive arts. These arts became to women what Eileen Boris has called "symbols of the self-expression possible within the family economy."[16] Indian pots, baskets, and blankets belonged in the long tradition of "women's arts" that had been so clearly and proudly demonstrated at the Columbian Exposition. No longer seen as savage arts, they were family arts endowed with inherent moral value, a value confirmed by their popularity among highly "civilized" and respectable white women of good breeding and taste, the very kind of women who were likely to organize and support efforts to help Indians.

The Indian Industries League's special concern for Indian women fit perfectly with a crucial aspect of the publicity given to Indian arts: It was directed largely at women. This fact can be seen in the pages of the *New York Daily Tribune*, which between 1891 and 1903 placed nearly every article about Indian arts on the daily woman's page. Candace Wheeler noted in 1901 that the drive to preserve Indian arts was being supported by women's clubs across the nation.[17] In New York City, for example, the General Federation of Women's Clubs ran the Woman's Exchange, a non-profit store carrying craft items made by working-class women in their homes. In 1901, this exchange generated much interest with its exhibit of Indian baskets collected in Washington by Mrs. Marion C. Pearsall, who studied and promoted Indian basketry.[18] Karen Blair argues that club-women championed American-made craft arts because they appealed to such a wide range of constituents: those who sought to beautify the domestic sphere, those who wanted to provide economic relief for poor women and immigrants, those who supported new professional arts opportunities for women, and those who pined with nostalgic patriotism for an "American" art. Thinking along these lines, which often intertwined, could lead one to conclude that Indian women were much like earlier American women in that they too shaped the domestic aesthetic with their own handiwork. One writer noticed this connection in 1891 when he remarked on the talent with which an Indian woman "in a vague, unconscious way adapts the pictures in her mind to the more practical needs of daily life," just as "our grandmothers wove blue and white linens into quilts, or as the same dear old ladies adapted nature in a less artistic way, in Rising Sun, Log Cabin, Pyramid and Crazy [quilt] patterns, for spare room comfortables." League member Constance Goddard Du Bois described precontact Indian women "always busy with this beautiful art-work [basketry] as American housewives in early days were with their spinning."[19]

Artist, domestic helpmate, independent New Woman—these images and others could be held simultaneously, and it seems impossible to say that any one was dominant or even that there was much conscious competition among these images. All were linked, however, by a revaluing of Indian women's labor that replaced the "squaw drudge" image with that of a domestic, primitive craftswoman. Essentially, one could not separate the aesthetic beauty of Indian women's arts from the women themselves. George Wharton James, who wrote about Indian baskets and blankets and lectured on the topic in Boston, found little to fault in the women who produced such beauty: "Let the white woman who has scorned the 'rude, dirty, vulgar, brutal, savage woman' take the finest and highest accomplishments of her race in needlework or any other 'refined' art and place it side by side with the art manifested in Indian basketry, and she may then, perhaps, begin to see how impertinent was her scorn, how ignorant her contempt." An honest examination of the Indian woman's work would uncover that she was not "ignorant, dull, stolid, brutal," but "sentient, poetic, religious."[20] The impact of these new ideas on the Indian Industries League would prove substantial.

Less than a decade after its founding, the league adopted this image of Indian female artistry to spur the consumption of Indian arts by white women. For a number of reasons, by 1900 the league had almost entirely abandoned the project of developing modern, civilized industries: Its financial resources were too limited to fund any but the smallest-scale industrial projects; the executive committee members' knowledge of civilized industries was limited, as was that of the fieldworkers who were to oversee these industries; men usually managed civilized industries, but the league's field contacts were women; the development of civilized industries that often employed men rather than women was logically at odds with the league's desire to help Indian women; the league's fundraising network consisted mainly of women, and they seemed most interested in funding work clearly directed at women; and finally, there appeared to be little public enthusiasm for this line of work. Facing the failure of its efforts to establish civilized industries among Indians, the league gradually began to support the production, distribution, and sale of arts made by Indian women.

Early assistance in these efforts came from the Office of Indian Affairs, which in 1900 instructed its field matrons to supply the Indian Industries League with information about the state of Indian arts in their areas. The league's response to the first batch of matrons' letters indicates the degree to which its decision to change focus reflected the perception that native industries were an "opportunity" not just for the Indians but for the league as well: "The committee expressed pleasure at the amount of industry which these letters reported on the part of the Indians, a state of affairs encouraging further efforts, and instructed the secretary to thank the commissioner for the opportunities opened through the co-operation of these matrons." President Lockwood reported that during the summer of 1901 the "League had been *prospecting* in regard to future work and had found on many sides opportunities which it had no funds to make use of" (emphasis added). The league's record books use the word "open" repeatedly in connection with native industries in the sense of "looking for openings" or "opening" an industry. Somewhat disturbingly, this rhetoric reveals the degree to which the Indian Industries League imagined Indians as raw resources that it could mine for its own benefit. True, the Indian artisans would profit when the league "opened" an industry in their tribe, but so too would the league, which was sensitive about the image it presented to other Indian reform organizations. Sparhawk reported peevishly that the 1901 Mohonk conference (an annual gathering of leading Indian reformers) gave barely five minutes to an account of the Indian Industries League's work and that the general impression among participants was that "the League was not doing much." Sibyl Carter had shown lace making to be quite remunerative for Indian women, and the league gave her occasional support, but one gets the impression that Carter had a firm claim on any successes associated with that industry.[21] The new opportunities in native arts, however, promised to give the Indian Industries League its own prominent image.

Selling Indian arts was not an entirely novel concept for Indian reform groups, although none had given the activity much prominence. Even Richard Pratt, the father of civilizing projects, had found it expedient to encourage his Plains Indian prisoners' industriousness by letting them sell ledger drawings, bows and arrows, and other Indian curios they made while imprisoned in Florida in 1875. The WNIA's annual reports from the 1890s indicate scattered instances of branch associations raising funds by holding sales of Indian goods that presumably had been sent by WNIA-supported missionaries.[22] Superintendent of Indian Schools William N. Hailmann (1894–1898) had recommended native arts as part of the Indian schools' curriculum, and he further suggested that if students were paid for their productions they would learn important economic lessons. Another Indian school, the Hampton Institute (Virginia), began to teach native arts in 1899 and to sell the students' work in the school's gift shop.[23]

Nevertheless, organizations that had been committed to assimilating Indians had to develop different marketing strategies than did Indian traders or the Fred Harvey Company, who made no claims about protecting Indians' interests or welfare. Commercial merchants presented Indian artisans as people from another time, as members of a vanishing way of life that the consumer could capture in an art object. The scarcity and fashionableness of such objects made them desirable, as evidenced in a Marshall Field department store advertisement for "rare specimens of Indian art" that were "much sought after for dens and other decorations." The advertisement created the false impression that the Indian goods for sale were collected in a distant past rather than produced recently for a growing market. Similar images were created in the Southwest, where the Fred Harvey Company managed the tourism side of the Santa Fe Railway's business. The Fred Harvey Company promoted the Southwest by romanticizing and packaging the local Native American cultures in a number of ways: stocking its hotel shops with Indian arts; arranging for native weavers and jewelers to demonstrate their skills in the train stations; running special excursions to Indian communities where tourists could buy wares directly from the artists; and creating postcards and advertising images that emphasized Southwestern Indians as artistic, domestic, and timeless peoples. Such imaging of Indian artisans tended to depoliticize their history and erase the economic significance of their participation in the art market. The artists and their work were turned into what Leah Dilworth has called a "spectacle" with tourists on one side and Indians on the other, with all possibility of communication and understanding reduced to the consumption of Indian arts.[24]

Although elements of these images inevitably crept into the reformers' descriptions of Indian artisans, the romanticization of an Indian past was minimized. Because the reform movement sought to bring Indians into the twentieth century, not lock them in the nineteenth, it needed to call attention to the ways that participation in the arts and crafts market stimulated Indians' industriousness and improved their economic prospects. Where the Fred Harvey Company could market Indian arts as exotic symbols of the Other, reformers had to represent those same arts as evidence of moral and social progress.

Most significantly, the apparent acceptance of Indian material culture had to be reconciled with long-standing "civilization" goals. Were "native" arts really "civilized" industries? If not, their fostering would obviously delay the Indians' assimilation. The Indian Industries League had been founded on the conviction that "the acquirement and practice of useful arts and industries are necessary to the civilization and elevation of the Indians in this country." Underlying this conviction was the implicit assumption that Indian cultures lacked arts and industries. Indeed, the league charter stated that "no industries exist" on Indian reservations, but its annual reports for 1900 and 1901 referred repeatedly to "native industries," and the league appeared eager to reevaluate the Indians' aptitudes. Sparhawk attributed inherent artistic ability to the Indian, which validated the league's new line of reform work: "Quickness and keenness of observation, artistic perceptions, power of attention and aptitude in execution this race has in a wonderful degree. We must give it an opportunity."[25] To a surprising extent, the league's reevaluation of Indian culture was framed in a reassessment of Anglo-American civilization, specifically of women's roles within that civilization.

The radical implications of this new line of work appeared as early as 1899, when Mr. and Mrs. Walter C. Roe of the Seger Colony, Oklahoma wrote to describe their "Mohonk Lodge," a "home, hospital, and workshop" that featured an "Industrial Room" where Indian women did traditional beadwork that the Roes then sold. Impressed with this program, the Indian Industries League began buying beadwork from the Roes and reselling it in Boston. The venture proved more successful than any the league had thus far undertaken. But, Walter C. Roe openly admitted that his work derived from a rejection of old reform attitudes, many of which had been concocted by people who did not really "know" Indians. He lamented that "the underlying mistake of our National policy toward the Indian has been the attempt to crush the Indian out of him." What might have been achieved, Roe wondered, if we had "treated the Indian more sympathetically as to his ideas, customs, arts, and even his dress and prejudices?" The Roes "put [themselves] into the place of [their] Indian sister" when searching for an appropriate industry to foster, and "decided in favor of the beadwork, as against either laundry-work or lace-making," reasoning that the former was "a beautiful art," whereas the latter two were despised by the Indian women. Increasingly, other observers agreed that the destruction of Indian cultures might be as great a crime as the destruction of Indians themselves.[26]

By the end of 1900, the Indian Industries League had heard from two more members who recommended that the organization devote itself to promoting native arts. Both women were members of WNIA branches and had written about why and how native arts should be fostered. They defended Indian culture from charges that it was savage, and in their advocacy of Indian arts they openly challenged certain assimilationist goals. Moreover, they offered careful arguments about why organizations run by and for women should take a special interest in Indian women's arts.

A dues-paying member of the league since 1896, Nellie Blanchan De Graff Doubleday (wife of Frank Nelson Doubleday, the New York publisher) urged an examination of the "opportunities and advantages of the basket industry for the Indians." Intrigued by Doubleday's suggestion, the league made her a member of its executive committee and requested her "to look into this industry and report upon the prospects of success should the League undertake it; also to see if there was any financial opening for the work." Doubleday replied that she had already secured a promise from William A. Jones, the commissioner of Indian Affairs, to put her in touch with Estelle Reel, the new superintendent of Indian schools, to discuss the possibility of teaching basket making in the government schools. Both government officials proved sympathetic to this plan and offered their support for the development of a basket industry among the Indians. Doubleday also offered practical advice about how to develop basketry industries, outlining in several pamphlets how eastern reform organizations could encourage, buy, and sell Indian arts for the benefit of Indian women.[27]

In addition to giving practical advice, Doubleday laid out a defense of why reformers should redirect their energies toward native arts. Doubleday acknowledged that the promotion of native arts seemed contrary to some of the main goals of late-nineteenth-century Indian reform work, but she argued that total assimilation was misguided both because it falsely posited Anglo culture as superior to Indian and because it robbed Indians and white Americans of important cultural resources. Contrary to the assimilationists, she firmly believed that the social and economic position of Indians could be raised through the encouragement of their arts. Additional new goals were to be considered too. By casting Indian arts as women's work, she suggested that a kind of gender allegiance demanded their preservation. Also important was the fact that in Indian women's art resided most of the cultural history of Indian tribes; encouraging the preservation of such art would ensure the preservation of a great store of knowledge that would otherwise vanish. Finally, Indian art, if encouraged, might reach unprecedented aesthetic heights and precipitate a new American art.[28]

Doubleday recognized that encouraging native arts would essentially help preserve the very Indian culture that only a decade earlier had been seen as both a barrier to assimilation and a symbol of savagery. Acknowledging the cultural meaning of Indian arts, she observed that "the intellectual and spiritual aspirations of the race [Indian]" were expressed "chiefly through the artistic handicrafts of the women." She also argued that the Indian basket was "the most expressive vehicle of the tribe's individuality, the embodiment of its mythology and folk-lore, tradition, history, poetry, art, and spiritual aspiration." Discouraging Indian women's arts effectively destroyed the tribes. Even forced allotment was a flawed policy because it was predicated on a false impression that Indian men headed households, when in fact Indian women were the heads of their families and already did most of the "industrious" work.[29] Doubleday believed that partial assimilation that allowed Indians to develop their own native industries would best benefit both Indians and the rest of the nation.

Doubleday's arguments against total assimilation stemmed from her understanding of recent studies of the role of primitive women in the development of civilization that had changed long-accepted assessments of Indian culture. Primitive women, she argued, were now recognized as natural "artists" from whose work all modern industries originated. The Indian woman should be encouraged in those arts, which had been shown to be the foundations of civilization: "With a more scientific appreciation of primitive woman's contribution to modern civilization, must come a sympathetic interest in the handicrafts of our Indian women."[30] Directed to an audience of white women, Doubleday's support of Indian women's arts revealed a belief that modern women had been cut off from that tradition and denied access to the "civilized" industries, which were run by white men. In this view, the preservation of Indian women's art symbolized a revival of women's creative power. There were no squaw drudges to be civilized, but only vibrant craftswomen to be nurtured and protected.

At the center of Doubleday's philosophy was a newfound conviction that Indian women had historically been both industrious and artistic, but that those traits had been crushed by white reformers. The first settlers found Indians practicing "many handicrafts which indicated intelligence, adaptability, art feeling and finger skill quite remarkable in an aboriginal people." But instead of supporting these native industries, whites had tried unsuccessfully to turn Indians to white industries. Fellow female reformers such as Sibyl Carter did not escape Doubleday's censure. She wrote (anonymously) that lace making had "evolved to meet the requirements of European aristocracy," not the needs of "aboriginal women upon a Minnesota reservation!" Worse, whites had corrupted native industries by trying to "improve" them: "I have failed to find one [native industry]—where one still exists—which has not deteriorated since our boasted civilization came in contact with it." This sounds like a classic conflict between the primitive and the civilized, but it is actually a conflict between women and men. Given that men produced nearly *everything* consumed by the industrialized culture, the blame for "our [white women's] over-conventional, inartistic houses" could be laid at men's feet.[31] Moreover, the sense of urgency in preserving Indian women's arts may well have stemmed not just from the oft-repeated fear that Indians were "vanishing," but also from Anglo women's own experience with the loss of their industries. Candace Wheeler, who led a decorative arts movement for women, used a similar rhetoric about the decline of needlework skills in the face of rapid technological change.[32] As Doubleday observed, the "beauty" one found in Indian women's baskets and other household arts could never be replicated by modern women.[33]

Finally, Doubleday's elevation of the craftswoman should be understood in contrast to the commercial Indian curio trade, which Marvin Cohodas argues was typified by "evolutionist schemes, arts and crafts ideals, and attempts to confine Native Americans within both ennobling and degrading stereotypes." To a certain extent Doubleday also drew on this rhetoric, but she differed from commercial promoters of Indian arts in her unrelenting attention to Indian women's present poverty and in her support for even arts of low quality. Her arguments and advice appealed to an audience used to a tradition of selling women's crafts to support various charitable aims.[34] More than simply memorials to a vanishing art, Doubleday's articles were calls to action. She advised concerned women to get their clubs to buy and resell Indians arts, encourage department stores to carry Indian goods, write articles for local newspapers, and demand that the government revise its Indian education policies to include the teaching of native arts. The profit potential was substantial: Doubleday claimed that the New York City branches of the WNIA had sold $18,000 worth of Indian arts, and she explained how in a year and a half an initial $75 investment in Indian baskets could be turned over until it reached $250. Such profits would ensure that "the rising generation of Indians will advance in thrift and prosperity far beyond any of its predecessors."[35] Whatever appeals to a romantic past may have laced Doubleday's texts, she promised a future for American Indians.

In 1903, Doubleday's friend Constance Goddard Du Bois, a member of the Indian Industries League's executive committee since 1901, persuaded it to assist her efforts on behalf of the Mission Indian basket industry. President of the Waterbury branch of the Connecticut Indian Association, the published author of an Indian reform novel, and an amateur anthropologist, for seven years Du Bois had supported Mary Watkins's work at Mesa Grande, an Indian community near San Diego, California.[36] Du Bois boasted impeccable reform credentials and was equipped with expert knowledge of the Mission Indians. She guided the league in its support of several field matrons among the Mission Indians, provided it with baskets, and alerted it to land issues facing the California Indians.

A tireless advocate for Indians, Du Bois labored to develop a new market for Indian baskets, one that could both bypass the exploitative commercial traders and support tribes who lived outside of existing markets. Like Doubleday and the Indian Industries League, Du Bois imagined that reform-minded white women would make ideal consumers. To reach these consumers, she often lectured at Indian association meetings, women's clubs, and churches, teaching her female listeners why they should buy and how they should evaluate the baskets that she offered for sale. Several of her lectures survive and, when analyzed in conjunction with other documentary evidence, they provide revealing insights into how an image of Indian artistry was constructed for a female, reform-minded audience.[37]

Like George Wharton James, Charles Lummis, and the other contemporary popularizers of Indian arts, Du Bois drew on anthropological research to establish the authority of her pronouncements. She opened her lectures by referring to the subject of ethnology in general, and then made references to specific anthropologists, often reading brief passages or showing illustrations from their texts. By placing her commentary within the context of scientific studies, she suggested the superiority of white knowledge. The Indians' cultures, seemingly impenetrable, could be understood and explained best by white observers. But Du Bois also subverted this anthropological authority in several respects. At one level, she insisted that scientific knowledge counteracted irrational racism, a significant concern for Indian reform groups. She also used the lecture format to express economic realities and political views absent in scientific publications. And, most important, she presented herself as a female researcher whose gender made her especially suited both to address women and to understand the female Indian artist.

For Du Bois, anthropology could combat negative stereotypes about Indians, including some that other reformers held. In one lecture, Du Bois began with a nod to the "humanizing" influence of anthropology, which when popularized could counteract the "race hatred and worse than that, race scorn, which is founded on ignorance and prejudice." Scientific study of Indians had "given breadth and vigor to our ideals concerning their [the Indians'] uplifting and betterment." Specifically, ethnologists had revised false stereotypes that had shaped Indian policy for the past century. In her lecture "Art and Industry among the Mission Indians" she drew on Otis T. Mason's work to make a case for the idea that Indians were industrious, not lazy, and that their women's handicrafts could be accurately categorized as "art." Ethnology had corrected the stereotype that Indians were "a naturally indolent race, disinclined to work of itself" by documenting the actual toil that survival had necessitated; the fact that this toil had been undertaken with beautifully decorated handicrafts "which [had been] raise[d] from drudgery to art" proved that Indians had "love of work and pride in successful production."[38] Policy measures intended to "make" the Indian "industrious" were obviously flawed unless they recognized that the Indians already had their own industries. Du Bois invited the women in her audience to demonstrate their scientific enlightenment by purchasing the Indian arts that she brought for sale.

Although Du Bois was able to promote anthropology in her lectures to reformers, she was unable to promote reform in her articles for anthropologists. Alfred Kroeber, editing the manuscript of one such article, crossed out a paragraph about basketry in which Du Bois mentioned its economic importance and her efforts to develop a market for it.[39] In her lectures, however, she faced no such censure, so she liberally interspersed her analysis of Indian arts with references to the poverty and oppression faced by their makers. Visiting Mesa Grande each summer had given her an acute sense of the Indians' desperate situation, and regular letters from Mary Watkins detailed the poverty and other troubles of the Indians who sold baskets and stories. Anthropologists often paid their native informants, and Du Bois was no different in this regard, but even when such payments were acknowledged in print, the economic necessity of those payments remained hidden. One of Du Bois's scientific articles, for example, mentioned her "philanthropic work," and others referred to the purchase of information, but in none did she indicate that the success of her annual summer research trips depended on her year-long support of the community through basket purchases as well as gifts of money, clothing, and supplies.[40] When addressing women's clubs and Indian associations, however, she could hold up a basket, mention its "half-starving" maker or describe the old woman who "lives in one of the poorest and remotest settlements . . . where the Indians are in a desperate condition on account of the encroachments of the whites upon the good land where they used to live," and go directly into an analysis of the basket's design.[41] Unfortunately, Du Bois did not address the moral implications of exploiting economic and political conditions to obtain objects and information that might otherwise have been retained, but at least she called attention to the plight of her Indian informants and basket suppliers.

As an amateur anthropologist, a reformer, and a woman, Du Bois brought a unique kind of authority to the lectern. Du Bois's intellectual credentials impressed all who knew her. Watkins *"grew tall"* with the pride of association when a local Indian agent remarked that Du Bois was "a *recognized power* and *authority*" (emphases in original) in the Indian field. Referring to membership in the Southwest Branch of the Archaeological Institute of America, Charles F. Lummis stated that aside from Alice Fletcher, Du Bois was the "only American woman I know who ought to be rated in such a list by virtue of personal achievement." Another friend and research associate, Ed H. Davis, described her as "the greatest brain force that he has met in a woman."[42] And Du Bois herself quietly reminded listeners of her authority by referring to her own field activities or displaying the objects, photos, and recordings that she had collected. Yet, she spoke not just for science, but also for humanity. Du Bois straddled the world of scientific exploration and the world of public service. She resembled the women in front of her in the sense that she also worked within women's organizations to promote social justice, but she differed in her professional credentials. The altruism of the reform world might have seemed like an uneasy partner to the objectivity of the scientific, but Du Bois presented the marriage as a strength.

Central to Du Bois's lectures was the idea that Indian arts were women's arts and as such were intrinsically significant to women everywhere, throwing light on the status, abilities, and duties of modern white women. The topic of basketry implied a female artist, but Du Bois stressed this point, consistently using feminine pronouns whenever she spoke of any Indian artist. In one lecture she even suggested that the mothering instinct, specifically the need for a baby carrier, spurred the invention of basketry.[43] Then, to heighten her audience's identification with the Indian woman, she explicitly contrasted white and Indian women. The contrasts followed much of the arts and crafts movement rhetoric in extolling the aesthetic virtues of the primitive, but they also generated an emotional basis for appreciation of Indian arts. In her lecture on "The Symbolism of Indian Basketry," Du Bois wasted little time getting to the fundamental question: "Have you ever stopped to think of what we have lost as women in the upward advance [of civilization]?" The question joined the audience together and established their special relationship to the topic at hand. In developing the answer ("native technical ability" and "individual creative power"), Du Bois invited her listeners to imagine a white woman in the California desert, gathering the basket maker's raw materials, spending three months weaving the basket, and all the time living "half starved; . . . in a shelter of boughs; . . . her heart wrung by gnawing grief; . . . her daughter with a young baby [lying] dying on the ground on a bed of ragged blankets soaked by a sudden cloud burst; . . . shapes of want and misery constantly before her eyes." The dramatic, emotional scene was calculated to arouse both admiration and pity for the Indian artist, crucial goads to financial support. Differences in technical ability also received attention, and in another lecture Du Bois detailed the complexity of a basket design and challenged her listeners: "If you wish really to appreciate the basket-maker's skill, please provide yourself with canvas and wools for the old-fashioned cross-stitch, and attempt to work a flower like this *without a pattern*" (emphasis in original).[44]

"Appreciation" could rightly be considered the overriding goal of these lectures. Du Bois needed her audience to appreciate the Indian and her baskets, to value them in some tangible way that would lead them to purchase some of the many objects that she had displayed on the tables at the back of the room. Her arguments followed the standard aesthetic claims made by arts and crafts connoisseurs, but she departed from the mainstream by investing the art objects with the stories of their creators, stories that consumers would never find in the department store or curio shop.

Why buy? Authenticity was one reason. Collectors of primitive arts had to trust the seller as to the origin of manufacture or they might end up with misidentified or perhaps even fake objects. Du Bois immediately assured her audience of both the authenticity and rarity of the baskets used to illustrate one lecture, noting that all were "California baskets of strictly aboriginal form and design" that could be found only in those New York City stores to which she had personally sold them. In her expert opinion, no other baskets boasted such "rich" colors and "varied" designs. Du Bois told the story of her search for the root used to create the unusual yellow dye used on one basket; triumphantly, she related that an analysis by "Mr. Coville of the Dept. of Agriculture in Washington" proved that the plant had "never before been used as a dye plant." Authenticity for the collector meant not just that a basket had been made by an Indian, but also that its design was "traditional." On this point Du Bois was adamant. Noting that "the ancient traditions of [the] tribes; and all this interesting knowledge, for which ethnologists would give a fortune, is hanging by a spider's thread," she claimed that "it is this which gives such value to Indian baskets, collected as mine have been in a region which has not come under the white man's influence." The designs themselves included elements that had "come down to the maker from very ancient times," and all of her bas- kets were "genuinely primitive."[45] The remoteness of the Indian weavers thus assured the authenticity and rarity of the baskets and gave them value. The purchaser bought contact with "real" Indians, with an ancient past.

As an expert, Du Bois could also verify the artistic quality of the baskets. During her lectures, she held up basket after basket, detailing both the ethnographer's and the connoisseur's appreciation of the subtlety of design. When she could not interpret a particular design, she declared that the "mystery" merely added to the value of the piece. Repeatedly, she used the words "art" and "artistry," and she declared that each purchase was "a real art investment," each basket "worth much more than a piece of fine porcelain or cut glass or silver." In fact, Du Bois declared that if she could afford to buy these baskets for her private collection, none would be available, as they would "decorate the walls, shelves and every nook and corner" of her home. Fortunately, she joked, the reasonable women in her audience did not suffer "this particular mental contagion."[46] Thus, Du Bois drew on her scientific authority to validate the value of the baskets, and she displayed the baskets themselves to stimulate desire for them. In these respects, her lectures somewhat resembled the sales strategies of the Fred Harvey Company, which led shoppers from instructional ethnographic exhibits to the sales shop itself.

There were, however, significant differences between the Santa Fe Railway tourist and the woman's club member, and Du Bois was careful to appeal to the special concerns of the latter. Collectors and tourists bought Indian arts for personal reasons, to satisfy individual desires or to bring home a memento. Members of the Connecticut Indian Association, however, expected their purchases to empower the women their organization had pledged to assist. Again, Du Bois's philanthropic work among the Indians was reassuring in this respect.

When the audience heard that "the chief living of the half-starving Indians of this region is derived from the basket-making," they surely felt a personal obligation to support this industry, regardless of whether they really wanted an Indian basket for the parlor. Du Bois pushed the idea that the Indian women would earn more money from their arts if Indian associations bought their work, thereby eliminating the large profit dealers and traders wrung from the Indians.[47] When Du Bois suggested to her Waterbury Indian Association that it patronize Indian weavers, she claimed that traders paid 75¢ for baskets they resold for $5; other times she was more conservative, estimating that Indians received one-quarter to one-half of the final sale price.[48] If the weavers could see some of this profit, their financial situation would greatly improve, and Du Bois openly admitted the place of "charity" in each purchase. Motivated by philanthropic feelings, women like Watkins bought both poor- and fine-quality baskets at relatively high prices, paying, as Watkins said, "with the idea of help more than the profit idea." Du Bois encouraged her lecture audiences to buy with the same spirit. Indeed, she sold in that spirit, paying an average of $3 for each basket (she bought $25 to $100 worth each month) and selling them for only slightly more and sometimes at a loss.[49] Any profits sponsored the purchase of more baskets or supplies, thereby ensuring that the Indian women's labor benefited both the individual maker and the larger community. In fact, the return on each sale increased beyond the dollar value of the basket in the sense that the Indian associations used the baskets as signs to attract not just purchases but donations, memberships, and promises of political activism.

Although the women at Du Bois's parlor sales bought mostly baskets made for the market, they also bought a narrative of Indian life that cast them in the role of saviors and protectors, of "friends" in a tradition going back to the first Quaker reformers. Arts bought within the community of Indian reformers were "authentic" in the sense that they connected the purchaser more directly to the maker than did a commercial basket that had gone through several middlemen before reaching the East Coast. This direct connection was established through the stories that accompanied each basket. These stories included recreations of the process through which weavers went to gather and prepare the basket materials. In her lectures, Du Bois illustrated each step in the basket-making process with a specimen of the plant used and a description of the landscape in which it was gathered. The buyer, although no weaver herself, could imagine the weaver's experience. The design on the basket itself had "its connection with a story which may never now be known to us," but Du Bois tried to persuade each maker to "send this message with her basket," messages that Du Bois faithfully communicated to her audience. Most intriguing, however, were the stories that Du Bois implied. For example, at one sale she included some 25¢ and 50¢ "rudely made sifting baskets and women's hats," which, although not beautiful, were a "bargain" when one considered their "old, old . . . half-starving" weavers, "of whom I could tell you many a long tale."[50] One imagines that after the lecture Du Bois shared these tales with interested listeners, perhaps even mentioning that she had sent six pairs of eyeglasses for the older weavers.[51] Certainly she knew them, for she had met many of these weavers, and Watkins wrote to Du Bois regularly with details of day-to-day life among the Indians. These stories, which helped the consumer see the significance of the basket—both economic and cultural—to its Indian maker, gave the basket an elevated value. When Du Bois lectured on Indian music, she assessed one recording as more valuable than the world's biggest diamond precisely because its singer held it sacred above all else.[52]

Even Du Bois's occasional use of the vanishing Indian rhetoric—her emphasis on "old" weavers and her warnings against the corruption of Indian arts by white contact—must be considered against the reality of her work for the Indians around Mesa Grande. There she and the Indian Industries League joined forces to support two young Indian women who, as government field matrons, were encouraging the old and young Indians in remote villages to produce baskets for the market.[53] Other white women in the same area were teaching and reviving basketry. Watkins wrote of one skilled weaver, Maria Antonia, who supported her three children by basket sales; and in a list of thirty-seven weavers from whom she bought, Watkins identified only nine as over forty years old.[54] The basket-weaving skill was not vanishing, at least in part because Du Bois gave so much energy to preserving it. She advocated the construction of day schools to preserve Indian communities, suggested the government pay Indians for their art, worked to protect native arts from white influences, and supported legal actions to defend Indian lands.[55] In short, the similarities between Du Bois's appeals and those of commercial promoters were far less significant than the actual work she tried to stimulate.

Spurred by Du Bois, the Indian Industries League also revised several long-standing attitudes toward Indian culture and assimilation policy. Old Indian women, once considered by Sparhawk to be evil hags bent on holding back progressive youths, were now sought out as teachers of Indian arts; contact between old and young Indian women was encouraged. Indians' material culture, once evidence of an unwillingness to assimilate, was now praised for its aesthetic beauty and practical utility and urged upon white consumers. Rather than modernize these arts, the Indian Industries League supported, sometimes with prize money, efforts to preserve traditional methods and materials. Forced allotment, once reformers' central assimilationist goal, was now opposed, especially in those cases where lands with crucial basket-weaving materials would be lost to the tribe. And the league tried, unsuccessfully, to establish a federal Indian arts and crafts board that would foster and promote Indian arts.[56]

Jackson Lears has argued that many of the antimodernist movements ended up offering personal redemption rather than lasting social solutions. One finds this confirmed, to a certain extent, in the turn-of-the-century popularization of Indian art. Most consumers bought Indian arts to improve themselves, not Indians, just as most promoters sought to benefit themselves, not Indians. The reformers' experience, however, points to another dimension of the commercialization of American Indian arts. With their parlor lectures, pamphlets, research, and prize money for excellent traditional baskets, the reformers might have seemed to differ little from commercial traders in dictating the shape of Indian arts. Yet, at another level, they bought with the idea that establishing an arts industry for Indian women would ensure their economic and cultural survival. This vision of an arts-based economic self-sufficiency may have been unrealistic, but it both reflected a desire to find creative, female-based solutions to the Indian "problem" and anticipated the efforts undertaken by a new generation of reform groups in the 1920s whose activities led to the New Deal–era establishment of a government Indian Arts and Crafts Board.

Notes

1. Papers of Constance Goddard Du Bois, Reel 4, no. 57, Huntington Free Library, New York (papers are hereafter cited as PCGD).

2. Among the numerous studies of Native American arts, Dilworth's stands out as a developed analysis of how Anglo preoccupations shaped public images of Native Americans; this chapter owes a significant debt to Dilworth's insights. Other important studies include Berlo; Cole; Jacobs; Mullin; and Rushing. For a recent essay that focuses on American Indian basketry, see Herzog.

3. This chapter is based on my dissertation. For the most part, I will use the words "civilized," "primitive," and "savage" without quotation marks, although it should be understood that these terms are simply those used in the primary texts I examine. I do not mean to imply that I accept any of these categories as accurate descriptions of reality. It is important, however, to realize that many of the people examined here used "primitive" and "Indian" interchangeably.

4. Quoted in Wanken, 238. For another study of the WNIA, see Mathes. Information about the 1892 WNIA meeting can also be found in Indian Industries League, *Record Book I,* 3 February 1894, 19 (hereafter cited as IIL). I wish to thank the Massachusetts Historical Society (Boston) for granting permission to quote from the papers of the Indian Industries League.

5. IIL, *Record Book I,* 23 November 1893, 9; 29 January 1894, 15.

6. IIL, *Record Book I,* 22 November 1894, 43. For studies, see Green, "The Pocahontas"; Smits; Riley; Albers and James; Maddox; and Coleman, 94.

7. Palmer, 22. Many studies emphasize the racist and imperialistic ideology behind the fair's anthropological exhibits, but most overlook the portrayals of primitive women. See, for example, Hoxie; Rydell, *All the World's a Fair* and "The Culture"; and Hinsley. Other studies examine the fair's predominantly conservative image of women, but overlook how this image was reinforced by the positive attention given to primitive women's domestic skills. See Sund; Banta; and Trachtenberg, 221. The exception is Weimann, who devotes a chapter to exhibits of primitive culture inside the Woman's Building. For a study of scientific racism and sexism, see Gould, especially 80, 115–18. Part of my discussion of the Columbian Exposition appeared originally, in a different form, in Trump, "Primitive Woman."

8. Lady Managers, "Preliminary Prospectus," 1891, quoted in Weimann, 393; Sara Hallowell, letter to Mrs. Palmer, January 1891, quoted in Weimann, 393; Weimann, 393.

9. Weimann, 393–425. Otis T. Mason, curator of the Smithsonian and author

of *Woman's Share in Primitive Culture,* designed the exhibition. For the space allotment, see the building schematic facing the table of contents in Elliott.

10. Quoted in Weimann, 416; McLaughlin ran the Cincinnati Pottery Club and invented a glazing method favored by the popular Rookwood Pottery. Wheeler, 59; Ellen Paul Denker and Bert Randall Denker, catalogue entries 55 and 56, in Kaplan, 170–71. The history of this idea is traced in Rodgers.

11. Corson, 715.

12. Fredericsen, 237. Fredericsen probably was referring to a speech Fletcher gave before the International Council of Women in 1888 to describe Indian women's rights (see Green, *Women,* 77); McDiarmid, 725. For an excellent study of how the woman suffrage movement used images of Indian women, see Landsman.

13. Goodale, "Some Lessons," 82–83. For a good introduction to Goodale's early work, see her *Sister to the Sioux;* "In 'Hopi' Clubdom."

14. Merrick; "The Position." For a similar but more forceful defense of Indian women's equality, see "Primitive Indian." The issue of Indian women's gender equality is still discussed among scholars today, some holding to the idea of Indian matriarchies, others arguing that words such as "autonomy," "complementarity," and "egalitarianism" best describe the nature of gender in Indian societies. See, for example, Klein and Ackerman, especially 230–49.

15. Mark, 236–37. Nancy Parezo has noted that by the 1920s "the respect for women noticed [by female anthropologists] in Puebloan cultures was a definite lure to women who realized they were not treated with equality in their own society" (356). Many white women in the early twentieth century entered the anthropological field by studying Indian women in the American Southwest (see Babcock and Parezo). Allen looks to American Indian cultures for feminist models of society; see 209–21.

16. Boris, 122. For a study that considers the interconnections among women's clubs, the arts, and social activism, see Blair.

17. Articles by Sparhawk and about the Indian Industries League appeared in the *Tribune,* as did regular reports on the New York City branch of the WNIA; "Arts Not."

18. "Art of Indian Basketry."

19. Blair, 83–85; "A California"; Du Bois, "Mission Indians," Reel 3, no. 26, p. 36, PCGD.

20. James, 269–70, 271. James lectured before the Boston Society of Arts and Crafts on 14 November 1902 (see "Notes," *Handicraft* 1 [December 1902]: 228). Babcock points out some of the darker implications of this "domestication" of Indians in her essay.

21. IIL, *Record Book II,* 1 November 1900, 62; 7 March 1901, 82; 3 October 1901, 93; 7 November 1901, 96. On the Sibyl Carter Indian Lace Association, see Duncan. For a thorough study of the field matron program, see Emmerich.

22. Pratt, 119, 126, 148, 157–62, 184; see Women's National Indian Associa-

tion papers, *Report of the Annual Meeting of the Women's National Indian Association, Dec. 6th and 7th, 1893,* Reel 1; *Our Missionary Report for 1896,* Reel 3, 49, Huntington Free Library, New York.

23. Hewes; Lindsey, 183.

24. Marshall Field and Company, full-page inside cover advertisement, *Brush and Pencil* 7 (December 1900); Dilworth, 79–80. Numerous studies of the Indian arts trade focus on the Southwest: see Tisdale for a thematic collection of articles; an introduction to the Fred Harvey Company can be found in Davies; more recent studies include Wiegle and Babcock and Howard and Pardue.

25. League charter, IIL, *Annual Report* (1900), 13; IIL, *Annual Report* (1901), 8. Jacobs points out that many female reformers encouraged Indian arts as a means of moral uplift, although she draws a sharper distinction between the "moral reformers" and the "feminist preservationists" than I think actually existed. Not only were both kinds of women members of organizations such as the Indian Industries League, but individual members often expressed contradictory ideas about their work.

26. IIL, *Record Book II,* 30 October 1899, 33; Roe, 178–79. Roe was the pastor at the Indian Mission Church in Colony, Oklahoma, where he and his wife had settled in 1897, and a vice president of the Indian Industries League from 1901 until his death; see his obituary, "Friend of Indian." The Seger Colony was under the supervision of John H. Seger; see his *Early Days* and Rairdon.

27. IIL, *Record Book II,* 4 October 1900, 60; 4 December 1902, 135; 3 January 1901, 68; see Doubleday, *Two Ways,* 15–18 and *Our Industrial,* 3, 6–11. Doubleday (1865–1918) remained on the executive committee through 1912, and although she never attended any meetings, she corresponded with some regularity and clearly served as an important contact, guiding the league toward money and people. For biographical information, see the following: *National Cyclopedia,* 400; Johnson and Malone, 392; Welker; Seaton. Reel joined the league's executive committee in 1902 and remained on it through 1910.

28. These arguments appear in the two Doubleday pamphlets cited in n. 27, as well as in Doubleday, "What the Basket" (this article appeared with the same title as the final chapter in White), and Doubleday, "Indian Industrial Development" (unattributed, but Du Bois confirms that it is a version of *Two Ways to Help the Indian*); see "Problem in Ethics," Reel 5, no. 72, PCGD.

29. Doubleday, "What the Basket," 561; *Our Industrial,* 1–2.

30. Doubleday, "What the Basket," 561.

31. Doubleday, *Two Ways,* 4–5; "Indian Industrial," 101; *Two Ways,* 6; *Two Ways,* 9. Doubleday's criticism of lace making seems wrongheaded, given that the Indian lace makers not only produced exceptionally fine and often innovative work but also sold it at a relatively good profit (see Duncan, 35).

32. McCarthy, 46.

33. Doubleday, "What the Basket," 561. If Doubleday noted any irony in the

fact that just a decade earlier the WNIA had been trying to persuade Indian women to adopt the trappings of the modern domestic home, she kept silent.

34. Cohodas, 88, see also 90, 102, 111, 113, 117; McCarthy, 40.

35. Doubleday, *Two Ways,* 15–18; *Our Industrial,* 3, 6–11.

36. IIL, *Record Book II,* 7 May 1903, 152; IIL, *Annual Report* (1904). Besides her Indian novel, *A Soul in Bronze,* Du Bois wrote several other novels on non-Indian topics.

37. The surviving lectures (undated, but probably written between 1903 and 1907) include the following: "The Symbolism of Indian Basketry," Reel 3, no. 38, PCGD; "Art and Industry among the Mission Indians," Reel 3, no. 38a, PCGD; and "Mission Indian Myth and Song," Reel 3, no. 27, PCGD. Many of Du Bois's other manuscripts about the Mission Indians appear to have been written as lectures, and in a date book for 1906 she records conducting Indian lectures and sales in several places.

38. Du Bois, "Symbolism," 1; "Mission Indian Folklore: The Culture Hero, Chaup," Reel 3, no. 25, p. 25, PCGD; "Art and Industry," 1.

39. See "Transcripts of Lowell Bean's Tape-Recorded Comments on the Constance Goddard Du Bois Papers at the Huntington Free Library," Reel 1, no. 4, p. 8, PCGD.

40. See Du Bois, "Mythology"; "Diegueno"; and "Religious."

41. Du Bois, "Symbolism," 6–7.

42. Watkins to Du Bois, 6 December 1901, Reel 1, PCGD; Lummis to Du Bois, 12 January 1908 [1909?], Charles F. Lummis Papers, Southwest Museum, Pasadena, Calif.; Watkins to Du Bois, 14 October 1903, Reel 1, PCGD. Watkins also feared that Du Bois's constant use of all her brain power was partly to blame for her persistent symptoms of "nerve strain."

43. Du Bois, "Art and Industry," 4.

44. Du Bois, "Symbolism," 2; "Symbolism," 4; "Art and Industry," 6.

45. Du Bois, "Symbolism," 1–2, 6, 9, 13.

46. Ibid., 7, 14.

47. Ibid., 7. Field workers who corresponded with the league reiterated this theme, and the league jealously guarded information about its basket suppliers. IIL, *Record Book III,* 28 September 1905, 54.

48. "Mission Indians," Reel 3, no. 26, p. 36, PCGD; Du Bois, "Symbolism," 14.

49. Watkins to Du Bois, 30 May 1900, Reel 1, PCGD; "Indian Workers and Record," Reel 4, no. 57, PCGD.

50. Du Bois, "Symbolism," 6–7, 14.

51. Watkins to Du Bois, 2 November 1897, Reel 1, no. 6, PCGD.

52. Du Bois, "Mission Indian Myth and Song," 3.

53. Rosalie Nejo was to do the buying, and her friend Frances La Chappa was to "instruct in better work and prettier" (Watkins to Du Bois, 29 September 1904,

Reel 1, PCGD). Watkins claimed that Rosalie could "teach basketry as well as I can and buy with more discretion" (Watkins to Du Bois, 5 December 1904, Reel 1, PCGD). See the Indian Industries League's annual reports for notes about its support of Nejo and La Chappa.

54. Watkins to Du Bois, 5 December 1904, Reel 1, PCGD; Du Bois, "Indian Workers and Record."

55. See draft of a letter from Du Bois to Estelle Reel, July 1898, Reel 5, no. 63, PCGD; Du Bois, "Symbolism," 12.

56. All of these efforts are described in the league's record books and annual reports.

Works Cited

Albers, Patricia C., and William R. James. "Illusion and Illumination: Visual Images of American Indian Women in the West." Pp. 35–50 in *The Women's West,* ed. Susan Armitage and Elizabeth Jameson. Norman: University of Oklahoma Press, 1987.

Allen, Paula Gunn. *The Sacred Hoop: Recovering the Feminine in American Indian Traditions.* Boston: Beacon Press, 1986.

"Art of Indian Basketry." *New York Daily Tribune,* 17 February 1901, 4.

"Arts Not to Be Lost." *New York Daily Tribune,* 8 April 1901, 5.

Babock, Barbara A. " 'A New Mexican Rebecca': Imaging Pueblo Women." *Journal of the Southwest* 32.4 (1990): 400–37.

Babcock, Barbara A., and Nancy J. Parezo, eds. *Daughters of the Desert: Women Anthropologists and the Native American Southwest, 1880–1980.* Albuquerque: University of New Mexico Press, 1988.

Banta, Martha. *Imaging American Women: Idea and Ideals in Cultural History.* New York: Columbia University Press, 1987.

Berlo, Janet Catherine, ed. *The Early Years of Native American Art History: The Politics of Scholarship and Collecting.* Seattle: University of Washington Press, 1992.

Blair, Karen J. *The Torchbearers: Women and Their Amateur Arts Associations in America, 1890–1930.* Bloomington: Indiana University Press, 1994.

Boris, Eileen. *Art and Labor: Ruskin, Morris, and the Craftsman Ideal in America.* Philadelphia: Temple University Press, 1986.

"A California Fad." *New York Daily Tribune,* 25 January 1891, 18.

Cohodas, Marvin. "Louisa Keyser and the Cohns: Mythmaking and Basket Making in the American West." Pp. 88–133 in *The Early Years of Native American Art History: The Politics of Scholarship and Collecting,* ed. Janet Catherine Berlo. Seattle: University of Washington Press, 1992.

Cole, Douglas. *Captured Heritage.* Seattle: University of Washington Press, 1985.

Coleman, Michael C. *Presbyterian Missionary Attitudes toward American Indians, 1837–1893.* Jackson: University Press of Mississippi, 1985.

Corson, Juliet. "The Evolution of Home." Pp. 714–18 in *The Congress of Women Held in the Woman's Building, World's Columbian Exposition, Chicago, USA, 1893,* ed. Mary Kavanaugh Oldham Eagle. 1894. Reprint, New York: Arno Press, 1974.

Davies, Cynthia. "Frontier Merchants and Native Craftsmen: The Fred Harvey Company Collects Indian Art." *Journal of the West* 21.1 (1982): 120–25.

Dilworth, Leah. *Imagining Indians in the Southwest: Persistent Visions of a Primitive Past.* Washington, D.C.: Smithsonian Institution Press, 1996.

Doubleday, Nellie. "Indian Industrial Development." *Outlook* 67 (12 January 1901): 101–102.

Doubleday, Nellie [Neltje Blanchan, pseud.]. *Our Industrial Work.* Philadelphia, Pa.: National Indian Association, 1903.

——. *Two Ways to Help the Indian.* Philadelphia, Pa.: National Indian Association, 1901.

——. "What the Basket Means to the Indian." *Everybody's Magazine* 5 (1901): 561–70.

Du Bois, Constance Goddard. "Diegueno Mortuary Ollas." *American Anthropologist* 9 (1907): 484–86.

——. "Mythology of the Mission Indians." *Journal of American Folk-Lore* 19 (April–June 1906): 145–64.

——. "Religious Ceremonies and Myths of the Mission Indians." *American Anthropologist* 7 (1905): 620–29.

——. *A Soul in Bronze: A Novel of Southern California.* Chicago: Herbert S. Stone & Co., 1900.

Duncan, Kate C. "American Indian Lace Making." *American Indian Art Magazine* 5 (May 1980): 28–35, 80.

Elliott, Maud, ed. *Art and Handicraft in the Woman's Building of the World's Columbian Exposition, Chicago, 1893.* Paris: Goupil, 1893.

Emmerich, Lisa. " 'To Respect and Love and Seek the Ways of White Women': Field Matrons, the Office of Indian Affairs, and Civilization Policy, 1890–1938." Ph.D. diss., University of Maryland, 1987.

Fredericsen, Kirstine. "Looking Backwards." Pp. 237–39 in *The Congress of Women Held in the Woman's Building, World's Columbian Exposition, Chicago, USA, 1893,* ed. Mary Kavanaugh Oldham Eagle. 1894. Reprint, New York: Arno Press, 1974.

"Friend of Indian." *Outlook* 103 (12 April 1913): 789–90.

Goodale, Elaine. *Sister to the Sioux: The Memoirs of Elaine Goodale Eastman, 1885–91.* Ed. Kay Graber. Lincoln: University of Nebraska Press, 1978.

——. "Some Lessons from Barbarism." *Popular Science Monthly* 38 (November 1890): 82–86.

Gould, Stephen Jay. *The Mismeasure of Man.* New York: Norton, 1981.

Green, Rayna. "The Pocahontas Perplex: The Image of Indian Women in American Culture." *Massachusetts Review* 16 (1975): 698–714.

——. *Women in American Indian Society.* Washington, D.C.: Smithsonian Institution Press, 1992.

Herzog, Melanie. "Aesthetics and Meanings: The Arts and Crafts Movement and the Revival of American Indian Basketry." Pp. 69–91 in *The Substance of Style: Perspectives on the American Arts and Crafts Movement,* ed. Bert Denker. Hanover, N.H.: University Press of New England, 1996.

Hewes, Dorothy W. "Those First Good Years of Indian Education: 1894 to 1898." *American Indian Culture and Research Journal* 5 (1981): 71.

Hinsley, Curtis M. "The World as Marketplace: Commodification of the Exotic at the World's Columbian Exposition, Chicago, 1893." Pp. 344–65 in *Exhibiting Cultures: The Poetics and Politics of Museum Display,* ed. Ivan Karp and Steven Lavine. Washington, D.C.: Smithsonian Institution Press, 1991.

"In 'Hopi' Clubdom." *New York Daily Tribune,* 13 October 1902, 5.

Howard, Kathleen L., and Diana F. Pardue. *Inventing the Southwest: The Fred Harvey Company and Native American Art.* Flagstaff, Ariz.: Northland, 1996.

Hoxie, Frederick E. *A Final Promise: The Campaign to Assimilate the Indians, 1880–1920.* Lincoln: University of Nebraska Press, 1984.

Jacobs, Margaret D. *Engendered Encounters: Feminism and Pueblo Cultures, 1874–1934.* Lincoln: University of Nebraska Press, 1999.

James, George Wharton. "Indian Handicrafts." *Handicraft* 1 (March 1903): 269–87.

Johnson, Allen, and Dumas Malone, eds. *Dictionary of American Biography.* Vol. 5. New York: Scribner's Sons, 1946.

Kaplan, Wendy. *The Art That Is Life: The Arts and Crafts Movement in America, 1875–1920.* Boston: Little, Brown, 1987.

Klein, Laura F., and Lillian A. Ackerman, eds. *Women and Power in Native North America.* Norman: University of Oklahoma Press, 1995.

Landsman, Gail H. "The 'Other' as Political Symbol: Images of Indians in the Woman Suffrage Movement." *Ethnohistory* 39 (Summer 1992): 247–84.

Lears, T. J. Jackson. *No Place of Grace: Antimodernism and the Transformation of American Culture, 1880–1920.* New York: Pantheon, 1981.

Lindsey, Donal F. *Indians at Hampton Institute, 1877–1923.* Urbana: University of Illinois Press, 1995.

Maddox, Lucy. "Bearing the Burden: Perceptions of Native American Women at Work." *Women: A Cultural Review* 2 (Winter 1991): 228–37.

Mark, Joan. *A Stranger in Her Native Land: Alice Fletcher and the American Indians.* Lincoln: University of Nebraska Press, 1988.

Mason, Otis T. *Woman's Share in Primitive Culture*. 1894. Reprint, New York: D. Appleton, 1899.

Mathes, Valerie Sherer. "Nineteenth-Century Women and Reform: The Women's National Indian Association." *American Indian Quarterly* 14 (Winter 1990): 1–18.

McCarthy, Kathleen D. *Women's Culture: American Philanthropy and Art, 1830–1930*. Chicago: University of Chicago Press, 1991.

McDiarmid, Clara. "Our Neighbors, The Alaskan Women." Pp. 723–26 in *The Congress of Women Held in the Woman's Building, World's Columbian Exposition, Chicago, USA, 1893*, ed. Mary Kavanaugh Oldham Eagle. 1894. Reprint, New York: Arno Press, 1974.

Merrick, Caroline E. "Personal Rights of Indian Wives." *The Woman's Journal* (8 March 1890): 78–79.

Mullin, Molly H. "Consuming the American Southwest: Culture, Art, and Difference." Ph.D. diss., Duke University, 1993.

National Cyclopedia of American Biography. 1913. Ann Arbor, Mich.: University Microfilms, 1967.

Palmer, Bertha. "The Growth of the Woman's Building." Pp. 9–22 in *Art and Handicraft in the Woman's Building of the World's Columbian Exposition, Chicago, 1893*, ed. Maud Elliott. Paris: Goupil, 1893.

Parezo, Nancy, ed. *Hidden Scholars: Women Anthropologists and the Native American Southwest*. Albuquerque: University of New Mexico Press, 1993.

"The Position of Indian Women." *The Red Man* (April 1889): 3.

Pratt, Richard Henry. *Battlefield and Classroom: Four Decades with the American Indian, 1867–1904*, ed. Robert M. Utley. New Haven, Conn.: Yale University Press, 1964.

"Primitive Indian Women." *New York Daily Tribune*, 27 October 1902, 5.

Rairdon, Jack T. "John Homer Seger: The Practical Indian Educator." *Chronicles of Oklahoma* 34 (Summer 1956): 203–16.

Riley, Glenda. *Women and Indians on the Frontier, 1825–1915*. Albuquerque: University of New Mexico Press, 1984.

Rodgers, Daniel T. *The Work Ethic in Industrial America, 1850–1920*. Chicago: University of Chicago Press, 1974.

Roe, Walter C. "The Mohonk Lodge: An Experiment in Indian Work." *Outlook* 68 (18 May 1901): 176–79.

Rushing, W. Jackson. *Native American Art and the New York Avant-Garde: A History of Cultural Primitivism*. Austin: University of Texas Press, 1995.

Rydell, Robert. *All the World's a Fair: Visions of Empire at American International Expositions, 1876–1916*. Chicago: University of Chicago Press, 1984.

——. "The Culture of Imperial Abundance: World's Fairs in the Making of American Culture." Pp. 191–216 in *Consuming Visions: Accumulation and Display of Goods in America, 1880–1920*, ed. Simon Bronner. New York: Norton, 1989.

Seaton, Beverly. "Nellie Blanchan De Graff Doubleday." Pp. 536–38 in *American Women Writers,* ed. Lina Mainiero. New York: Frederick Ungar, 1979.

Seger, John H. *Early Days among the Cheyenne and Arapahoe Indians.* Ed. Stanley Vestal. Norman: University of Oklahoma Press, 1956.

Smits, David D. "The 'Squaw Drudge': A Prime Index of Savagism." *Ethnohistory* 29.4 (1982): 281–306.

Sparhawk, Frances. *Onoqua.* Boston: Lee and Shepard, 1892.

——. *Senator Intrigue and Inspector Noseby: A Tale of Spoils.* Boston: Red-letter, 1895.

Sund, Judy. "Columbus and Columbia in Chicago, 1893: Man of Genius Meets Generic Woman." *Art Bulletin* 75 (September 1993): 443–66.

Tisdale, Shelby, J., ed. "Southwestern Indian Art Markets." Special edition of *Journal of the Southwest* 38.4 (Winter 1996).

Trachtenberg, Alan. *The Incorporation of America: Culture and Society in the Gilded Age.* New York: Hill and Wang, 1982.

Trump, Erik. "The Indian Industries League and Its Support of American Indian Arts, 1893–1922: A Study of Changing Attitudes toward Indian Women and Assimilationist Policy." Ph.D. diss., Boston University, 1996.

——. "Primitive Woman—Domestic(ated) Woman: The Image of the Primitive Woman at the 1893 World's Columbian Exposition," *Women's Studies* 27 (1998): 215–58.

Wanken, Helen M. " 'Woman's Sphere' and Indian Reform: The Women's National Indian Association, 1879–1901." Ph.D. diss., Marquette University, 1981.

Weimann, Jeanne. *The Fair Women.* Chicago: Academy Chicago, 1981.

Welker, Herbert H. "Doubleday, Neltje Blanchan De Graff." Pp. 508–509 in *Notable American Women, 1607–1950,* Vol. 1, ed. Edward T. James. Oxford, U.K.: Oxford University Press, 1971.

Wheeler, Candace. "Applied Arts in the Woman's Building." Pp. 59–69 in *Art and Handicraft in the Woman's Building of the World's Columbian Exposition, Chicago, 1893,* ed. Maud Elliott. Paris: Goupil, 1893.

White, Mary. *How to Make Baskets.* 1902. Reprint, Detroit, Mich.: Gale Research, 1972.

Wiegle, Marta, and Barbara A. Babcock, eds. *The Great Southwest of the Fred Harvey Company and the Santa Fe Railway.* Phoenix: Heard Museum, 1996.

6

Saving the Pueblos

Commercialism and Indian Reform in the 1920s

CARTER JONES MEYER

DURING THE 1920s, when the federal government intensified its efforts to detribalize and assimilate American Indians, a small but influential group of Anglo intellectuals, many of whom lived in the southwestern United States, began a massive campaign to save native cultures from the threat of destruction. Based on their highly romanticized appraisal of the Pueblo Indians in New Mexico and Arizona, these intellectuals reasoned that native cultures possessed "secrets of life" that modern American culture lacked, among them deeply rooted beliefs in communalism and the principle of unity between man and nature. For zealous crusaders like John Collier, a leader of the protest, reform of U.S. Indian policy seemed imperative if these secrets were to be saved, but some who became involved in the campaign, notably writer Mary Austin and archaeologist Edgar L. Hewett, also believed that political reform of this magnitude could not be accomplished without an attendant education campaign that would enlighten the public about the value of Indian cultures in American life. A two-pronged strategy of this nature would not only thwart the policy of assimilation, thus saving the Indians from certain destruction, but also provide an essential foundation for the regeneration of an American culture that all believed was being crushed by urban-industrial growth and the stifling effects of mass culture. According to Hewett, director of the School of American Research and the Museum of New Mexico in Santa Fe, immediate action was critically important. An "insistent pressure" was needed, he wrote in a virtual call-to-arms, "through every possible channel of influence for increased knowledge of the Native American race, for appreciation of its unique culture and for the recognition of its value and rightful place in the political, economic and cultural development of the future in America."[1]

The immediate catalyst for this ambitious campaign was the controversial Bursum bill, drawn up in 1922 to help settle an increasingly antagonistic dispute between the Pueblo Indians of New Mexico and non-Indians who had wittingly taken up residence on their lands. Although introduced in the U.S. Senate by Holm Bursum, New Mexico's Republican senator, the bill was originally drafted by Secretary of the Interior Albert Fall, a fierce advocate of private ownership and development of public-domain lands who would shortly be indicted for illegal actions in the Teapot Dome scandal. Written to embody Fall's views, the bill proposed to officially recognize the claims of non-Indians who had resided on Pueblo lands since 1900; those who had assumed claims after this time could, with the approval of a special court and the Secretary of the Interior himself, purchase their holdings at market value.[2] Whereas proponents of the bill believed it was the most efficient way to settle disputed land claims and defuse any possible conflicts between racial groups, whites who considered themselves friends of the Indians saw it as part of a much more insidious plot to "loot the Indians of every bit of the land and resources they still had," according to Collier. Passage of the bill would undermine the regeneration they imagined might result from saving Indian cultures from the ravages of the assimilation policy, which had dominated Indian affairs since passage of the Dawes Act in 1887.[3]

Those who became involved in the campaign to defeat the Bursum bill shared a deep disdain for its architects and the rigidly ethnocentric Indian policy that informed it. Ultimately, however, they held American culture itself responsible for what was happening to the Pueblos. Austin, best known for her studies of the Western landscape, notably in *The Land of Little Rain* (1903), criticized Americans' aesthetic narrow-mindedness as she despaired over the impact of urban-industrial development and material "progress" on their ability to adapt to the natural environment. She chafed in particular at the hegemony of the eastern literary establishment, which exalted the borrowed traditions of European literature and consequently failed to acknowledge the strengths and desirability of an authentic American literature derived from the rhythms of the land. Austin was especially critical of New York, the seat of this urban narrow-mindedness. "It [New York City] was not simple or direct enough," she wrote in her autobiography; "bemused by its own complexity, it missed the open order of the country west of the Alleghenies. It was too much intrigued with its own reactions, took, in the general scene, too narrow a sweep. It lacked freshness, air and light. More than anything else it lacked pattern, and I had a pattern-hungry mind."[4]

Hewett, a prominent archaeologist and educator, worried that the lack of public interest in preserving America's ancient past was reflective of a larger tendency toward Anglocentrism, which denied the legitimacy and relevance of prehistoric Indian civilizations as it exalted the achievements of the white man in the post-Columbian era. "We of the white race have been so long dominant that we have accustomed ourselves to look upon every people less advanced than ourselves in material agencies, as an 'inferior' race, forgetting that it takes several factors to constitute a fully developed, civilized people, and that in some respects the peoples whom we have called primitive, or savage, or uncivilized, have been far in advance of ourselves."[5] Like Austin, Hewett questioned the cultural myopia that seemed so entrenched in early-twentieth-century America, and he viewed the Bursum bill as one of its more odious manifestations.

The disappointment each of these reformers felt toward modern American culture was reinforced by their contact with Indian cultures and especially the Pueblos. Hewett and Austin had been some of the first to see in the Pueblos' holistic way of life an antidote to the deficiencies that seemed so abundant in their own culture. Austin first encountered Indians in the early 1890s, when she lived in the Owens Valley of California and spent long hours among the Paiutes who lived near her home. Befriending some of the women of the tribe, she was able to gather valuable material on their creation myths and views of the land, which she later incorporated in short stories for *The Land of Little Rain*. In these stories, Austin established the predominating theme of her desert literature, celebrating not only the economy of the desert environment but also the Indians who, through centuries of adaptation, lived in harmony with it. "Live long enough with an Indian," she marveled in "Shoshone Land," "and he or the wild things will show you a use for everything that grows in these border lands."[6]

Austin's experiences among the Indians of California, in combination with extensive study of native songs and poetry—as translated or "re-expressed" by whites—led her to believe that a new American poetry might be developed from the song cycles and rhythmic patterns of the Indians. She was convinced that, to be truly authentic, poetry, and by extension all art, should be an expression of the land. Because the Indians' rhythmic patterns seemed to correspond so well with the actual rhythms of nature, it followed that their verse forms were the appropriate model for a new, distinctly American poetry inspired by the natural environment. Although this theory was not to receive full articulation until the publication of *The American Rhythm* in 1923, Austin used it in the broken verse of her play *The Arrow Maker* (1911). In 1918, she provided an outline of the theory in her introduction to *The Path on the Rainbow,* an anthology of American Indian verse edited by George Cronyn, which was the first of its kind to be published without an accompanying explanatory text. More than 350 pages in length with poetry arranged by geographical regions, *The Path on the Rainbow* attempted to establish an Indian poetic tradition that modern American poets might use as a source for their own work. Austin was convinced of the book's literary importance: "Arresting as single examples of it are, a greater interest still attaches to the relationship which seems to develop between Indian verse and the ultimate literary destiny of America." Austin believed that study of this critical relationship was imperative, because "the whole instinctive movement of the American people is for a deeper footing in their native soil."[7] By 1922, when the Bursum bill controversy attracted the attention of many in America who had never before considered the value of the Indians, Austin was already considered a leading voice on the subject.

Austin also developed an interest in preserving Indian art, believing that it embodied a special vision lost to modern American culture: "It concerned itself entirely with the principle of the conscious unity in all things, the gesture of a rhythmic beauty to interpret the significance of the common things, the ploughing and watering and planting of the corn, the fine moralities of nature." The Indian is an artist, she concluded, "because he is sensitive to the spirit of existence. Art for him is a logical necessity."[8] Austin's emergent passion for native art was no doubt fueled by Edgar Hewett, whom she met in Santa Fe in 1918 and who offered her an overwhelming amount of material with which to work in the native artifact collections of the School of American Research. Although there is no record of their conversations, they must surely have discussed their common desire to preserve and promote traditional Indian art and to increase, more generally, public appreciation for native cultures. Clearly, Austin was energized by Hewett's work and by the collections to which she had access: "The school here has put every facility at my command and the field is so rich that I lie awake at nights fearing somebody may take it away from me."[9] Consumed by her desire to dominate the field, she began to host teas at the Museum of New Mexico, where she introduced her ideas on the development of an indigenous American literature and on the value of Indian art for modern culture.[10] Austin believed every effort was needed to protect this art. To do so would lead not only to the resurrection of a handicraft culture threatened by the machine age, but also to a renewed interest in the environment as the focal point of American life. As the foremost interpreter of native literary and artistic expression—at least in Austin's own mind—she would lead the way.

Hewett became interested in Indian, and specifically Pueblo, culture after making periodic visits to ancient Indian settlements in New Mexico in the 1890s. Although a secondary school teacher in Colorado at this point, Hewett dreamed of a career in archaeology, no doubt inspired by the Swiss-born ethnologist Adolph Bandelier, who had only recently discovered cave dwellings at the Rito de los Frijoles in New Mexico (later to be known as Bandelier National Monument). In 1898, as president of the fledgling Normal College at Las Vegas, New Mexico (now New Mexico Highlands University), Hewett began conducting archaeological excavations at the Pajarito Plateau near Santa Fe and organized the New Mexico Archaeological Society to cultivate support for his projects. Five years later, he left his career in college administration to pursue archaeology professionally, beginning work for a Ph.D. at the University of Geneva and conducting research for the Archaeological Institute of America. An important part of Hewett's work was to conduct a survey of the Mesa Verde cliff dwellings in southwestern Colorado. Through personal contact with John F. Lacey, congressman from Iowa and chairman of the House Committee on Public Lands, Hewett recommended that Mesa Verde be preserved as a national park and that an American antiquities act was needed to ensure that the nation's ancient heritage was protected from archaeological vandalism. The American Antiquities Act, passed by Congress in 1906, is a tribute to Hewett's tireless efforts on behalf of this cause.[11]

One of Hewett's greatest triumphs occurred in 1907, when he was able to convince the Archaeological Institute of America to establish its American school in Santa Fe, only a short distance from some of the richest archaeological sights of the Pueblo country. Eastern-university-trained archaeologists had initially opposed the decision, regarding Santa Fe as a cultural and intellectual wasteland. However, Hewett's insistent lobbying at the institute enabled him to win this most important battle and gain needed recognition for his projects. As a reward for his work, Hewett was appointed first director of the school and the Museum of New Mexico as well, an educational adjunct that was to be housed with the school in the Spanish-built Palace of the Governors, located in the heart of Santa Fe and commonly regarded as the oldest public building in America (1610). Restoration of the structure under Hewett's direction would serve as the cornerstone of a massive revival of Pueblo-Spanish-style architecture throughout Santa Fe and would lead ultimately to its reinvention for the t⌐ market as "The City Different."[12]

As director of the School of American Research and the Museum of New Mexico, Hewett embarked on a massive promotional effort on behalf of Santa Fe and the Southwest. At the heart of it was a celebration of the city's and the region's Indian, Hispanic, and Anglo heritage. The museum was established as a center for regional arts, for example, providing studios and exhibition space for talented painters who were able to capture the tricultural dynamic of the area. Then, in 1919, Hewett and his associates recreated the Santa Fe Fiesta, an elaborate three-day pageant derived from celebrations dating back to 1712 but that now assumed a distinctly modern identity emphasizing spectacle. Processions, reenactments, and Indian dances, encompassing the epic history of the Southwest, served as educational displays for tourists and residents alike, aiming to forge a new regional identity and pride while filling city coffers. Hewett intended that the Indians of New Mexico and Arizona be an important focus of the event. He and his staff at the School of American Research worked diligently to ensure their participation, meeting frequently with the Indians themselves to convince them that the Santa Fe Fiesta was as much their celebration as it was for the Anglos and Hispanics. The Indians were encouraged to stage ceremonies "in their primitive beauty, in accordance with their own traditions and their religious significance," so that spectators might gain at least a glimpse into Indian life. There was apparently some hesitancy among the Indians, who had seldom if ever "staged" ceremonial dances outside of ritual calendars and away from the pueblos. Yet, according to the school's *El Palacio* magazine, careful deliberations, sometimes "as formal and impressive as the negotiating and signing of a World treaty," with the added incentive of financial remuneration, led many to accept the invitation and to participate in the fiesta.[13] Thus, Santa Fe's premier event, in addition to celebrating invented regional traditions, became an important venue for the transformation of Indian ceremonial dances into a form of educational entertainment neatly packaged for the consumption of a public lured to Santa Fe by the romance of its Indian past.

Hewett was the mastermind behind this transformation. By 1922, he was widely regarded, like Austin, as a leading interpreter and promoter of Indian cultures, past and present. Through the School of American Research and the Museum of New Mexico, Hewett worked to publicize the latest archaeological findings regarding the ancient inhabitants of the Southwest, but also took some of the first steps to preserve and protect contemporary Indian cultures, which he believed were threatened not only by the assimilation policy of the federal government, but by the dominance of a modern culture that held little regard for traditional ways of life. In the Indians of today, Hewett wrote, "the culture of the past survives, dormant, inert, perhaps smoldering and capable of being fanned into flame."[14] Like Austin, he believed that the Indians possessed superior ways of viewing the world from which the white man might learn: "Perhaps in nothing else does the superiority of the Indian race appear to such advantage as in its outlook on nature and life," he added, echoing Austin. "The Indian conceived himself to be, not a master of creation, ordained to conquer and rule all other creatures, but rather a single factor in the whole scheme of life. . . . It was this singularly fine outlook upon the world, the exact antithesis of the egocentric point of view of the Caucasian, that accounts for all the major achievements of the Indian."[15] As this observation suggests, Hewett viewed American Indians, particularly the Pueblos, through the same romantic lens as did Austin. He freely employed noble-savage rhetoric to emphasize both the value of the Indians in modern society and the degeneration of that society because of its indifference to their holistic view of life. To save Indians from destruction would mean the rebirth of American culture itself.

Others involved in the campaign to reform U.S. Indian policy in the 1920s, including John Collier, Mabel Dodge Luhan, and Elizabeth Shepley Sargeant, used similar rhetoric to defend their position. Using the Pueblos as their standard of cultural perfection, they condemned ethnocentrism and chastised the acquisitive, materialistic character of modern society that tended to commodify both land and people. Yet, what Hewett and other critics accused American society of perpetrating might easily be applied to Hewett's own work on behalf of the Indians and the formulation of regional identity. The neatly packaged Indian dances of the Santa Fe Fiesta, for example, do represent to some extent the commodification and exploitation of native cultures by the dominant society. But Hewett, of course, never considered this to be the case. Instead, he believed his promotion of the Indians was less an instance of exploitation than it was an affirmation of the legitimacy of Indian cultures in modern American society, an idea apparently lost on the Bureau of Indian Affairs. The noble-savage rhetoric he employed, although sentimental and at odds with the social and economic realities of Indian life in the early twentieth century (which Hewett knew well, given his position), became a means by which to manipulate public opinion in support of Indian self-determination, a hallmark of Indian reform efforts in the 1920s and a special concern of Hewett himself. "It is what [the Indian] does for himself that makes for his future character and progress," he wrote in defense of this position. "A sound policy is to leave him alone in most of his personal affairs, merely giving him the opportunity to select and adapt what we have to offer under the guidance of his own judgement."[16] Although the conflation of this policy proposal with romantic conceptions of Indianness is deeply ironic, because noble-savage imagery worked against the Indians' welfare by reducing them to idealized Others, Hewett believed it was an effective way to convince the public of the Indians' ability to determine their own lives. Their special knowledge of nature and man's place within it, he posited, entitled them to nothing less.

Given their admiration for Indian cultures and their desire to save them, particularly the Pueblos, it is not surprising that Austin and Hewett were initially sympathetic to the massive campaign that aimed to defeat the Bursum bill and usher in a new era in Indian affairs predicated on self-determination and cultural renewal. Leaders of the campaign included Collier and Mabel Dodge Luhan, the famous New York salon organizer who had recently taken up residence in New Mexico and had taken as her fourth husband a Taos Pueblo Indian. These leaders planned to blanket the leading magazines and newspapers of the day with articles defending the Pueblos and attacking the federal government for the gross injustice of its Indian policy. Collier and Luhan also arranged an extensive publicity tour in Chicago and New York for Pueblo representatives who were planning to appear at congressional hearings on the bill. Perhaps the most impressive moment of that tour came on the floor of the New York Stock Exchange, where drum beating and a Pueblo dance brought to a standstill the nation's most bustling financial center.[17]

The primary aim of the campaign was to educate the public about the bill itself, the ethnocentric policy that informed it, and the threat each posed to the survival of Pueblo culture. The leaders knew as well that the public must learn the value of Pueblo culture for the future of America itself. As Luhan counseled the many artists and writers who joined the cause, "The national love for Indians is now up in the public conscious-ness. . . . Give Americans more of the Indian life, more knowledge of the beauty and wholeness of that almost secret nation within a nation."[18] Austin and Hewett, of course, had come to this conclusion much earlier and were deeply engaged in promoting the Pueblos at the time of the campaign.

As early as 1919, Austin began developing a strategy for preserving and protecting Indian arts and crafts. In a letter to Secretary of the Interior Franklin K. Lane, she proposed that the federal government establish a department of arts and letters that would be responsible for spreading appreciation of native art in schools and through the press, preserving its sources in Indian culture, and developing an effective strategy for marketing the art throughout the United States.[19] Lane's reply was not positive— no doubt owing to the fact that Austin had essentially demanded that the federal government suspend its policy of assimilation. However, her letter remains significant for its articulation of a bona fide strategy for promoting Indian arts and crafts.

While the Bursum bill controversy raged in 1922 and 1923, Austin continued to press for an organization that would preserve and promote the best examples of Indian arts and crafts, even as she became embroiled in the more immediate politics of defeating the Bursum bill. She found support for this idea among her colleagues in Santa Fe, who organized the Pueblo Pottery Fund in 1922 (renamed the Indian Arts Fund in 1925) to help protect the best examples of Pueblo pottery through creation of a permanent collection, which Hewett agreed to house in the basement of the Museum of New Mexico.[20] All agreed that there was great need for such an organization. According to Austin, Pueblo pottery, and by extension all of Indian art, was "falling into desuetude through the indifference of ignorance."[21] White traders who worked the tourist market were encouraging Indians to produce only the cheapest trinkets for sale to the public. Because demand at this level was high and also quite profitable, the artists were being pressured to produce merchandise in a slapdash manner, thus corrupting what Austin considered America's last handicraft culture. Missionaries and federally operated schools also contributed to this cultural destruction by purposely isolating Indians from the spiritual sources of their art. In their zeal to impose Christian morality on a "heathen" population, for example, missionaries, sanctioned by the federal government, discouraged traditional religious visions, which had inspired and guided creation of the best Indian art. In addition, the federal government began a series of crackdowns on ceremonial dances in the 1920s, primarily at the urging of missionaries who found in these dances sexual promiscuity and an indulgence in drugs (notably peyote) and alcohol that would cause Indians to sink into "immorality" and "irreligion."[22] Schools, too, discouraged native artistic expression as part of the assimilation process. The extent of these restrictions is nowhere more evident than in an official circular sent to all day schools by C. J. Crandall, head of the Northern Pueblo Agency in Santa Fe: "I recommend and trust that this freehand and uninstructed drawing be abolished and that no pictures of Indian dances, Indian customs, warriors, etc., be permitted to be encouraged."[23] Austin was certain that only through a concerted drive to stop practices like these would Indian art, and by inference an Indian identity, survive.

She and her colleagues in the Indian Arts Fund supported efforts to reform federal Indian policy as a means toward this end, but they also believed that the creation of a permanent collection of native art would ensure the survival of a unique aesthetic expression from which all Americans would benefit. In collecting and preserving the finest examples of pottery, jewelry, weavings, and to some extent paintings, members of the fund hoped to assist young artists in restoring ancient Indian perspectives and styles that assimilationists and the tourist trade had partially succeeded in destroying. This collection would rekindle an Indian identity, provide much needed income for those living near or below the poverty line, and help to educate white Americans in the appreciation of an indigenous art form far superior to the cheap imitations passed on to tourists as "authentic" Indian art. Austin was confident that Americans would recognize in this art some of their own ideals: "home, security, communal labor, happy evenings by the fire, the satisfaction of achievement." Native art "stirs a fundamental Americanism in us, something subconsciously associated with these things . . . something real and experiencable" that would remain "permanently popular." "But the moment the thread is broken which binds Indian art to American experience," Austin warned, "it will become as merely traditional to us as Egyptian or Persian or Gothic art are to-day."[24] The goal of the Indian Arts Fund thus became twofold: to collect and preserve the best examples of Indian art as educational tools for young native artists and to take steps to make Indian art a vital, redeeming part of modern American life.

Austin became an active crusader on behalf of the Indian Arts Fund, making speeches nationwide and soliciting funds for it throughout the 1920s and until her death in 1934. She offered the organization land she owned in Santa Fe for the construction of a museum and arranged to have the royalties from a revision of Frank Hamilton Cushing's *Zuni Folk Tales* (1930) she had produced with Frederick Webb Hodge given to the Indian Arts Fund for additional purchases of Indian art.[25] She also donated to the fund her own collection of Pueblo paintings, which she had begun to amass in 1918 and that included the works of artists who went on to great fame, including Awa Tsireh (Alfonso Roybal) of San Ildefonso Pueblo. Ironically, Hewett's School of American Research also began collecting these paintings and, in fact, became instrumental in the development of Pueblo painting during this time. Austin purchased some of these works from the Indians who were given studio space by the school and later helped to organize exhibits of them at the Museum of New Mexico.[26] These exhibits "excited general interest and created a demand. . . . The demand grew and the quality of the paintings increased. They were in no way related to white men's work; they remained thoroughly Indian, exquisitely done and colored in accordance with the Indian philosophy of color." Confident of their worth, Austin concluded that they "extend the whole range of pictorial art in America."[27]

Hewett had similar concerns about arts, crafts, and the survival of Indian cultures but did not work through the Indian Arts Fund to achieve his goals. Instead, he used his own position as director of the School of American Research and the Museum of New Mexico to organize the Southwest Indian Fair, an annual event first held in 1922 as part of the Santa Fe Fiesta. Indians were already an integral part of the fiesta, but Hewett, in creating the fair, obviously wanted something more for them. In particular, this new venture aimed to bolster the Indians' economies through the exhibition and sale of their best arts and crafts. Hewett believed this was critically important to the restoration of their self-respect as a people. In a revealing display of paternalism that belies his support of Indian self-determination, he wrote, "They must be helped to understand and prize their citizenship, and the help that is accorded them should be of such character that it will not impair their self esteem. They have special abilities which can be made of great service to them and to us." The Southwest Indian Fair was an important way by which to achieve this. "The Pueblos are in no way averse to the practice of their fine old arts and industries, but the incentive therefore has been small; consequently the finest of their old arts and crafts were degenerating, even disappearing."[28]

Under Hewett's direction, members of the school's staff traveled to the pueblos to help the Indians improve their work, "not assuming that we could teach them anything with reference to their art, but leading them through proper encouragement to improve it."[29] At San Ildefonso, for example, a pueblo that had specialized in the production of blackware pottery (so called because of the special firing process that gave to the pottery both its black color and its high polish), school staff members assisted potters like Maria and Julian Martinez, who quickly rose to prominence as artists and whose work became prized possessions of museums and collectors alike. Of course, the essential element in this success was the development of a market for the art, and the Southwest Indian Fair helped establish it.

The fair, which opened on September 4, 1922, exhibited a vast array of Southwestern Indian arts and crafts, including weaving, pottery, painting, beadwork, and jewelry. Exhibitors, who were categorized by pueblo, competed for prizes that were awarded by members of the museum curatorial staff. (Competition was a foreign concept to the Indians, but organizers of the fair either disregarded this fact or believed it was an important first step in modernizing the Pueblos' economies.) Those winning first place received a $5 prize; second place garnered $3. A more dubious award in some respects was the Albert Bacon Fall Trophy Cup for best tribal display, especially given the fact that Fall, through the Bursum bill, was at that moment seeking to extinguish title to Pueblo lands.

The Southwest Indian Fair program outlined the objectives of the exhibition as the encouragement of traditional Indian arts and crafts, the establishment of markets and reasonable prices for Indian products, the authentication of all handicrafts, and the protection of the Indian artists in their dealings with white traders and buyers.[30] Beyond this, however, organizers of the event over the next few years felt it necessary to explain the larger implications of the fair. The Santa Fe Fiesta program for 1926, for example, explained that the motive for the exhibition

> was the obvious fact that there is a danger of losing to the world the priceless heritage of distinctive Indian art unless something is done to keep it alive. . . . An endeavor is being made to secure for the Indians a fair return for their work, to lead them to discover that their arts and handicraft are wanted, and that people are willing to pay enough for them to make it worth while to engage in this line of endeavor. When this is done the question of how to prevent these priceless arts from disappearing from the earth, will be solved.[31]

Hewett argued that the work done by the School of American Research through the Southwest Indian Fair significantly improved the economies of the Pueblos. Citing San Ildefonso, where success was perhaps greatest due to the pottery of the Martinezes, he stated, "An official inquiry shows that all the families of San Ildefonso put together derived from the production of their farms in the year 1923 slightly over $3300. The pottery making industry can be brought up to several times that amount in a comparatively short time." The Martinezes alone made more than $200 a month from their work, and the demand for their pottery far exceeded their ability to produce it. Hewett went on to boast that the School of American Research now received inquiries "by the car lot." But fearing that this would lead to accusations of commercialism, he explained that there was no intention of meeting such a demand, "for that would imply a degree of commercialization that would remove it from the realm of fine art. The intention is to preserve it as a purely aesthetic production, each piece a true work of art without duplication." If demand is high, Hewett added, then more artists needed to be developed.[32]

Between 1922 and 1926, under the aegis of Hewett and the School of American Research, the Southwest Indian Fair became a popular attraction for visitors to Santa Fe at the same time that it played an important role in the Pueblo pottery revival of the 1920s. New attractions were added with each passing year. In 1925, for example, the fair included a production of "The Sunset Trail," by Charles Wakefield Cadman, a leading member of the "Indianist" school of composers who achieved national renown in the early twentieth century by incorporating Indian themes and melodies into his popular ballads and operas. "The Sunset Trail" was an especially romantic depiction of the early struggles of the Plains Indians against the reservation system. Perhaps the greatest sensations of the opera were the classically trained Indian singers Tsianina Redfeather and Oskenonton. According to the Santa Fe *New Mexican,* the audience could not get enough of them; the audience leaned forward "in their seats, to see better the unusual spectacle of real Indians singing in opera."[33] In addition, a special tour to Santo Domingo Pueblo was arranged so that visitors could view the Green Corn Dance. According to the *New Mexican,* it was an immensely successful event as far as attendance was concerned; cars flooded the roads leading to the pueblo and trains made special stops to drop off passengers. "As usual," the article concluded, "the crowds piled up on the roofs and under the portales until it looked as if some of the Indian houses would collapse under the strain."[34]

Hewett felt fully justified in promoting Indian cultures in these ways. In fact, he came to believe that these were the only legitimate ways to educate the public about the merits of Indian cultures while reforming the Indian policy that threatened them. Clues to this thinking can be gained through Hewett's increasing frustration with the confrontational, often manipulative tactics used by John Collier to defeat the Bursum bill and then, in 1924, Collier's defense of Indian ceremonial dances that the Bureau of Indian Affairs sought to restrict. Hewett was especially incensed by the All Pueblo Councils Collier organized to gain the support of the Indians for his agenda. They smacked of paternalism, he thought; Collier, as an outsider, "was appallingly ignorant of Indian psychology and character" and the way in which they were conducted was "as foreign to Indian procedure as those of the political convention of past years which we have discredited and discarded." Having attended one, Hewett complained that "The whole thing was a demonstration of modern propaganda methods, the highly systematized procedure that we have seen in operation in this and other countries during the past decade, and which we brand as subversive of our form of popular government."[35] If Indian self-determination was the goal of reformers in the 1920s, Collier, as a leader of the movement, seemed woefully, even dangerously, off track.

Austin, too, became increasingly irritated by Collier's reform agenda, which seemed too focused on politics and not enough on culture. Although she chaired the publicity committee of Collier's American Indian Defense Association in hopes that her presence within the organization would lead to support for an Indian arts and crafts program, she was consistently disappointed. It is no wonder, then, that Austin became involved in the Indian Arts Fund by 1924. Here, she felt, she could better achieve her vision of preserving and protecting Pueblo art while establishing a broader foundation for an indigenous American aesthetic. Later in the 1920s, when Collier at last began to develop a program for Indian arts and crafts, which became the ill-fated Frazier-Leavitt bill, Austin expressed annoyance, primarily because he had not consulted her and other members of the Indian Arts Fund: "Why do you not, before rushing ahead with these things, consult the Indian Arts Foundation. . . . They would be the natural reference in such matters. . . . the best known, most experienced and best financed group in this field. And here I am, lecturing far and wide on Indian arts, who learn of this measure only after it has been determined upon, and given definite form."[36] Convinced of her own authority and leadership in the field, Austin could not tolerate the competition of others. In fact, at the very time Collier began work on his program for Indian arts and crafts, Austin was busily lobbying the Hoover administration, notably Indian Commissioner Charles J. Rhoads, for a more supportive Indian arts policy that would acknowledge the Indian Arts Fund as the leading authority on the subject. In an open directive to Rhoads, published in 1929, Austin again challenged the assimilation policy, citing a changed public attitude toward Indians as an important reason:

> The public at large has now come to realize that the Indian is a community asset. . . . Within the last ten years . . . Indian art has taken its place among the things that Americans talk about both at home and abroad, go to see, collect, and take into account in summing up the sources of American culture. In other words, we have come to realize that our Indians mean more to us as Indians than as imitation whites—a change in attitude which can no longer be ignored in our public policy toward them.[37]

That the Indian Arts Fund had played a fundamental role in this transformation was obvious to Austin. She expected that it would be obvious to federal officials, as well, who were to defer to her and other experts in the organization in all matters relating to native arts. After all, she surmised, the "official mind" displayed "confusion" and "honest ignorance" when it came to understanding the sources of Indian art.[38]

In her struggle for dominance in the field of Indian arts and crafts, Austin faced formidable competition from Hewett as well as Collier. Always in search of new funding for the Museum of New Mexico and School of American Research's many projects, for example, Hewett began in 1926 to court John D. Rockefeller Jr., who had expressed interest in funding a museum in Santa Fe. After visiting the collections of the Indian Arts Fund, still housed in the basement of the museum, where Hewett could better control them, Rockefeller chose to finance the organization and offer it better exhibition space in the new Laboratory of Anthropology, which was to be entirely separate from the museum and school and therefore beyond the control of Hewett himself. According to Austin, members of the fund insisted that the new museum be a "living" one, "for the benefit of Indians and the pouring of their capacity into the stream of American life." Rockefeller's assurance that he had been looking for just such a mission helped formalize the arrangement.[39] News of the agreement must have been a severe blow to Hewett and his supporters; indeed, they are reported to have accused Indian Arts Fund members of disloyalty.[40] Disloyal or not, the Indian Arts Fund won important recognition for its work, and Rockefeller's funding helped establish its legitimacy among organizations dedicated to the preservation of Indian arts and crafts.

The competition, criticism, and infighting that marked the Indian reform movement of the 1920s, particularly within the area of arts and crafts preservation, led reformers to offer exaggerated assessments of their own work on behalf of the Indians. Reflecting on his contributions later in life, Hewett wrote,

> Keenly realizing how nearly impossible it is for the white man to get deeply into the spirit of the Indian, I have felt it a duty to make an effort to do for the race what it has never attempted to do for itself, namely, to interpret it to those under whose control it has fallen. . . . There is a dearth of exegesis of the Indian world, of his position in the world picture. The spiritual stature of the Indian is all but unknown. For the sake of the truth of history it should be better understood.[41]

If Hewett's work on their behalf ever exhibited commercial tendencies, he would not admit it. "There should be a destiny for the American Indian more honorable than to be exploited as material for stirring fiction and spectacular exhibition," he explained in *Ancient Life in the American Southwest* (1930). "His is a race of splendid works and noble characteristics—a people who, in spite of the appalling adversities of the last four centuries, may be blending with its conquerors and at the same time preserving its own arts [that] look forward to a future on the high plane of its ancient traditions."[42]

Austin, too, made exaggerated claims regarding her role in educating the public about the merits of Indian cultures. Having studied native beliefs extensively—although always from the outside and always from a Western perspective—she believed there was no one better qualified for the task: "No editor who has published my work will deny that I have done much to secure for all classes of Indian books a proper public, nor, I think will anyone at all acquainted with the matter take exception to my claim to have made a noticeable difference in the general American interest in our Indian Arts."[43] Whereas Hewett at least acknowledged the difficulty, if not impossibility, of outsiders fully understanding the mind of the Indian, Austin made no such admission. She seems never to have questioned her expertise in the field of Indian arts and culture nor her ability to penetrate the native worldview.

That Austin and Hewett *did* make a difference in Americans' general knowledge of Indian cultures cannot be denied. At a time when the assimilation policy threatened tribal identities and many in the United States assumed that the Indians, as a people, were shattered and vanishing, Austin and Hewett were some of the first whites to suggest otherwise. Through their work, Americans learned that Indian cultures were still vital and had value in American life. In taking this position, they challenged the ethnocentric assumptions of their day, which posited the superiority of Anglo society and culture. Through the Indian Arts Fund and the Southwest Indian Fair, in particular, Austin and Hewett helped develop native artists and boosted pueblo economies while they offered Americans an alternative vision of life in the modern era, one predicated on a deep spirituality born of the land and of communal responsibility. They counseled respect for Indian points of view and argued for greater self-determination in the handling of their affairs. If new attitudes toward the Indians could be forged, Austin and Hewett buoyantly predicted, modern American culture itself would be renewed.

In spite of these remarkable steps away from the cultural myopia of their time, however, Austin and Hewett were still captives of it. They continued to view Indians as exotic Others and worked to keep them that way. In preserving Indian arts and crafts, Austin and Hewett believed they were preserving a way of life and spiritual outlook that were superior to their own and that held answers to its problems. Hewett's elaborate displays of Indians at the Santa Fe Fiesta and the Southwest Indian Fair tended to reinforce their separate, highly romanticized image in spite of his belief that the events were helping to carve a place in American society for the Indians. That these were commercial ventures, in spite of their assertions to the contrary, cannot be denied. Indian cultures were put on sale as a means of educating the public and ultimately reforming an ethnocentric Indian policy determined to destroy Indianness as a precondition for assimilation. The aim of the new policy initiative was self-determination for the Indians, but the selling of their cultures by well-meaning white patrons like Austin and Hewett seems to have compromised this intention. Their paternalistic approach, in instructing the Indians in "good" pottery, weaving, or painting styles or in shepherding them about in staged dances and pageants, suggests that they still conceived of Indians as childlike, needing the guidance of those who considered themselves more advanced, at least in their understanding of the complex machinations of modern society. To some extent this may have been true, but it was still at odds with the rhetoric of self-determination that permeated Indian reform in the 1920s. Moreover, the abundant paternalism of the movement was matched only by the competition and egotism of those involved. While Austin and Hewett professed to have the Indians' best interests at heart, their constant assertions that they

were the only ones who really knew the Indians and that their organizations were the only legitimate ones dedicated to saving Pueblo cultures
undercut the thrust of their work and brought confusion to the reform
campaign. Had Austin and Hewett been able to set aside their egos and
focus on their common interests, they may have garnered more influence
on federal policy.

The complex responses of these reformers to Indian affairs in the 1920s
cannot be resolved. Rather, it is better to concede their incongruities and
acknowledge Austin and Hewett as transitional figures in the early phase of
a larger cultural reorientation in twentieth-century America predicated on
the shift from an Anglocentric to a multicultural ideal. Although their work
with the Pueblos helped establish a foundation for this reorientation, they
could not fully abandon their own power and authority within it. Thus, the
gains Austin and Hewett may have made were compromised. It remained
for native activists of the postwar era, notably in the Red Power movement,
to pick up the threads of these earlier reform efforts and fashion them into a
new, more emboldened campaign for Indian self-determination.

Notes

1. Hewett, "Statement," 48.

2. *Congressional Record,* 67th Cong., 2nd sess., 11 September 1922, 62, Part i,
12, 323–25.

3. Collier, 128.

4. Austin, *Earth,* 349.

5. Hewett, "The Unknown," 30.

6. Austin, *The Land,* 59.

7. Cronyn, xv–xvii.

8. Austin, *Earth,* 362.

9. Quoted in Fink, 185.

10. See *El Palacio,* 7 December 1918; 9 December 1918; and 5 February 1919.

11. Frost, 57; Chauvenet, 56–57.

12. For an in-depth study of the architectural invention of Santa Fe, see
Wilson.

13. *El Palacio,* 15 September 1924, 132–33. In at least one fiesta during the
1920s, organizers brought in seventy-five Pueblo Indians as participants. For ten
days away from their villages, not including transportation, they were paid $3,000.
See Box 54, Edgar L. Hewett Papers, Fray Angelico Chavez History Library, Museum of New Mexico, Santa Fe (hereafter cited as ELHP). Some of the dances that
were staged included the Basket, Eagle, Deer, Buffalo, and Bow and Arrow Dances

and Shalako ceremony. Spectators viewed the dances in "kivas"—performance centers loosely based on the ceremonial chambers used by Pueblo Indians—and received programs that described the meaning and significance of each dance. For a broader history of historical pageantry in America during the early twentieth century, of which the Santa Fe Fiesta was an important part, see Glassberg.

14. Hewett, "The Native," 17–18.

15. Hewett, "The Unknown," 11–12.

16. Hewett, "Present," 8.

17. Collier, 132; *New York Times,* 15 January 1923, 28. The role of John Collier in the campaign to end assimilation is well covered in Philp; Kelly. For information on Luhan's role, see Rudnick.

18. Luhan, n.p.

19. Austin, "To Franklin K. Lane."

20. In 1925, members of the Indian Arts Fund included Kenneth Chapman, curator of the Museum of New Mexico and a founding member of the earlier Pueblo Pottery Fund; Mary Austin; arts patron Amelia E. White; Mabel Dodge Luhan; writer Elizabeth Shepley Sargeant; archaeologist Alfred V. Kidder; and Frederick Webb Hodge, representing the Museum of the American Indian in New York City. See Indian Arts Fund, Inc.

21. Austin, "Indian," n.p.

22. The Board of Indian Commissioners' recommendations on Indian dances, made to Commissioner Charles Burke, are in "Board of Indian Commissioners, Minutes of the Fall Meeting, Mohonk, New York, October 20–21, 1920," Records of the Board of Indian Commissioners, RG 75, National Archives, Washington, D.C.

23. Circular no. 59 from C. J. Randall to Day School Teachers, Northern Pueblo Agency, Santa Fe, 9 February 1926, Box 22, Mary Austin Papers, Huntington Library, San Marino, Calif. (hereafter cited as MAP).

24. Austin, "Indian," n.p.

25. Austin, *Earth,* 361; Hougland, 59–60.

26. Austin, *Earth,* 361; Brody, 74.

27. Austin, *Earth,* 361.

28. Hewett, "Letters," 14.

29. Ibid., 15.

30. Hewett, "The Unknown."

31. Ibid., 14.

32. Hewett, "Letters," 15–16.

33. Newspaper clipping, "Cadman Drama 'Sunset Trail' Thrills 1,000 at the Museum," 7 August 1925, Box 54, ELHP.

34. Newspaper clipping, "Thousands of Spectators at the Green Corn Dance," 5 August 1925, Box 54, ELHP.

35. Hewett, "Letters," 6–8. Hewett did not mention Collier by name in this

attack, but the inference is very clear. Hewett's view of Collier's work as subversive propaganda is remarkably similar to the criticism Albert Fall leveled at Collier in the defeat of the Bursum bill. "Such propaganda as this," Fall said in testimony on the bill, "if allowed to go entirely unchecked, will eventually break down this democratic Government of ours; if we are to have a Government by propaganda, and not by the three departments of the Government, the present conditions in soviet Russia would constitute a political paradise, compared to what we might have here." See U.S. Senate, *Hearings on S. 3865 and S. 4223,* 67th Cong., 4th sess., 1923, 225. It may be that Hewett, ever mindful of the political scene that could make or break his work, chose to adopt at least the language of U.S. government officials to distance himself from Collier's radicalism and protect his own projects, for which he needed state funding.

36. Austin, "To John Collier." The Frazier-Leavitt bill grew out of an Indian arts and crafts marketing plan that Collier had drawn up with James W. Young, vice president of the J. Walter Thompson advertising agency and a member of the board of the American Indian Defense Association. The legislation introduced in the House by Republican Scott Leavitt of Montana and in the Senate by Republican Lynn Frazier of North Dakota was officially known as the Indian Cooperative Marketing Board bill. It proposed a U.S. government trademark on all genuine Indian products and a corporation with the exclusive right to use it. It also authorized the president to appoint an Indian Cooperative Marketing Board, consisting of three people, which would in turn form the corporation, composed of Indians, to buy, sell, deal in, own, and promote the production of Indian goods through $500,000 of nonvoting, preferred stock and 3,000 shares of no-par, nonparticipating but voting common stock. All profits would be paid to the treasurer of the United States, who would in turn distribute the monies to the various tribal funds. The Frazier-Leavitt bill was defeated in 1930, in part because of the Hoover administration's lack of support for federally sponsored corporations and also because of the hard realities of the Depression, which made it difficult for lawmakers to justify the initial appropriation of $10,000. When Collier became commissioner of Indian Affairs in the Roosevelt administration, he resurrected many of the ideas behind the Frazier-Leavitt bill, which became a foundation for the Indian Arts and Crafts Board (1935). For information on the Frazier-Leavitt bill and the Indian Arts and Crafts Board, see Schrader. For additional information on the struggles between Austin and Collier regarding Indian arts and crafts, see Stineman, 174–79.

37. Austin, "Why Americanize," 171–72.

38. Ibid.

39. Austin, *Earth,* 362.

40. Chauvenet, 199–200.

41. Hewett, "The Native," 17–18.

42. Hewett, *Ancient Life,* 27–28.

43. Mary Austin, incomplete book review rebuttal, Box 36, MAP.

Works Cited

Austin, Mary. *Earth Horizon*. New York: The Literary Guild, 1932.

——. To Franklin K. Lane. 16 January 1919, Box 1, MAP.

——. "Indian Arts and Crafts." Unpublished manuscript, n.d., n.p., Box 26, MAP.

——. To John Collier. 31 January 1930, John Collier Papers, Sterling Library, Yale University, New Haven, Conn.

——. *The Land of Little Rain*. Albuquerque: University of New Mexico Press, 1974.

——. "Why Americanize the Indian?" *Forum* (September 1929): 171–73.

Brody, J. J. *Pueblo Indian Painting: Tradition and Modernism in New Mexico, 1900–1930*. Santa Fe: School of American Research Press, 1997.

Chauvenet, Beatrice. *Hewett and Friends: A Biography of Santa Fe's Vibrant Era*. Santa Fe: Museum of New Mexico Press, 1983.

Collier, John. *From Every Zenith*. Denver: Sage Books, 1963.

Cronyn, George W., ed. *The Path on the Rainbow*. New York: Boni and Liveright, 1918.

Fink, Augusta. *I-Mary*. Tucson: University of Arizona Press, 1983.

Frost, Robert H. "The Romantic Inflation of Pueblo Culture." *The American West* (January/February 1980): 5–9, 59–60.

Glassberg, David. *American Historical Pageantry: The Uses of Tradition in Early Twentieth Century America*. Chapel Hill: University of North Carolina Press, 1990.

Hewett, Edgar L. *Ancient Life in the American Southwest*. Indianapolis: Bobbs Merrill, 1930.

——. "Letters on the Pueblo Indian Situation." *Papers of the School of American Research*. Santa Fe: Archaeological Institute of America, 1925.

——. "The Native American Race in the Drama of History." Annual address to the School of Research of the University of Southern California, 12 January 1939, Box 46, ELHP.

——. "Present Condition of the Pueblos." *Papers of the School of American Research*. Santa Fe: Archaeological Institute of America, 1925.

——. "Statement of the Director of the School of American Research for the Year 1922." *El Palacio* (15 February 1923): 47–52.

——. "The Unknown Centuries." *Santa Fe Fiesta Program*, pp. 6–13, 1926, Box 54, ELHP.

Hougland, Willard, ed. *Mary Austin: A Memorial*. Santa Fe: Laboratory of Anthropology, 1944.

Indian Arts Fund, Inc. *Quiet Triumph: Forty Years with the Indian Arts Fund, Santa Fe*. Fort Worth, Tex.: Amon Carter Museum of Western Art, 1966.

Kelly, Lawrence. *The Assault on Assimilation*. Albuquerque: University of New Mexico Press, 1983.

Luhan, Mabel Dodge. "The Indian Speaks," ts., n.p., Mabel Dodge Luhan Papers, Yale University, New Haven, Conn.

Philp, Kenneth. *John Collier's Crusade for Indian Reform*. Tucson: University of Arizona Press, 1977.

Rudnick, Lois. *Mabel Dodge Luhan: New Woman, New Worlds*. Albuquerque: University of New Mexico Press, 1984.

Schrader, Robert Fay. *The Indian Arts and Crafts Board*. Albuquerque: University of New Mexico Press, 1983.

Stineman, Esther Lanigan. *Mary Austin: Song of a Maverick*. New Haven, Conn.: Yale University Press, 1989.

Wilson, Chris. *The Myth of Santa Fe*. Albuquerque: University of New Mexico Press, 1997.

7

Marketing Traditions

Cherokee Basketry and Tourist Economies

SARAH H. HILL

IN THE SPRING OF 1942, the Philbrook Art Center in Tulsa, Oklahoma opened an exhibition of Native American baskets donated by local collector Clark Field.[1] Of Field's more than 1,000 baskets, 55 were Cherokee; 21 baskets came from the Eastern Band of Cherokees in North Carolina and 34 from the Cherokee Nation of Oklahoma.[2] Field's collection provides an opportunity to explore various processes that individually and collectively engaged Eastern and Western Cherokee women in the first half of the twentieth century. The baskets inform us about their makers' work, environments, and concepts. Their different forms and functions signal the weavers' efforts to develop varied markets. The baskets' commercial appeal points to consumer values of non-Native buyers, like Field. As museum pieces, they testify to the interest in Indian objects shared by art patrons and scholars. Their carefully recorded prices reveal Native economies in the early years of Indian tourism. Finally, the basket market that linked Field with Eastern and Western Cherokee weavers attests to the commercialization of Indian basketry by buyers, governments, and reformers. As a microcosm of market processes, the collection contains, as Clark Field acknowledged, "a hint of the whole pattern of life" of weavers, and of the early era of Indian tourism.[3]

Among Cherokees, women were the traditional weavers.[4] Every identified basket weaver of the Cherokee containers was female, and Field stated that with few exceptions, "it is the Indian woman, not the man [,] who makes baskets."[5] Cherokee women were the customary weavers because they required so many baskets for domestic tasks such as food preparation.[6] Basket sifters, winnowers, and sieves were common Cherokee household items, along with food servers, storage containers, and gathering and carrying baskets. The functions identified for Field's Cherokee baskets confirm that women's manufacture, use, and sale of traditional baskets persisted well into the twentieth century. The Western Cherokee baskets included those made for corn sifting, sofkey preparation, egg gathering, and storage.[7] Similarly, the Eastern collection contains sifters, gatherers, and storage baskets. These functions reflect the daily lives and long-held customs of their makers (figs. 7.1 and 7.2).

By the early twentieth century, however, Cherokee women were also producing nonutilitarian vessels to appeal to buyers.[8] Only ten of the thirty-four Western baskets were identified by function, suggesting that more than two-thirds were decorative and were probably created for sale. Moreover, one Western container was labeled "fruit basket," a form and name specifically designed for marketing. The baskets' absence of wear also implies they were made for sale rather than as utility wares. The Eastern baskets are comparable. Only six of the twenty-one Eastern baskets have identifiable functions, and two of them are sewing containers, a type weavers developed for non-Native buyers.[9] As with the Western baskets, few Eastern containers show signs of use. The pristine condition and decorative appearance of the majority of Cherokee baskets indicate that weavers were diversifying from utilitarian wares and creating basket types they personally did not use to engage a non-Native market.

A long history exists for shared basket forms among Eastern and Western Cherokee women, particularly for utility containers, which demonstrates the persistence of commonly held values across time and space.[10] In addition to making baskets representative of their shared past, however, Eastern and Western Cherokee weavers increasingly experimented with forms as the economic importance of marketing increased. Twentieth-century basket weavers recognized that innovation provided a way to become known to buyers.[11]

Size was one aspect that weavers varied. Field bought an Eastern miniature only 2 inches high and a Western storage basket that was the largest he had ever seen (nearly 2 feet high).[12] Weavers varied other formal attributes as well. The Field collection includes a unique interlaced, double-woven basket; a double weave in an unexpected material; several atypical shapes; uncommon lids; baskets with unique handles; and one whose "pattern or shape" Field characterized as "unusual."[13] Although he asserted that weavers made baskets "either for utilitarian use or for ceremonial use," Field also acknowledged that Western Cherokee containers "are made, as a rule, for sale."[14] His purchases underscore women's success in marketing unusual as well as customary forms.

FIGURE 7.1. An oak-splint burden basket (ca. 1941) woven by Katie Lossie, Western Cherokee. Gift of Clark Field, The Philbrook Museum.

Whereas forms indicate either shared values or individual choices, weaving materials represent women's adaptations to specific environments.[15] "The materials used in any particular basket," wrote Field, "reflect the locale of the tribe which produced it, for the Indian used materials that were at hand."[16] The geographic and social separation of Eastern and Western Cherokee weavers can be seen in their basket materials. In the Southern Appalachian environment of the Eastern Cherokees, weavers had long preferred river cane and white oak for utilitarian baskets.[17] When seeking markets, however, they began turning to different materials.

Field purchased six Eastern baskets made with Japanese honeysuckle, an introduced vine that twentieth-century weavers used in response to economic pressures. In the late 1920s, Lucy Nola George popularized honeysuckle weaving and claimed she "knew of only one woman who used the honeysuckle vine as a basket weaving material." Competing for limited markets, she "felt that my chances of helping provide for my family's needs would be better if I worked with this material."[18] The uncommonness of the material appealed to George and, in turn, to buyers. In contrast to river cane or white oak containers, honeysuckle baskets are

FIGURE 7.2. Left: A hickory-splint sifter (ca. 1936) woven by an unknown Eastern Cherokee. Right: A hickory-splint sifter (ca. 1890) woven by an unknown Eastern Cherokee. Gifts of Clark Field, The Philbrook Museum.

more suited for decoration than work (fig. 7.3). As buyers' interests increasingly turned to home beautification, the popularity of such delicate containers increased. In addition to the honeysuckle baskets, two of Field's Eastern Cherokee baskets are woven with raffia, or rattan, an imported, light, and fibrous material popular for ornamental wares.[19] Although Eastern weavers continued to make utility baskets with traditional vegetation, their incorporation of different materials for sales baskets asserts their interest in marketing.

In the West, however, material innovation was less common, pointing to different ecosystems and attitudes. Following their forced removal to Indian Territory, Western Cherokee women found little river cane for their baskets. They came to rely instead on a locally abundant plant called buckbrush, along with the more familiar materials of white oak and hickory. In Field's collection, the predominant Western basket material is buckbrush (twenty-two examples), with remaining materials identified as hickory (two), white oak (two), river cane (one), and ash (two).[20] Western Cherokee weavers' reliance on buckbrush throughout the century after Cherokee removal contrasts with Lucy George's eagerness to experiment with honeysuckle and leads to questions about market processes. What differences existed in twentieth-century markets for Eastern and Western Cherokee baskets? Who participated in the development of those markets? How did markets affect Eastern and Western weavers?

Field began collecting Native American baskets during the arts and crafts revival, a movement "with intellectual and social as well as economic ramifications."[21] The revival brought attention to Eastern Cherokee

FIGURE 7.3. A honeysuckle "cracker basket" with lid and decorative curlicues by Lucy N. George, Eastern Cherokee, Qualla Arts and Crafts Cooperative. (Photograph by Ron Ruehl)

weavers as Southern Appalachia became a focus of crafts revivalists. Social missionaries considered handiwork an essential economic resource for mountain artisans and, equally important, an antidote to the modern ills of the American public. They believed handicrafts enhanced social and recreational life in rural communities, while reconnecting industrialized America with its lost past and the natural world. Establishing programs to satisfy their own moral imperatives, these social missionaries determined to "improve" Appalachian crafts, expand markets, and link rural producers with urban purchasers. Revival merged with reform as enthusiasts celebrated the benefits of handicrafts, but superimposed their own standards to increase product marketability. In his 1937 promotional study of Southern mountain crafts, sociologist Allen Eaton claimed that "baskets can be made with sufficient uniformity to be satisfactorily sold from samples."[22] As revivalists developed craft markets, they contended it was necessary to "subject the work to a degree of regulation by those sponsoring the revival."[23] To control the crafts they revived, leaders of the movement resolved to "maintain the quality expected by outside purchasers and to guarantee the filling of orders" by recruiting experts "to improve methods of work and to establish standards."[24] Generally, the "experts" were college-educated, middle-class, white women engaged in social reform, uplift, and education.[25] Because local artisans were not considered experts, they were excluded from the arenas of political and economic power.

Emphasizing forms of the pre-industrial past, revivalists established Appalachian production centers and craft guilds to promote handicrafts. They concentrated on poor whites as an "exceptional population" who had saved crafts that "our forebears brought across the sea."[26] Yet, revivalists also acknowledged the handiwork of the Eastern Cherokees, whose reservation lay in the midst of Appalachia. Valuing Cherokee basketry for its antiquity, beauty, and usefulness, Eaton cited claims of ethnologists that basketry's "best expression has been obtained by primitive people." He concluded, "there is general agreement that the American Indian has created the finest baskets in history."[27] Although revivalists concentrated on white Appalachians, their activities affected Cherokees as well.

From 1901 to 1934, revivalists initiated more than thirty Appalachian craft enterprises. Seven craft centers opened less than 50 miles from the Cherokee Reservation, and each center created new markets for Eastern weavers.[28] Cherokees sold baskets to the directors of the centers, who then marketed them to the public. Weavers who met the experts' standards were invited to join guilds and cooperatives, where they gained access to markets generated by revivalists' publicity. The Cherokee weavers participated in craft demonstrations, markets, and fairs that attracted buyers. At the same time, however, they became subject to production standards imposed by guild authorities. Revivalists governed the craft centers, set prices, and controlled distribution. As a result, weavers who benefitted from expanded markets and exposure were simultaneously impeded by restricted choices and prices. Their independence, expressed in basket form and function, contrasted sharply with their dependence on craft centers for acceptance and then for reimbursement.

No such revival appeared in the Cherokee Nation or the surrounding Ozark Mountains. For Western Cherokee weavers, market development for their work came through the interests of agents such as Indian reformers. Like revivalists, Indian reform activists created programs to address the economic and social problems of very specific populations.[29] And, like their counterparts in the revival, they exalted crafts as part of the solution. With comparable zeal, the reformers sought to control production while they expanded markets. Racism colored their rhetoric, for reformers believed that Indians had not yet attained the standards of civilization represented by white Americans. The goal of the reform movement was to reverse oppressive government policies and lead Indians from their so-called degraded state. Economic advancement was the first step.

Reform activists regarded Indian crafts as the means to economic independence. "There are possibilities in all the Indians' industries," wrote Neltje Doubleday, "but his [sic] unrivalled [sic] baskets might easily become his greatest staple, a joyous source of self-support."[30] Reformers emphasized the oldest customs of weaving and rejected all innovations, especially the use of commercial materials such as dyes. Scorning "the little aniline-dyed, sweet-grass affairs we are wont to associate with the little half-breeds in the East," Doubleday and other activists demanded the promotion of Indian markets and the revitalization of Indian basketry.[31] Reformers called for basketry instruction in Indian schools and philanthropic intervention in the market as components of "a new and enlightened policy in the Anglo-Saxon's dealing with subject races."[32] Such racism was commonplace in the early-twentieth-century reform movements.

With the prodding and support of reformers, various commercial centers began to market Indians' wares. The successful "Indian department in the most popular department store in New York City" was matched by a comparable outlet in Marshall Field's Chicago store. Relying on "many helpers in the field," activists like Doubleday also linked buyers directly with Native American artisans, offered "cash prizes for the revival of nearly lost arts," purchased basket collections for museums, and published articles on the value of "Indian industries." Transformation of Indians into imitators of "civilized" whites remained a priority, and Doubleday decried the difficulty of filling orders "among unorganized aboriginal women without the faintest idea of time and system."[33] Among reformers, regard for Native arts did not necessarily engender respect for the artisans.

The Indian reform movement constituted a powerful political lobby, and in the early decades of the twentieth century, Cherokee girls in government boarding schools like Sequoyah in Oklahoma or the Cherokee Boarding School in North Carolina soon encountered a curriculum that included instruction in Indian basketry. When Superintendent of Indian Schools Estelle Reel introduced weaving into the required course of study, she wrote that "of all Indian work, basketry must take the lead since the demand for this article is great everywhere."[34] Federal Indian policy aimed to connect Indian labor and world markets, and Reel notified Indian agents that basketry "must be revived by the children of the present generation, that they may take their rightful place among the leading basket makers of the world and supply the demands of the markets for such baskets."[35] As a result of the reform lobby, the government determined to play an explicit role in the commercialization of Cherokee baskets. Training Indian girls was a beginning, and market development for their work was left for later initiatives.

In the wake of reform and revival activities, public interest in Indian objects burgeoned. Collectors sought out Native artisans to negotiate prices, production, and form. In North Carolina, Fred Olds made recurring visits to the Cherokee Reservation to purchase baskets for his own collection and for a new Raleigh museum. Clark Field journeyed far beyond Oklahoma to amass his life's collection of more than 1,000 baskets. Popular books and articles revealed the power of the collecting impulse with photographs of homes crammed with dozens and even hundreds of Native American baskets.[36] California collector George Wharton James tapped the interests of the larger public in his journal for "lovers of the Indian basket and other good things."[37] *The Basket* included basketry articles, book reviews, photographs, and instructions for making Indian baskets. Removed from their context—the weaver, her heritage, and her environment—Indian baskets became objects of fashion, "attractive ornaments for library and parlor," as one news article proclaimed.[38]

Like reformers, collectors tended to value pre-industrial traditions of weaving, and they particularly disdained commercial dyes. James demanded dismissal of "every intrusion of foreign color." He contended weavers would reject commercial dyes "did they not think white purchasers preferred them."[39] Such assertions reveal the tensions existing in the commercialization of basketry. Revivalists, reformers, and collectors were eager for a basket market, but they simultaneously condemned its influence on weavers. Those who made and sold baskets continued to exercise choices about materials, forms, and functions, but they faced increasing economic pressure to adapt to the expectations of reformers and collectors.

The promotion of Indian basketry linked various agents of change. Revivalists wanted to standardize handicrafts to improve the lives of makers and buyers. Reformers promoted Native arts as a way to bring Indians into conformity with their own standards. Collectors, more interested in objects than artisans, contributed to a heightened interest in Indian art rather than culture. Scholars constituted a fourth group who entered the basket market and played a part in its development. Among those promoting indigenous traditions, anthropologists were the most prominent.

By the early twentieth century, public interest in Indians was sweeping the country. Because virtually all Indians were moved onto reservations, they came to represent the vanishing past, a remnant of what could never be recovered. With a sense of urgency about cultural loss, anthropologists sought Indian myths, customs, lore, and objects such as baskets.[40] Edward Palmer, James Mooney, M. R. Harrington, and Frank Speck were among the scholars who obtained extensive collections of Cherokee containers.[41] Although they purchased new forms, such scholars attributed greater authenticity to baskets that represented earlier periods. Mooney claimed an Eastern Cherokee rib basket was "an imitation of civilized patterns, and tho' quite pretty represents no Indian idea."[42] In actuality, the basket represented a weaver's choices about how to make a particular container.[43]

As scholars bought directly from weavers, they and their sponsoring museums expanded the basket market. Harrington sold to the American Museum of Natural History, the National Museum of the American Indian, and the New York State Museum. Palmer's and Mooney's collections went to the Smithsonian, and Speck's baskets to the Milwaukee Public Museum and the Museum of the University of Pennsylvania.[44] Out of the hands of the weavers, baskets circulated among different institutions and buyers. The Chicago Field Museum sent material to Marshall Field's Indian department, and Speck sold twelve of his own Eastern Cherokee baskets to Clark Field.[45] From museums and scholars to outlets and collectors, disparate strands of revival, reform, intervention, education, and collection began to converge in the 1930s' commercialization of Indian baskets.

When Clark Field purchased his first Cherokee basket in Kenwood, Oklahoma, John Collier had been Commissioner of Indian Affairs for three years. As part of the New Deal for Native Americans, Collier called for the development of Indian arts. To enhance impoverished reservation economies, he implemented several recommendations initially made in the survey of "economic and social conditions of the American Indian" compiled in 1927 by the Brookings Institute for Government Research.[46] The report's opening sentence established the problem: "An overwhelming majority of the Indians are poor, even extremely poor, and they are not adjusted to the economic and social system of the dominant white civilization."[47]

Commonly called the Meriam Report, the survey readily acknowledged the importance of women's work, emphasizing that "baskets of distinctive character are made by the women of tribes in every section of the United States."[48] In a series of proposals for economic relief, women's work and market development were explicitly connected: "prosperity" on reservations "depends upon family earning power rather than upon the ability of the father alone."[49] Women's baskets represented a source of "family earning power," but only if they satisfied non-Native buyers. "Women," according to the report, "are able to follow at home traditional arts highly respected by discriminating white customers."[50] The proposed government policy, which was subsequently implemented by Collier, was commitment to a tourist economy. Indian women were to remain at home on reservations and produce traditional goods for "discriminating" white tourists. Under Collier, the goal of assimilating Indians into the dominant culture was reversed and the era of Indian tourism began in earnest.

The Meriam Report had recommended that the Indian Office undertake "the development of Indian handicrafts" by standardizing and marketing them.[51] It ignored the possibility of Native initiative and advocated government supervision of artisans to guarantee products that were both "characteristically Indian" and "of good workmanship."[52] When Collier assumed office in 1933, his programs executed the kinds of reforms included in the Meriam Report. The federal government undertook to supervise artisans and to standardize and market their work.

Marketing potential differed between Eastern and Western Cherokee weavers. Eastern Cherokees lived in close proximity to one another on lands that were the functional equivalent of a reservation. A government agent had been assigned to the Eastern Cherokees for more than a half century, supervising the local Cherokee Boarding School. Eastern weavers sold baskets through the government agent and also directly to white tourists who visited the school. The annual Cherokee Fair, with a successful basket market, was one of the most popular gatherings in North Carolina. Following one fair in the 1920s, the agent reported that "every available basket" was sold and "there was a riot when the selling began."[53]

In 1932, the agent and several boarding school employees joined the Southern Highland Handicraft Guild, an Appalachian crafts revival organization. Weavers attended guild functions to demonstrate weaving and sell baskets. That same year, the Cherokee Council agreed to include a crafts salesroom in their proposed new Council House (see fig. 7.4).[54] Eastern Cherokees awaited the opening of the adjacent Great Smoky Mountains National Park and "the opportunities that the great forthcoming tourist traffic will offer."[55]

Tourism promised economic relief that Eastern Cherokees desperately needed. The 1934 Cherokee Agency reported that Cherokees lived in "considerable poverty," with "poor housing, low standards of sanitation,

FIGURE 7.4. Carolyn Foreman with baskets and other purchases, Eastern Cherokee Reservation in North Carolina, September 1932. (Photograph courtesy of the Archives and Manuscripts Division of the Oklahoma Historical Society)

and wrong kind of diet."[56] Many homes had unsafe water supplies and no sewage disposal.[57] Although subsistence farming provided for immediate needs, "clothing and household furnishings are very meager."[58] Little cash circulated on the reservation, and "many homes have no cash income other than that obtained from sale of baskets and pottery."[59] These were the circumstances in which Lucy Nola George initiated honeysuckle weaving to support her family, and these same conditions empowered craft centers and buyers to set basket prices.

Western conditions differed in several ways. Western Cherokees lived scattered across thirteen counties in eastern Oklahoma, beyond direct federal supervision. The government school in the Cherokee capitol at Tahlequah did not attract tourists seeking Indian souvenirs. No annual fair drew regional visitors. With no local outlets, weavers marketed their wares from household to household or to stores as far away as Arkansas.[60] Basket markets were so obscure that the Meriam committee claimed "native handicrafts seem to have disappeared almost completely."[61] Western Cherokees had neither a council house for displays nor a council to support artisans' work. The superintendent reported that "there is at present no form of tribal government for the Cherokee Nation. There is no chief. The tribal lands are gone except for 365.87 acres."[62] Virtually no tourism trade existed for Western Cherokees, and no nearby parkland attracted travelers.

The average annual cash income per family in the northern part of the Cherokee Nation was approximately $95. According to geographer Leslie Hewes, Cherokee farmers lacked "sufficient cash income to buy clothing and other necessities." The Cherokee Nation "had notably less land in hay, pasture, fruits, and vegetables" relative to neighboring counties. Settlements were scattered, "farm buildings are poorer, and towns are less well developed." With substandard housing and "an economy not well suited to present conditions," Western Cherokees were hardly in a position to develop and sustain tourist markets, nor were weavers able to command better prices.[63]

Although Eastern and Western Cherokee market potential differed, government initiatives followed similar courses. In 1933, the Western Cherokee superintendent undertook "to dispose of Indian products for the benefit of Indians."[64] He had sold approximately $460 worth of Navajo rugs and $10.90 worth of "baskets and miscellaneous items for local Indians" in the past year and was actively "creating a local market for Indian products." In his annual report, Superintendent Landman predicted greater success the following year.[65] When the first "all-Indian fair" took place in "the Cherokee hills" in 1934, Landman "sold Indian products, including Navajo rugs, jewelry, pottery, [and] Cherokee baskets" for the sum of nearly $2,000, which provided his evidence that "the local markets for Indian products was better."[66]

To revive Native industries, the government sent Works Progress Administration workers "into the Cherokee hills to encourage the Cherokees to make baskets." Oklahoma historian Carolyn Thomas Foreman subsequently asserted that weavers readily sold sturdy baskets in urban areas "and many patterns of buckbrush wickerwork were sold in Muscogee."[67] By 1937, the Bureau of Indian Affairs publication *Indians at Work* celebrated the revival of Native arts in Oklahoma, attributing its success to the artisans' growing awareness that crafts "have an excellent exchange value in the commercial world." The article also pointed out that it was difficult "to convince the basket makers that vegetable dyes are to be preferred over aniline because the general public is more easily captured by brilliant colors."[68] Regardless of the weavers' ability to sell baskets they colored with commercial dyes, government agents joined reformers, revivalists, collectors, and scholars in discouraging such innovations. Yet, weavers persisted in choosing commercial dyes, an indication of their continuing resistance to outside control and a determined expression of independence.

In addition to influencing adults, Collier's policy of stimulating craft production altered Eastern and Western Cherokee school curricula. Home economics classes proliferated in government schools and included courses in loom weaving, a craft promoted by the Southern Appalachian revivalists earlier in the century. The Bureau of Indian Affairs sent Berea College graduate Edna Groves to teach loom weaving to girls in the Eastern Cherokee Boarding School and to their mothers in local community clubs.[69] Home economics supervisor Gertrude Flanagan reorganized school programs to include craft instruction and revised the academic requirements to emphasize "vocational work" such as loom weaving.[70]

Flanagan also hired Cherokee weaver Lottie Queen Stamper to teach basket making, which became a popular and enduring elective.[71] "The teaching of basketry has taken surprisingly well," the 1937 superintendent reported, "and quite a group of girls are planning to take this as their major craft activity."[72] Stamper's students sold their baskets at local fairs, to craft shops, and to tourists who traveled through the reservation to get to the Great Smoky Mountains National Park. As the government's home economics instructor, however, Gertrude Flanagan set the prices. Buyers contacted her, or the agent, to procure baskets at prices they agreed upon.

Similar programs began among Western Cherokees. In 1938, the Indian Service employed New York textile weaver William Ames to introduce loom weaving at the Sequoyah Indian School. Two years later, Ames extended loom weaving and other classes to adults in surrounding Cherokee communities.[73] Recalling his classes with Ames, contemporary Cherokee John Ketcher acknowledged that he liked loom weaving so much he rejected all other vocational classes. After graduating, Ketcher became Ames's assistant and helped establish and run the community classes.[74]

Because Western Cherokees lacked sales outlets, Ketcher and three other graduates formed the Sequoyah Indian Weavers Association to organize production and markets. They converted a surplus army barracks to a weaving and display room, where they sold blankets, tweed clothing, rugs, and baskets made by several hundred association members.[75] Adjacent to the display room, Cherokee artisans Emmet Knight and "a fullblood Cherokee woman" named Beaver taught pottery, woodworking, and basketry. Ketcher also employed Native artisans as community instructors, so that weavers earned money from teaching as well as making baskets. Visitors came in tour buses to the outlet, but the community centers were too isolated to be effective markets.[76]

Regardless of government programs; vocational instruction; Native teachers; the attention of scholars, reformers, collectors, and revivalists; and the Cherokee weavers' resourcefulness, basket prices remained appallingly low. Buyers and government supervisors determined prices, and weavers capitulated to earn money whenever possible. For the thirty-three baskets Clark Field bought from Western Cherokee weavers, prices ranged from $2 to $15. Nearly half cost only $3 each. Although Field professed a preference for "authentic specimens made for actual use," he paid less for traditional containers than for unique pieces.[77] Similarly, he paid from $1 to $25 for Eastern baskets. Twelve cost $5 or less, and the highest price was paid to a merchandizer rather than a weaver.[78] The persistence of basketry in a market that paid little and demanded conformity testifies to the weavers' needs for money.

Following World War II, the Eastern Band continued to pursue tourism. The number of reservation craft shops and motels increased annually, providing basket markets along with seasonal opportunities for wage work. Outside of the tourist season, however, Eastern Cherokees struggled economically. To establish a year-round sales outlet and raise prices for their crafts, artisans formed a cooperative association, which became the most successful Native cooperative in the country. Members were paid as they delivered products and were also given annual dividend checks. For the first time, weavers who belonged to the cooperative could market baskets all year. And from the beginning, baskets were the most popular cooperative sales items.[79]

Nonetheless, real economic improvement came slowly. As the government crafts specialist, Gertrude Flanagan continued to impose standards. She discouraged the use of commercial dyes in diverse ways, including refusing to allow aniline-dyed baskets in the annual fair basket competition.

Gradually, Eastern Cherokee weavers returned to natural dyes, which were difficult to procure and process. Yielding to Flanagan's requirements meant a greater expenditure of time and effort, thus effectively reducing the weavers' profit. Flanagan also continued to set prices. She maintained an office in the cooperative, influencing weavers' choices about production and design until she retired in the mid-1950s. She then advised the new shop manager to keep a ceiling on basket prices.[80]

Craft initiatives continued in the Cherokee Nation in similar ways. John Ketcher returned from military service and resumed work with Ames and the community centers. The number of weavers increased; in 1947, according to Carolyn Foreman, 163 basket makers sold a total of 1,370 baskets, or an average of 8 baskets each.[81] Marketing in urban areas, Ketcher and Ames organized craft shows at Oklahoma City shopping malls for members of the Five Civilized Tribes. The success of early shows led to similar efforts in Tulsa, and then, according to Ketcher, "a lot of other towns took it up." Weavers eventually participated in craft shows as often as once a week, which enabled them to make direct contact with buyers.[82] Baskets of buckbrush dyed with commercial dyes continued to be popular. "Prominent women from Tulsa" drove to Eucha, Oklahoma to buy baskets from weavers and personally assisted them in marketing. "No other project," reported Foreman, "has benefitted them [the Western Cherokees] as much as has weaving and basketry, and it has raised the standard of living among them to a noticeable degree."[83]

Regardless of the notion that basketry raised living standards, as Foreman claimed; that discriminating whites respected Native work, as the Meriam Report promised; or that basketry would become a joyous source of self-support, as Doubleday predicted, Cherokee women did not earn a minimal living wage for their weaving. Eastern basket prices rose so slowly that contemporary weavers remember clearly when every basket brought less than $5. Even in the 1990s, when a honeysuckle basket cost $25 and elaborate, river cane double weaves as much as $1,000, weavers did not earn minimum wage. Basketry cannot guarantee a regular income and is entirely dependent on adequate supplies, ready buyers, and time to weave. Tourism remains seasonal, except for casino gamblers, who are not interested in cultural objects. Also, in contrast to other parts of Indian country, the Eastern Cherokee Reservation attracts family tourists, who resist paying more for handwoven containers than for machine-produced trinkets. Knowledgeable and affluent collectors do patronize a small minority of weavers, but for most Eastern Cherokee women, basketry continues to be a way to earn extra money. No one supports herself on weaving.

Western Cherokees have had even less success. In the 1960s, according to anthropologist Albert Warhaftig, Western Cherokees were "miserably poor," with a median per capita income of $450 to $650 per year. Welfare subsidized more than half of all Cherokee households and available jobs were limited, seasonal, or part-time.[84] In such deprivation, income from basket sales could be important, but the scarcity of outlets handicapped the weavers. According to a 1968 hearing before the Indian Education Sub-committee, the Tahlequah Agency reported that thirty-two trainees at the Mulberry Craft Center had earned a total of $500 and that a combination of basket weavers, cane makers, bead workers, doll makers, "and other small craftworkers" earned $2,546.[85]

In the absence of crafts cooperatives or tourist industries, Western Cherokee weavers have been unable to raise basket prices; with few exceptions, contemporary weavers make only from $15 to $50 per basket. John Ketcher is one of many who doubts that tourism will ever become a reliable, dependable industry for Western weavers "because Tahlequah is not on a main road to anywhere." Money for baskets, he maintains, will never be more than supplemental income.[86] Few outlets have been established in the Cherokee Nation's population centers, and according to the Cherokee Nation Department of Education, "very few traditional basket-weavers are practicing in Oklahoma at the present time."[87] The promise of markets was never fulfilled.

Clark Field's basket collection allows us to view multiple processes at work in the lives of Cherokee weavers. In the first half of the twentieth century, women contributed income to their impoverished households by selling baskets they created with local vegetation. There were few outlets, however, and no viable way to market their wares. Varying non-Indian enterprises encouraged basketry as a means to moral uplift, economic stability, or cultural preservation, and each promised economic relief to Eastern and Western Cherokees.

Operating independently, each intervening agency determined to standardize the artisans' work to develop markets. Nonetheless, Eastern and Western Cherokee weavers continued to make choices about basket forms, and the Field collection indicates that they did not restrict themselves to customary shapes, designs, functions, or materials. Moreover, the weavers' long refusal to abandon commercial dyes, even though this would allow new marketing opportunities, expresses their determination to retain some degree of control over their product. Among Eastern Cherokee weavers, the establishment of their own cooperative as their first year-round market and the influence of the government's representative during the cooperative's early years finally led to the decline of commercial dyes. The market shaped by "experts" brought change in one significant aspect of Eastern Cherokee basket form.

Tourism brought a degree of economic relief to Eastern Cherokees, but it has not been adequate to support full-time basket production. Tourism may have contributed to the tradition's viability, however, as baskets continue to sell well in the cooperative and local stores. The proximity of the Great Smoky Mountains National Park has guaranteed annual tourism. Western Cherokee weavers have had fewer marketing opportunities, little tourism, and less intervention from reformers and revivalists. Weavers have persisted in the use of commercial dyes, but the overall number of weavers has declined. Although the Western Cherokee population is perhaps twenty times greater, Eastern Cherokees can claim twice as many practicing weavers.

Nonetheless, basketry has proven to be an extraordinarily resilient art, withstanding environmental change, economic strain, and a century of cultural intervention. In the East and West, women have continued to weave baskets, express a degree of independence from non-Cherokee influences, and seek markets wherever possible. Field believed that "by the year 2000 there will be NO Indian baskets being woven."[88] This brief examination suggests the imprudence of attempting to control Cherokee weavers, to guarantee their markets, or to predict the future of their basketry.

Notes

1. Born in Dallas in 1882, Clark Field became an Oklahoma journalist in 1900 and a traveling salesman in 1904. After starting his own stationery company in 1917, he began collecting Native American pottery and baskets. In 1942, he donated most of his baskets to the Philbrook Museum of Art and became a part-time curator. Two decades later, Field published *The Art and the Romance of Indian Basketry,* a brief catalogue of his Philbrook exhibition.

2. In his foreword to Field's publication, Philbrook director Donald G. Humphrey stated the collection contained "more than a thousand specimens." Field noted that the collection was "rated by the U.S. Indian Arts and Crafts Board as the most outstanding Indian basket collection in North America." His catalogue docu-

mentation includes the year, location, and price of each basket and occasionally the name of the weaver. See Humphrey; Field, 26.

3. Field, 1.

4. For examples of Native American women as basket weavers, see Hill, "Weaving History" and *Weaving New;* James, *Indian Basketry,* 9, 13; Mason, 7–8; Schlick, 5; Tanner, 17. For comments on male and female weavers among the Pomo, see Abel-Vidor et al., 19.

5. Field, 2.

6. Prior to the nineteenth century, Cherokee women also created ceremonial baskets, but following their removal from Southeastern tribal lands and attendant cultural dislocations the use of ceremonial baskets disappeared. See Hill, *Weaving New,* 45–49.

7. Sofkey is the traditional corn mush of the Cherokees.

8. Weavers assigned functions to sale baskets that related primarily to household decoration rather than to traditional Native American household tasks. The sieve, for example, was marketed as a dresser tray.

9. Philbrook Native American collections assistant Therese Mathews (personal communication, 13 August 1998) stated that most of Field's Cherokee baskets are ornamental and appear to have been made for sale.

10. For discussion of the concept of material goods as expressive of cultural beliefs, see McCracken, 57–70; Prown; Lubar and Kingery, 3.

11. See Hill, *Weaving New,* for extended discussions of the Eastern Cherokee weavers' efforts to create and sustain markets by innovating with forms, functions, materials, and designs.

12. The Eastern basket, original catalogue number 407, is 2 inches high with a 2-inch diameter. The Western basket, original catalogue number 194, is 21 inches high with an 18-inch diameter. Field's comment about the large size appears on the catalogue card for the Western basket.

13. Philbrook Field Collection catalogue number 331.

14. Field, 2, 30.

15. Buckbrush *(Ceanothus cuneatus),* now considered a traditional material for Western Cherokees, does not grow in Southeastern ecosystems. River cane *(Arundinaria* spp.), the most traditional material of Southeastern weavers, is generally not available to Western Cherokees. The difference in material and related difference in weaving techniques exemplify cultural distinctions between the two populations. For full discussion of Southeastern Cherokee selection of weaving materials in changing environments, see Hill, *Weaving New.*

16. Field, 1.

17. See Hill, *Weaving New,* 35–184.

18. "Basketry of Lucy George"; also in Hill, *Weaving New,* 193.

19. In the catalogue notes, the raffia vine is incorrectly identified as honeysuckle. It lacks the joints that are characteristic of honeysuckle vines.

20. Material for four of the baskets is not identified.

21. Davidson, 3. Heir to the English arts and crafts movement of Morris, Carlyle, and Ruskin, the American revival began in the final decades of the nineteenth century and was revitalized in the 1930s and again in the 1960s. Useful studies include Barker; Boris; Eaton; Goodrich; and Triggs. Important critiques of the movement are Whisnant; Becker.

22. Eaton, 178.

23. Ibid., 264.

24. Ibid.

25. Whisnant, 11–13; Becker, 73–75.

26. Eaton, 37.

27. Ibid., 30, 166.

28. Ibid., 59–91. The five North Carolina centers included four in Asheville and one in Brasstown. Across the Appalachian Mountains, two initiatives were undertaken in Sevier County, Tennessee.

29. Other reform organizations included the Sequoya League, Indian Rights Association, Mohonk Conference, Women's National Indian Association, Indian Industries League, American Indian League, National Indian Defense Association, Indian's Hope Association, and the Boston Indian Citizenship Committee.

30. Doubleday, "Aboriginal," 85.

31. Ibid., 84. New England tribes such as the Penobscot had long traditions of sweet-grass basketry and by the early twentieth century often applied commercial dyes to their wares.

32. Doubleday, "Aboriginal," 83.

33. Doubleday, "Indian," 102.

34. "Cherokee Basketweaving," 56.

35. Ibid., 54.

36. James, *Indian Basketry,* 21, 75, 100, 190, 260.

37. James, *The Basket,* title page.

38. Holden. For additional texts that consider Indian baskets as decorative items, see Foreman, 16; James, "Indian Basketry in House Decoration."

39. James, *Indian Basketry,* 230.

40. For a full discussion of the development of this assumption, see Dippie.

41. See, for example, Duggan and Riggs; Speck, *Decorative Art.* Even though Mooney contacted Western Cherokees, he neither collected baskets from them nor mentioned their basketry in his notes.

42. Mooney Collection catalogue notes.

43. For example, Cherokees devised a new technique for lid attachments. They burned holes in the interior of the basket handle with a hot nail, then pressed the ends of the lid frame into the holes. Moreover, the weaver of the basket Mooney referred to had attached the lid on one side only and had created a

secondary support base made of ribs for the basket, both of which were entirely "Indian ideas."

44. Speck correspondence file.

45. Field Museum Cherokee Collection catalogue notes. The Field Museum had purchased the collection acquired by anthropologist Frederick Starr in 1894. Accession notes disclose the "transfer" of the detachable lid of a river cane basket.

46. Institute, viii.

47. Ibid., 3.

48. Ibid., 32.

49. Ibid., 532–33.

50. Ibid., 533.

51. Ibid., 651.

52. Ibid., 651.

53. Henderson.

54. Spalsbury.

55. National Archives Records Administration (hereafter NARA), Cherokee Agency, Box 32; "Preliminary," 4.

56. Ibid., 8.

57. Nesbit and Surgeon.

58. McDaniel.

59. Ibid.

60. Foreman, 33.

61. Institute, 645–46.

62. NARA, Annual Report, m1011, Roll 39, 4.

63. Hewes, 281.

64. NARA, Annual Report, m1011, Roll 40, 18.

65. Ibid., 18.

66. Ibid., 20–21.

67. Foreman, 31–32.

68. Ataloa, 41.

69. Groves.

70. Flanagan and Stevens.

71. Stamper, 1.

72. Foght, 17 June 1937.

73. Baldwin, 76–77. The Sequoyah Indian School began in 1871 as the Cherokee Orphans Asylum to educate children orphaned by the Civil War. After a 1903 fire destroyed the building, the Cherokee government moved the school to Salina. In 1914, the school was again opened in Tahlequah and sold to the federal government, which ran it until 1985. The name was changed to the Sequoyah Orphans Training School in 1940 ("The Sequoyah School").

74. John Ketcher, personal communication, 17 August 1998.

75. Foreman, 16.

76. For a report of tour buses, see Baldwin, 78.

77. Field, 31.

78. Philbrook Field Collection catalogue notes.

79. Foreman, 11.

80. Author interview with Betty Craig Dupree, 27 November 1990.

81. Foreman, 21, 23.

82. Ketcher, personal communication, 17 August 1998.

83. Foreman, 21–23, 31.

84. Warhaftig, 414.

85. United States, 982.

86. Ketcher, personal communication, 17 August 1998.

87. "Cherokee Basketweaving," 1.

88. Field, 2.

Works Cited

Abel-Vidor, Suzanne, Dot Brovarney, and Susan Billy. *Remember Your Relations: The Elsie Allen Baskets, Family and Friends.* Berkeley, Calif.: Heyday Press, 1996.

Ataloa. "The Revival of Indian Art in Oklahoma." *Indians at Work* (15 June 1937): 37–43.

Baldwin, Cinda K. R. "The Sequoyah Indian Weavers Association." *Journal of Cherokee Studies* 9, no. 2 (1984): 76–88.

Barker, Garry G. *The Handicraft Revival in Southern Appalachia, 1930–1990.* Knoxville: University of Tennessee Press, 1991.

"Basketry of Lucy George." Exhibition catalogue. Cherokee, N.C.: Qualla Arts and Crafts Cooperative, 1970.

Becker, Jane S. *Selling Tradition: Appalachia and the Construction of an American Folk, 1930–1940.* Chapel Hill: University of North Carolina Press, 1998.

Boris, Eileen. *Art and Labor: Ruskin, Morris, and the Craftsman Ideal in America.* Philadelphia: Temple University Press, 1986.

"Cherokee Basketweaving." In Cherokee Nation Department of Education. *Course of Study for the Indian Schools of the United States: Industrial and Literary.* Washington, D.C.: Government Printing Office, 1901.

Cherokee Collection Catalogue Notes. Field Museum of Natural History, Chicago.

———. National Museum of the American Indian, New York.

———. Smithsonian Department of Anthropology, Washington, D.C.

Clark Field Collection Catalogue Notes. Philbrook Art Center, Tulsa, Okla.

Davidson, Jan. "Foreword." Pp. 1–47 in *Mountain Homespun*, by Frances Louisa Goodrich. Knoxville: University of Tennessee Press, 1989.

Department of Anthropology Catalogue Notes. Smithsonian Institution, Washington, D.C.

Dippie, Brian W. *The Vanishing American: White Attitudes and U.S. Indian Policy.* Middletown, Mass.: Weslyan University Press, 1982.

Doubleday, Neltje De G. "Aboriginal Industries." *Southern Workman* (February 1901): 81–85.

——. "Indian Industrial Problems." *Southern Workman* (February 1902): 99–105.

Duggan, Betty J., and Brett H. Riggs. *Studies in Cherokee Basketry.* University of Tennessee Occasional Paper no. 9. Knoxville: Frank H. McClung Museum, 1991.

Eaton, Allen H. *Handicrafts of the Southern Highlands.* 1937. Reprint, New York: Dover Press, 1973.

Field, Clark. *The Art and the Romance of Indian Basketry.* Tulsa, Okla.: Philbrook Art Center, 1964.

Flanagan, Gertrude, and C. D. Stevens. To Harold Foght. 7 November 1934, Box 65, NARA.

Foght, Superintendent. To Commissioner of Indian Affairs. 17 June 1937, Box 10, NARA.

Foreman, Carolyn Thomas. *Cherokee Weaving and Basketry.* Muskogee, Okla.: Star Printing, 1948.

Goodrich, Frances Louisa. *Mountain Homespun.* 1931. Reprint, Knoxville: University of Tennessee Press, 1989.

Groves, Edna. To Superintendent Page. 17 September 1930, Box 7, NARA.

Henderson, Superintendent James. To Nellie Denny. 30 September 1921, Box 14, NARA.

Hewes, Leslie. "The Oklahoma Ozarks as the Land of the Cherokees." *Geographical Review* 32 (1942): 269–81.

Hill, Sarah H. "Weaving History: Cherokee Baskets from the Springplace Mission." *William and Mary Quarterly* 3rd ser. 53 (1996): 115–36.

——. *Weaving New Worlds: Southeastern Cherokee Women and Their Basketry.* Chapel Hill: University of North Carolina Press, 1997.

Holden, C. F. "Baskets in the Home." *Placer Herald* (Calif.), 10 January 1891.

Humphrey, Donald G. "Foreword." In *The Art and the Romance of Indian Basketry,* by Clark Field. Tulsa, Okla.: Philbrook Art Center, 1964.

Institute for Government Research. *The Problem of Indian Administration.* Baltimore, Md.: Johns Hopkins University Press, 1928.

James, George Wharton, ed. *The Basket: The Journal of the Basket Fraternity, or Lovers of the Indian Basket and Other Good Things.* Pasadena, Calif.: The Basket Fraternity, 1904.

——. *Indian Basketry.* 1909. Reprint, New York: Dover Press, 1972.

——. "Indian Basketry in House Decoration." *Chatauquan* (September 1901): 619.

Lubar, Steven, and W. David Kingery, eds. *History from Material Things: Essays on Material Culture.* Washington, D.C.: Smithsonian Institution Press, 1993.

Mason, Otis Tufton. *American Indian Basketry.* 1904. Reprint, New York: Dover Press, 1988.

McCracken, Grant. *Culture and Consumption.* Bloomington: Indiana University Press, 1990.

McDaniel, Grace. To Superintendent Foght. 25 September 1934, Box 32, NARA.

Mooney Collection Catalogue Notes. Smithsonian Department of Anthropology, Washington, D.C.

Nesbit, W. W., and P. A. Surgeon. To Superintendent Foght. 28 September 1934, Box 32, NARA.

National Archives Records Administration (NARA). RG 75, National Archives, East Point, Ga.

——. Annual Report of the Superintendent for the Five Civilized Tribes. 31 July 1934–30 June 1935, m1011, Roll 39.

——. Annual Report. m1011, Roll 40.

——. Cherokee Agency ser. 5, Gen. Rec. Corr. Boxes 14, 29.

——. Cherokee Agency ser. 6, Gen. Rec. Corr. Boxes 7, 9, 10, 32, 65.

——. "Preliminary Organization of Activities." 1934. Cherokee Agency ser. 6, Gen. Rec. Corr. Box 32.

Prown, Jules David. "Mind in Matter: An Introduction to Material Culture Theory and Method." *Winterthur Portfolio* 17.1 (1982): 1–19.

Schlick, Mary Dodds. *Columbia River Basketry.* Seattle: University of Washington Press, 1994.

"The Sequoyah School." *Cherokee Advocate* (February 1996): 1.

"The Sequoya League." *Southern Workman* (April 1902): 102–103.

Spalsbury, Superintendent. To Commissioner of Indian Affairs, 28 April and 21 December 1932, Box 29, NARA.

Speck, Frank. Correspondence file. Milwaukee Public Museum, Milwaukee, Wis.

——. *Decorative Art and Basketry of the Cherokee.* Bulletin of the Public Museum of the City of Milwaukee 2, no. 2, 1920.

Stamper, Lottie. Autobiography 1, ts. Qualla Arts and Crafts Cooperative, Cherokee, N.C.

Tanner, Clara Lee. *Apache Indian Baskets.* Tucson: University of Arizona Press, 1982.

Triggs, Oscar Lovell. *Chapters in the History of the Arts and Crafts Movement.* 1902. Reprint, New York: Arno Press, 1979.

United States Committee on Labor and Public Welfare. *Indian Education Hearings.* 90th Cong., 1st and 2nd sess. on the Study of the Education of Indian Children, part 2. Washington, D.C.: Government Printing Office, 1969.

Warhaftig, Albert L. "Making Do with Dark Meat: A Report on the Cherokee
Indians in Oklahoma." Pp. 409–510 in *American Indian Economic Development,*
ed. Sam Stanley. Chicago: Aldine Press, 1978.

Whisnant, David E. *All That Is Native and Fine: The Politics of Culture in an American
Region.* Chapel Hill: University of North Carolina Press, 1983.

8

Crafts, Tourism, and Traditional Life in Chiapas, Mexico

A Tale Related by a Pillowcase

CHRIS GOERTZEN

THE ROCKING CHAIR IN OUR Mississippi home holds a pillow. I bought its colorful cover in May 1997 in San Cristóbal, the only sizeable city in the highlands of Chiapas, Mexico. I was there to continue research for a book on the relationship of crafts and festivals with tourism in Indian southern Mexico. As part of that research, I took pictures of the pillowcase. Later in the visit, I returned to the shop and reexamined the piece with a tourist's eyes. It was well-crafted and reasonably priced, featured colors that drew but did not jar the eye, bore a region-specific and attractive pattern that could later evoke memories of this trip, and would pack easily—all characteristics of the perfect souvenir.

One month before I began writing this essay (at the end of 1997), I read newspaper accounts of paramilitary gunmen indiscriminately slaughtering forty-five men, women, and children in one of the hamlets belonging to the *municipio* of Chenalhó, just 37 kilometers into the mountains from San Cristóbal. The attacked settlement was sympathetic to the Zapatistas, whereas the attackers supported the ruling party, the PRI (Institutional Revolutionary Party); whether the national government or just the arch-conservative local authorities sympathized with the attack remains unclear. Had the gunmen's trucks traveled just a few minutes in a different direction, they would have entered the municipio home to the weaver of the central panel of my pillowcase, San Andrés Larrainzar. The elegant traditional craftsmanship embodied in that object, the tourism that sponsored its creation, and the wanton violence of the highlands' latest atrocity all express the working of the same intertwined factors.

Politics and Tradition in Highland Chiapas

Chiapas, the southernmost state of Mexico, was for a long time the least accessible state. It remains one of the two states with the highest concentrations of Indians (the other being Oaxaca). And, although Chiapas is arguably the state with the richest natural resources, it also is home to the largest populations of the desperately poor and the illiterate.[1] Highland Chiapas, together with the Yucatán Peninsula, neighboring Guatemala, and Belize, is home to the about 3 million descendants of the Maya Indians. As is true throughout Indian areas of Central America, principal urban populations are *Ladino* (roughly synonymous with *mestizo*—of mixed European and Indian blood—but Ladino also includes genetically pure Indians who have moved to the city and adopted mestizo culture). Surrounding villages include some Ladino merchants and more Indians, and the countryside is Indian.

Highland Chiapas is stunningly beautiful. The mountains rise to a height of more than 9,000 feet, whereas valleys such as that cradling San Cristóbal are at around 7,000 feet. The elevation yields a temperate climate gentle to visitors, but the vistas and climate are not the primary attraction: It is rather the Indians, whom outsiders perceive as representatives of an ancient and intriguing way of life and as creators of handsome and unique crafts. Indeed, it is not just at first glance that the modern Maya seem more closely tied to tradition than any other substantial population in Mexico, but their "authenticity" is not entirely voluntary. The characteristics that anthropologists and tourists find so fascinating resonate with a colonial and modern history unmatched in Mexico in terms of ill treatment of Indians and, consequently, of friction between the few Ladinos in power and the many Indians forced to endure endless injustices.

Spaniards arrived in upland Chiapas in 1524 and founded San Cristóbal four years later. They settled in the city center, while groups of Indian allies from elsewhere in Mexico occupied surrounding barrios.[2] The colonial era here—as throughout Mexico—saw Indians decimated by foreign diseases, further ground down by forced labor and taxes, and dispossessed of most of their arable land. Although most of Mexico has experienced some ideological liberalization and land reform, any change that might adversely affect the Ladino property owners who dominate local government has been resisted in Chiapas. And the minimal reforms that have slipped past the obduracy of the rich have been more than offset by population growth: Between 1950 and 1990, population more than tripled, despite massive outmigration. When Porfirio Diaz moved the state capital from San Cristóbal to the lowland city of Tuxtla Gutiérrez in 1891, it was because this right-wing dictator found the elite of San Cristóbal too conservative![3] Friction has bubbled into open conflict here more regularly than anywhere else in the country, notably in the rebellions of the 1530s, an uprising in the 1780s inspired by a religious vision, the so-called caste wars of the late 1860s, unrest linked to bootlegging in the late 1950s, and the Zapatista uprising that commenced in 1994. What is most unusual about the most recent violence is that it attracted the attention of the press, thus pressuring Mexico's central government into intervention.

Today, San Cristóbal is a town of about 100,000 surrounded by more than 1 million Indians. For most of this century, life in the highlands combined subsistence agriculture with seasonal labor in the lowlands, sources that today are no longer able to sustain booming populations. Authority remains vested in a complex system that is at once religious and civil. Men raise their standing in the community by assuming expensive religious obligations when they can in what anthropologists call a cargo system.[4] For instance, one man might pay for flowers for a year's heavy calendar of festivals, another sponsor fireworks, another musicians' strings, and so on. The system thus substitutes enhancements in prestige for economic betterment: It promotes financial leveling.

Each village pastes a Catholic veneer onto traditional local beliefs and customs in its own way.[5] To illustrate this point, I will quote from the locally composed guidebook to Chamula, the nearest village to San Cristóbal and the most visited. Most of the brochure concerns religious customs, both because these permeate modern Mayan life and because colorful, exotic religious practices (along with inexpensive crafts) are what sends scores of tour buses roaring into the village each month. The guidebook states that Saint John the Baptist and his brothers began to build the main church in the eighteenth century. When they found caches of suitable stones, they would say "Get up, stones, and walk!" Generally, the stones would obey. When the stones behaved in any distinctive manner, that inspired the naming of that location. For example, "once upon a hill they told the stones to walk, but the stones walked very slowly and then stood still. That's why today there is a place called Ch'ahtontik, or 'Lazy Stones.'" And, from a section describing prayer: "To accompany the prayer 'Almighty God, give us our daily bread' we use small and large candles. For 'All of the Saints' we use white, tallow, and green, a half liter of *posh* [locally distilled hard liquor], 5 bottled sodas, 6 eggs, dried fish, and dried beef jerky."[6]

Most of the tourists who read these words belong to one of two general categories. Young people, carrying backpacks and traveling alone or in small groups, take *combis* (vans serving as buses for the local populace) from the main market in San Cristóbal to the square in Chamula. More visitors, especially affluent Europeans, arrive en masse in tall buses for brief tours. Each tourist will want to enter the church, which requires buying a ticket. The Indians need tourist dollars, but clearly do not welcome intrusions into their lives and religion. Ticket sellers speak some Spanish, but no other European tongue, and are absolutely neutral in bearing—they will sell tickets and brochures, but not offer other services or pretend friendliness. It is forbidden to take pictures in the church (a guard searches all bags for cameras), and photography anywhere in the village is repeatedly discouraged, although beggar girls offer to pose outside of the church for a fee. To pass more than a few steps into the church entails the purchasing of candles. Mass is not said—instead, small groups of Chamulans kneel on the stone floor, attach and light their candles in a row on the floor before them, set offerings down, and address personal incantations to the saints whose statues line the walls. Thousands of stoically tolerated outsiders witness this each year.

Villages like Chamula and Zinacantan fit classic definitions of peasant life: Culture is inward looking and carefully circumscribed, social life is intense and largely egalitarian, and religion is critical in the social control of wealth. Nevertheless, the sense of community in even these intensely conservative highland villages is clearly on the wane.[7] It is tempting to believe that it is only recently that this traditional culture came under siege, but that would not merely be false, it would obscure a critical factor in the formation of the threatened culture. It is likely that the religion-centered skein of local identities and associated expressive culture—including crafts—has been intensified over many centuries as a cumulative defensive reaction to this culture being threatened. To become sympathetic with this interpretation, we must shelve romantic views of this tradition as, in the words of George Collier, "vestigial or residual [in favor of seeing it] as constituting a dynamic response that Indians make to their peripheral position in a larger, changing system."[8] Indeed, the villages nearest to San Cristóbal, which one might expect to be the most assimilated, are actually the most adamantly distinctive.

Tourists constitute the third wave of outsiders invading highland Chiapas during the twentieth century. The first group of new intruders, initially a trickle but cumulatively powerful in effect, were Protestant missionaries. When the second wave, anthropologists, arrived in substantial numbers in the 1950s, they found that one of their first important tasks was to demonstrate that they were not yet another beachhead of evangelists. Evon Z. Vogt, the distinguished leader of the Harvard Chiapas Project, found that he and his colleagues had to overcome Indians' initial wariness by conspicuously smoking and drinking at every opportunity.[9] Perhaps the barriers that scholars had to penetrate before being permitted to study modern Mayan religion had been exacerbated by missionary activity. After all, when Protestants advocated abandoning the Catholic and local religious festival system—an argument with immediate economic appeal, because festival support was so expensive—they were fomenting overturning all authority, because religious and civil authority were and are so thoroughly intertwined.

Tourism was slow to arrive in San Cristóbal. Guidebooks about Mexico published before World War II almost never even mention Chiapas.[10] Graham Greene did make of point of traveling to San Cristóbal in 1938, but found it a challenging destination. The mountains of Chiapas seemed "like a prison wall" that he conquered only by undertaking what proved to be a "hellish mule ride."[11] Although the Pan-American highway arrived in 1946 and was paved in 1950, sheer distance continued to impede the flow of travelers. Tourism would not boom until well into the 1970s with the growth of air travel. About three-fourths of today's visitors are Europeans who fly to Tuxtla Gutiérrez, then take buses for the harrowing two-hour climb to San Cristóbal.

Tourism is an intense and isolable modern alternative to daily life. Some approaches to being a tourist feature reduced mental activity and responsibility through emphasizing physical pleasure, thus justifying Huxley's assertion that "we read and travel not that we may broaden our minds, but that we may pleasantly forget they exist."[12] Conversely, MacCannell describes "sightseeing" as "a kind of collective striving for a transcendence of the modern totality, a way of attempting to overcome the discontinuity of modernity, of incorporating its fragments into unified experience."[13] There is a flavor of a pilgrimage here, which Graburn makes more explicit. He notes that "holiday" formerly meant "holy day," when much of a year's travel would be spent going to religious festivals. Other travels have replaced these over time, but some of the ritual and the hunt for life's deeper meanings remain.[14] Of course, today's tourist-pilgrims vary in how much intelligence and industry they can or care to muster. Also, and of critical importance, the quest that MacCannell and Graburn describe is often— perhaps usually—mixed in individual tourists with the "switching-off" that topped a survey by Krippendorf of German tourists' motives for travel.[15] Cohen put this diplomatically: Whereas some tourists are discriminating (his nobler categories are "experimental" and "experiential"), "recreational tourists, who seek in the Other mainly enjoyable restoration and recupera- tion and hence tend to approach the cultural products encountered on their trip with a playful attitude of make believe, will entertain much broader criteria of authenticity."[16]

Tourists who journey to San Cristóbal can indulge in some "switching off" because this is a beautiful location with a relaxing climate and a well- developed infrastructure of hotels and service employees. But most of these tourists, whether carrying backpacks or Italian leather luggage, *do* come on a romantic quest to view an embodiment of an earlier, presumably better— and to them certainly more exotic—way of life. My experience with this population—and I belong to it some days—is that they are intellectually active and curious during their visits, mean well in a general way, and certainly do not want to hurt the culture on which their "holiday" focusses. But, to the Indians, the sheer affluence of these visitors is disturbing: The contrast between the standards of living of visitor and visited is incompre- hensible and cannot but inspire envy and suspicion.

Constant visits from even the best-intentioned outsiders must continue to take a toll in the collective morale of highlands Chiapas Indians. Over time, these visits must inspire mixed feelings about the very ways of life admired by those whom the Indians see as bizarrely rich but profoundly ignorant visitors. In short, this latest group of outsiders, tourists, are drawn to the Indians of Chiapas by the exoticism and "authenticity" of aspects of culture that, ironically, are to a considerable degree surface symptoms of those Indians' long-term defensive response to ill treatment. What may be new to a significant degree is the nature of the threat to culture.

The oligarchy of landowners took the Indians' property, and some- times their very lives. But these oppressors despised or ignored Indian culture, which therefore remained the Indians' own, a locus of spiritual refuge. Are Indians now being forced to market this line of defense? When they accept money to let tourists learn about their religion and sell crafts bearing deep cultural significance, are they now yielding up their souls? The answer to this is far from simple. A short response detailing ways in which tourists are prevented from interfering overly with local religious practice would include the frequent proscribing of photography, rationing entrance into churches, and the barrier of language—it is a rare tourist who can tune into prayers spoken in Tzotzil or any other modern Mayan language. I hope that one of the scholars well-versed in the religions of the area will someday pursue this line of inquiry. I will concentrate here on what we can learn about the maintenance of and changes in traditional life from how craft items are designed, made, and sold.

One Pillowcase as a Site of Negotiation

Craftspersons who sell their creations to outsiders *may* be allowed to express tradition in the best ways they know how, but *must* make things that fit or can shape the expectations of their customers. The Indians who thus market hard-won skills and enduring symbols know that the arbiters of the effectiveness of their efforts are those customers. It is nearly impossible to have a conversation with a craftsperson that escapes this commercial shadow, and perhaps it is willful and unseemly to insist on chatting about aesthetics and techniques when the wolf is so near to many of their doors. Nevertheless, each craft object represents a negotiation in which images of authenticity (and of beauty) theoretically might match, might conflict, or might be possible to reconcile. Craftspersons may be willing to bend a little (or a lot), although, paradoxically, their customers might prefer that no yielding take place. As McKean noted, it is "especially in the performing and plastic arts" that "tourists expect the perpetuation of ancient traditions."[17] The ideal craft object is arguably authentic, precisely the right balance of the understandable and the palatably mysterious, and, of course, attractive.

Although tourists in highland Chiapas are preoccupied with authenticity, they generally lack detailed knowledge to inform their judgements. In fact, although both Indian craftspersons and tourists harbor complex notions about what is important in tradition, neither group articulates those feelings easily. I believe that the best window on the negotiation of authenticity as embodied in the craft object is the testimony of the object itself. The witness at hand is the aforementioned pillowcase, an untraditional object handwoven in traditional ways presenting a modern version of an ancient, sacred design, an object made with the tourist in mind. Should we consider its existence a symptom of another layer of colonization, in which the craftsperson must debase his or her work to earn a living? Or is it a natural and healthy outgrowth of tradition?

We can approach answers to these questions through a careful "reading" of the details of this "text." This examination will reveal a series of artistic decisions that stake out common ground between craftsperson and customer, this task guided by an intermediary, the director of textiles for a cottage industry. At the same time, we witness departures from tradition that follow familiar paths within the process of intensification, the accruing of visual impact that generally takes place when craft tilts toward art. I propose to examine and contextualize these factors: the fact that a sacred design decorates this pillowcase; the identity of that design; the size of this version of the design; the number and choice of colors appearing on the pillowcase; techniques of weaving; and how this pillowcase was designed and marketed. Figure 8.1 illustrates this pillowcase in its new home, and figure 8.2 focusses on the design filling the case's central panel.

SACRED DESIGNS ON AN ORNAMENTAL PILLOWCASE

Patterns such as the one on this pillowcase have as their primary home *huipiles,* elaborately handwoven blouses on which carefully ordered series of sacred designs present religious maxims or tales in a visually attractive way (see fig. 8.3). Modern Maya Indians do not consider a functional pillowcase—that is, a piece of bed linen—as a showcase for ornament or for religious narrative and generally do not have large enough dwellings to accommodate couches with decorative pillows. However, such a product does fit into a traditional category of woven goods, that of the sampler. This category has its origin in the desire for practice and for experimentation, for exploring the effects of various combinations of patterns and of colors without devoting the amount of time needed to finish a huipil (which can be up to a year). Samplers may have no other intended function at the outset. They may end up as small tablecloths, sides of purses, and so on; a pillowcase is a plausible use for such a piece. In short, samplers offer an arena in which sacred patterns can escape the weight of tradition and the narrative logic that governs their use on huipiles.

THE IDENTITY OF THIS DESIGN

This particular sacred pattern is common in its home municipio, San Andrés Larrainzar. Whereas some designs have up to four distinct meanings, this one corresponds to a single, slightly fluid meaning.[18] Its short title (each

FIGURE 8.1. A pillowcase from San Cristóbal, Chiapas highlands, Mexico. (Photograph by Chris Goertzen)

design also has narrative implications) is variously rendered as "man and woman," "father and mother," or, most commonly, "ancestors." The man's arms reach toward the heavens, while the woman's curl toward earth. In this and many versions of the design, the woman's arms are in several pairs, the lower sets representing corn. The narratives associated with the titles also vary. Each pattern represents an episode in the stories told through the ordering of patterns on huipiles. In a catalogue of photos of rugs at La Albarrada (see Paternalistic Cottage Industries section for a precís of this organization), this sentence accompanies the pattern: "Los antepasados que sobrevivieron el diluvio obedecieron a dios y sembraron maiz" (The ancestors who survived the deluge obeyed God and cultivated corn). A more extended narrative appears in a short description of these patterns that the government-sponsored store Casa de Artesanias hands out. This brochure gives the sentence quoted at La Albarrada, then proceeds: "The ancestors protect society and, through dreams, teach the proper way to live. They are supernatural beings like the saints."[19]

Just as both the short title and narrative implications of this pattern exist in slight variations, so does the pattern itself. The model of the pattern

FIGURE 8.2. A closeup of the design on the central panel of the pillowcase. (Photograph by Chris Goertzen)

kept in the mind of the craftsperson is fluid, stored "in dreams." When a pattern exists in many versions, the simpler versions are the most sacred.[20] The form on this pillowcase is near the complicated end of the spectrum, thus more suitable in a forum that is primarily decorative.

When presented in a series of patterns on a huipil, a row of "ancestors" often is a border. Figure 8.3 shows such use on a contemporary huipil from San Andrés, one of many very similar—but never identical—huipiles for sale in the summer of 1997 in the San Andrés section of Sna Jolobil (described below in the Cooperatives section). Perhaps the fact that "ancestors" repose on an edge of many arrays of patterns makes it especially easy to break it off for a solo appearance (although the principal pattern on this and many huipiles, the diamond standing for the universe, and a handful of other visually distinctive patterns also can be employed as the only design on samplers such as pillowcases). More likely, it is the custom of using "ancestors" as a border and as an accent that makes it seem natural for that pattern to act as a symbol or distillation for the family of patterns. The design has an impeccable pedigree in tradition, but by using only the design the visual effect is amplified and emphasized. Intensification through selection thus helps turn an authentic craft that had been as much aimed at the soul as at the eyes into satisfactory art for outsiders.

Another reason that "ancestors" is an apt design to appear alone is because it can be considered broadly representative in one sense: it includes some reference to all basic graphic approaches to shaping these designs. Morris places these in four categories: (1) diamonds representing earth and sky as a unity; (2) undulatory forms (e.g., snakes) representing earth; (3) "forms with three vertical lines which symbolize the foundation of the world, the community and its history"; and (4) representational figures.[21] That "ancestors" is representational helps at least some part of its message to translate easily; the pairing of a man and a woman can nowhere seem

FIGURE 8.3. A contemporary *huipile* (handwoven blouse) from San Andrés section of the cooperative Sna Jolobil. (Photograph by Chris Goertzen)

meaningless. In addition, "ancestors" includes the ground graphic elements of diamonds, curves, and sets of three vertical lines in logical locations within the total design. Diamonds make up the man's and woman's heads, and more diamonds align vertically with their heads, assuring their place in the universe. The lower pairs of limbs on the woman's body, which represent corn, curve: The corn issues from the earth. Last, because men have always dominated religion in Mayan society, it is the male figure who reaches upward, who touches three vertical lines with each arm and with his head, and whose very body is composed of three vertical lines. In short, "ancestors" presented alone can substitute for a series of many patterns because it really is many patterns in one.

THE SIZE OF THIS VERSION OF THE DESIGN

The design as worked out on this pillowcase is significantly larger than is common, especially on huipiles. Of course, this pattern never gets as small as the most diminutive uses, of, say, the diamond (universe) pattern, because "ancestors" has relatively many elements and contours, even in its simplest incarnations. Its large embodiment here pleases customers because the resultant impression is bold, actually hovering nicely between seeming pictorial and receding into a texture. And this size is not *too* out of line with tradition: Often, this particular pattern is made larger than neighboring patterns when it decorates the border of a huipil. Craftspersons to whom time is money also must welcome larger designs because they are easier and faster to execute.

A certain flexibility in the shape and size of each design is built into tradition. As mentioned briefly above, craftspersons do not do new work from sketches or any concrete plan, but rather "from dreams" that do not include exact thread counts. Dreams partake of the supernatural and offer a sacred endorsement of what an outsider might call creativity. The guidance of dreams also helps the weaver to get around a potential practical difficulty: Changing the size of a design by certain increments often entails adjustments in shape. This is because weaving, unlike painting, must obey mathematical constraints: The weaver can make an image taller or wider by the thickness of three, four, or five threads, but not by three and a half or four and a half. If, for instance, a design in one realization is one-third as wide as it is tall, and its height is increased by the thickness of two threads, a faithful maintaining of proportion would require widening it by two-thirds of a thread. The weaver must instead widen the pattern by one thread or not at all, either fattening the figure or slimming it.

THE NUMBER AND CHOICE OF COLORS
APPEARING ON THE PILLOWCASE

That there are just three colors on the panel of the pillowcase is unusual in historical perspective, but does fit into one of a trio of modern trends. The general practice until rather recently was for crafts such as huipiles to employ most or all readily available colors. In the case of a typical huipil from San Andrés, the field (background) was white or off-white cloth, the dominant color set onto the field likely red (or sometimes black), then perhaps a half-dozen other colors appeared as accents.

At some point the number of colors of dye or of thread available increased well past the number that could reasonably be included on a given article, and self-conscious choice became a larger part of the process of selecting colors. Some of today's craftspersons choose to cleave to densities of information that were typical in earlier decades. Indian weavers who sell through the prestigious cooperative Sna Jolobil frequently follow this "classical" approach. They hold to the letter of tradition—the earlier average number of colors and of patterns—rather than the spirit, which was to exploit most or all of the available selection. Many discriminating tourists pay premium prices for these carefully made older-style exemplars. These huipiles stand out because of the high level of craftsmanship, illustrating intensification through virtuosity. A second choice adopted by modern weavers is to increase the visual impact of a given article by making patterns somewhat more dense and using somewhat more colors than before. The governing principle here is "the more the merrier," that is, "the more authentic details and colors the more authentic the piece"—intensification through addition. The approach yields products that are real eye-catchers in more than a few of San Cristóbal's boutiques, but that may seem garish back in Milwaukee.

The third general option is to go the opposite direction, to pare down visual complexity by employing fewer colors and patterns than had been typical historically. This choice, common in both cooperatives and boutiques, yields crafts that may not demand as much attention as those in the above groups, but rather offer a carefully rationed fillip of the exotic, while matching or complementing a customer's color scheme at home. Pillowcases like mine follow this model, a carefully measured intensification through selection. It is important to note that each of these three avenues represents a historical rupture. The unselfconscious continuing of age-old tradition that tourists would prefer to imagine that they are witnessing and purchasing and that salesmen claim is in force is not really among the options.

The picture is further complicated by the history of the types of dyes and thus of available hues used in woolen weavings in the Chiapas highlands, a history with approximate parallels elsewhere in Mexico. Craftspersons used natural dyes for most of the history of weaving. When synthetic dyes for wool and synthetically dyed, ready-made cotton thread became available a few decades ago, natural dyes were rapidly abandoned throughout the highlands. The new hues were brighter, offered more variety, took much less time to apply, and were more colorfast. The recent return to the use of natural dyes and to synthetic colors that look like those produced by natural dyes resulted from outside intervention.

Ambar Past, an American, first came to Chiapas as a culture-oriented tourist in the early 1970s, found each visit lasting longer, then settled there. She arrived eager to take up traditional weaving employing organic dyes, which she was dismayed to find had completely fallen out of use in the highlands. Past asked weavers in the municipio in which she had settled (San Andrés Larrainzar) about their grandmothers' dyeing techniques, and soon was experimenting with old and new mordants (metallic compounds that combine with organic dyes to keep them from decomposing and fading). Originally working on her own time and nickel, Past soon received support (support that an Indian would not have known how to seek) from FONART, UNICEF, and INI to study and eventually teach the use of these dyes.[22] At first, she had to pay her skeptical Indian associates to work with the natural dyes, which they did not like, as they found them relatively subdued and "sad."[23] But their reluctance vanished when tourists bought articles thus dyed. By 1976, Indian women trained in the use of natural dyes (by this outsider, who had synthesized some of these same women's memories of their ancestors' practices) had joined forces with weavers and had begun doing their own teaching. At this point Past could bow out, moving on to activities I will describe in the next section of this essay.[24]

Tourists' romantic enthusiasm for natural dyes refracted back into the municipio, and soon other villages were employing natural dyes on weavings for their own use as well as on sale garments. This illustrates a process that McKean witnessed in Bali, one he termed "cultural involution," in which a combination of economic necessity and social conservation brought crafts that had been made newly conservative for the sake of tourists back into local culture with that transformation intact.[25] Today, a new synthesis is under way, with natural dyes (and colors like those made from these dyes in purchased, factory-dyed, cotton thread) still dominating somewhat in practice and overwhelmingly in rhetoric—but with favorite synthetic dyes used too, if sparingly. My pillowcase is made of purchased cotton thread in synthetic colors approximating ones available in natural dyes—but these will not fade, and the cotton is more comfortable than locally produced wool.

White is the traditional background color for many types of highland weaving, and bright red a common accent, but the other color on my pillowcase, an extremely dark purple, has no historical precedent in either of the natural dye periods or in the time during which synthetics reigned. Its effect is of an enlivened black. Of course, the broad impression of dark patterning bearing bright accents, all on a white field, is right on target. The only surprise is that the traditional black is supplanted by an improved, vibrant version. I cannot imagine that this bothered the weaver at all. The few colors work together beautifully. I believe that the use of very dark purple offers a complexity that informally goes a ways toward balancing the untraditional absence of a richer palette.

TECHNIQUES OF WEAVING

The pillowcase consists of a decorative panel woven on a backstrap loom by a woman—the backstrap loom is usually women's territory—with that panel set into a larger piece of cloth woven on the colonial pedal loom, normally the province of men. The backstrap loom can be set up almost anywhere. It is a small loom suspended in the air, with one end extending to a loop wrapped around the weaver's back—hence the name of the loom—and the other tied around a tree or to a nail at a convenient height. Such looms can accompany women as they mind children, sit in the market, and so on. There are limits to the size of cloth that can be made on a backstrap loom; larger pieces must be woven on the nonportable pedal loom, on which the sequence of thread crossings is more complex. The visual result of employing these two weaving techniques is that the texture of the cloth in the panel and that of the broader field contrast subtly and pleasantly.

The gendered division of labor on this pillowcase has precedents in the world of textiles in Chiapas and parallels elsewhere in tourist crafts. The most direct precedent is in the traditional assembly of women's outfits. Carefully decorated huipiles have long been made on backstrap looms by women, while the plain blue cloth used typically for skirts has traditionally been woven on pedal looms by men. And cooperative efforts abound today. Rugs made by men are from yarn dyed by women, and, reversing the order of participation, the marvelous wooden animals and devils of Oaxaca are generally carved by men and painted by women. Which gender dominates which craft does have implications in the dynamics of family life—a topic that I will discuss up near the end of the chapter.

HOW THIS PILLOWCASE WAS DESIGNED AND MARKETED

I found all of the authenticity-oriented craft outlets in San Cristóbal by first finding a few—partly by chance and partly through asking at the tourist office—then soliciting recommendations in each for other similar or complementary establishments. In answer to my more specific request to be referred to a store that did new things imbued with tradition, several managers of good stores or cooperatives pointed me toward Kun Kun. This turned out to be what I now think of as a fair-minded, paternalistic enterprise, which, while run by highly educated outsiders, was founded and is operated with the primary goal of improving the welfare of Indians. This and similar cottage industries try to operate in a manner that respects tradition and awards adequate (quite modest, but in the local context, nonexploitative) living wages to its employees. The director of textiles, Maddalena Forcella (an Italian married to the store director, Mexican anthropologist Luis Joel Morales), was friendly and forthcoming during my visits. She made many of the style decisions outlined in the previous paragraphs. In our discussions of these, she was not disposed to analyze as I have, but rather evinced an intuitive grasp of how to locate useful middle ground between her weavers and potential customers. To design an article for sale, she first selects an old pattern, feeling that, on the one hand, customers prefer designs with an explainable history and, on the other, that the craftspersons she employs may work more carefully with a design that they consider meaningful (although, she reiterated, her own first criterion is that the design be attractive). Forcella also decides which colors to employ and purchases and disperses the cotton thread. She said she simply chooses colors that looked good to her. I noticed that all of the textiles in the store had a mixture of traditional and new colors roughly parallel to those on my pillowcase and always were in just one or two hues (either completely or over a white background).

Kun Kun, which produced ornamental tiles before adding the line of textiles, now supports about 300 Indians on the textile side, including shepherds, spinners, and weavers (most of these people in the municipios, but about 20 in production and sales on the premises in San Cristóbal). I asked who had made the pillowcase that I had purchased. Forcella did not offer the weavers' names—middlemen tend not to, thus guarding craftspersons' privacy, and, not incidentally, their own function—but said that the central panel was woven by a woman living in Bayalemó (a small hamlet fifteen minutes from the center of the municipio of San Andrés Larrainzar). The man who did the rest of the cloth worked on a pedal loom in the store in San Cristóbal. His home municipio was not mentioned, I suppose because it would not have mattered, that is, his part of the job drew on a regional rather than a village-specific tradition. My sense was that all concerned in the manufacture and sale of this craft object were content with how things had been done and that, despite tremendous gulfs of various kinds between craftsperson and customer, this was a nonstressful transaction in terms of aesthetics, identity, and money. But to what degree can this interaction stand for others between Indian and tourist?

Craft Outlets and Crafts in San Cristóbal:
Marketing Subcomandante Marcos

Tourists who get off buses in San Cristóbal immediately have opportunities to purchase crafts. As they walk along the few streets in this small city that join the main tourist destinations, tourists are never out of view of such opportunities. Imagine a lowercase letter t on which the right-hand (east) side of the crossbar extends twice as far as the left. The bus station is at the bottom (south end) of the t, where downtown San Cristóbal's busiest street meets the Pan-American highway. The tourists walking north to-ward the *zócalo* (the square, at the crossing of the t), pass restaurants, ho-tels, and plenty of souvenir shops. The best boutiques, along with many of the top hotels and restaurants, line up on the crossbar of the t, especially on its eastward extension. The main street above the square (the top of the t) passes the largest churches (near which stand the top textile coopera-tives and the open-air craft market) on the way to the main market. And wherever the tourists walk, they will be hounded by hawkers carrying woven crafts.

A survey of these various types of craft outlets and what they offer may reveal to what degree and for how many Indians the processes that created or infuse my pillowcase are at work (see table 8.1). In the course of this sur-vey, certain themes are always present, if not always foregrounded. These themes concern the desires and capabilities of the parties in the craft trans-action. Tourists want crafts to combine authenticity and attractiveness. Their capabilities to interact with a craft object include how much under-standing they can muster, what prices they can afford, and what sizes they can transport. Craftspersons need remuneration for their work and access to the sales site (transportation, type and location of shop) and would like to do their work in a way reinforcing ethnicity, allowing creativity, and maintain-ing dignity. The abilities they bring to bear include craftsmanship (in the sense of learned skills); some combination of memory, research, and imagi-nation; and, ideally, some modest capital, so they can take the time to make larger items or to wait to be paid for finished crafts that are on consignment (rather than accepting the pittances paid by most middlemen).

COOPERATIVES AND GOVERNMENT-SPONSORED STORES
THAT REFERENCE MUSEUMS

A handful of textile cooperatives and government-sponsored stores offer the crafts that are in appearance the most "authentic," the closest to how

TABLE 8.1 *Survey of Craft Outlets in San Cristóbal*

Type of outlet	Cooperatives and government-sponsored "museum" stores	Paternal cottage industries in new niches	Boutiques and souvenir stores	Spaces in Santo Domingo market	Hawkers and street vendors
Goods for sale	Mostly textiles, both *huipiles* and samplers	Specialized: sampler textiles, tiles, paper, etc.	Textiles plus broad array of other types	Blouses, etc.; dolls, pottery, miniatures	Woven belts, wrist-bands, other cheap items
Attitude toward authenticity	"Classical"; conservative, literal (artificial?)	Use knowledge as point of departure	May assert authenticity (dubiously)	Cheaper goods; symbolize authenticity	Items hastily made using authentic techniques
Where goods were made	Mostly in Indian *municipios*; some on premises	Mostly in San Cristóbal; some in municipios	San Cristóbal, municipios, and Mexican cities	Chamula, San Cristóbal, Guatemala	Chamula, San Cristóbal
Quality of goods	Excellent; can be very expensive	Excellent, varied prices	Adequate to very good	Poor to adequate	Poor
Middlemen between Indians and tourists	Foreign or upper-class; likely romantic and well-educated, with altruistic intent; perhaps in government; later: Indians		Mestizo businessmen; left-wing snowbirds	None or contacts with Guatemalan refugee camps	None
How much money goes to Indians	Modest; if better, may have to wait for sale	Modest, may have aspects of cooperatives	Minimal to slightly more	Minimal	Subsistence at best

items were made and looked a few generations before the advent of tourism. Painstaking work with an explicit pedigree means high prices, so locations must be central enough that even the tourists with the least leisure, the Europeans whose package tours devote just a day or two to San Cristóbal, will enter these outlets. All three of San Cristóbal's main cooperatives are between the square and the market, within a block or so of the big churches; Sna Jolobil (Tzotzil for "Weaver's House") is the most successful partly because it has the best location.[26]

These outlets share a critical element in their histories: the involvement of one or several educated, altruistic intermediaries. The "best" transactions, that is, those most satisfactory in remuneration and mental comfort to the Indian craftsperson and in aesthetics and authenticity to customers, have been arranged through the cumulative diplomacy of the most skilled culture brokers. Here, Sna Jolobil again stands out. Walter F. "Chip" Morris, who now runs the most interesting museum-library-hotel in the city, Na Bolom, has long been the central scholar of modern Mayan textiles. During his earlier employment with FONART, he put together Sna Jolobil and contributed to its ethos. Then he left it in the hands of a capable group of Indian women; that his name does not appear in the cooperative's publicity helps with its image of authenticity.

Outlets in this category explicitly market authenticity by displaying artifacts and offering information in ways referencing museums. The Casa de Artesanias, for example, has a small side room containing a dozen dioramas illustrating life in specific municipios, several of these displays including statues of Indian women at backstrap looms. The customer can compare the huipiles the statues wear (and the textiles on the looms) with those for sale. Few on the racks actually match those in the museum alcove, but an implicit endorsement takes place: The people with the inclination and knowledge to mount a knowledgeable exhibition would certainly sell authentic textiles. Sna Jolobil follows a double "museum" strategy. First, the entire wall space—in the luxuriously roomy former cloister next to the Santo Domingo church—is devoted to a series of sets of huipiles labeled conspicuously by municipio. These and piles of similar garments stacked below the educational display are all for sale (at premium prices). Second, one of the cooperative managers sets up her backstrap loom just outside the door, becoming an ethnic demonstration and living advertisement. The salespeople in such stores have been trained (first by the seminal middleman, then by each other) not to be aggressive—as they are with one another in the market, and thus tend to be with tourists—but rather to wait patiently for customers to ask questions. Thus, authentic-looking goods join museum-style exhibitions and outsider-style sales etiquette, a winning combination.

This category of craft outlet focuses on the local central craft of textiles in its most complex and traditional form, the huipil. However, samplers in the forms of pillowcases, napkins, and so forth are available for the customer who cannot afford a huipil or would not expect to wear one. Samplers do not seem out of place in huipil-dominated stores, but rather become part of a visual sequence: Indian women with religious patterns on their blouses, then similar garments bearing similar patterns for sale, then those patterns on other pieces of cloth useful to customers. Morris feels that Sna Jolobil has found its own style, basically "classical."[27] I think that he and the European customers have inspired a sort of nostalgic romanticism among the members of the cooperative. Last, I would note again that the basic folkloric process of intensification is at work here, not in a crowding of effects within given items, but through the impact of stunning craftsmanship and in the close juxtaposition of so many different beautiful garments.

PATERNALISTIC COTTAGE INDUSTRIES SEEKING
NEW MARKET NICHES

This category of outlet overlaps considerably with the cooperative. They share a type of important middleman, and the privately operated paternalistic cottage industry often gets grants from branches of the Mexican government and from foreign foundations. Customers are once again looking for something truly special, but with an essence weighted toward the spirit rather than the letter of authenticity and toward the unique item. In other words, tradition has now become a historical and local anchor for kinds of artistic play familiar to customers from fashion in their home countries. Kun Kun, the source of my pillowcase, is such an outlet. It was supported during its first years by a Swiss foundation, Pequeño Sol. The sampler textiles that constitute the second rung of offerings in the cooperatives here assume center stage and have been transformed as outlined in the discussion of my pillowcase.

Ambar Past, after ramrodding the reintroduction of natural dyes in the highlands and, as an outgrowth of this activity, stimulating the growth of the cooperative system, settled down in San Cristóbal and founded the most interesting of this category of outlets, Taller Leñateros. She speaks of her several dozen Indian and mestizo associates as "experimenting together," although it is clear that the impetus is largely hers. For instance,

Past paid Indian women to paint images from their dreams, which they had not done before, resulting in a wonderful book in which these paintings alternate with song lyrics, *Conjuros y Ebriedades: Cantos de Mujeres Mayas.* Her atelier produces silkscreens, woodcuts, paper made from recycled paper with interesting flowers or other vegetable materials added, crafts that combine these, and a bilingual (Tzotzil-Spanish) manual on making and using natural dyes, *Bon: Tintes Naturales.* The attraction of this wild riot of crafts is both aesthetic and historical—not in the sense of reproducing old things, but rather in encompassing change over millennia in single items, for example, a T-shirt bearing a strangely elegant, silkscreened illustration of a Mayan god (pictured largely as in the ancient codices) happily astride a small motorcycle.

One of the government-sponsored cottage industries supports an even wider range of endeavors. La Albarrada, classified as a *centro de desarrollo comunitario* (essentially a vocational school), has divisions for textiles; saddle-making; marquetry; making tortillas, baked goods, and candy; a vegetable nursery and one for flowering plants; and so on. The center's most interesting project began in the 1980s. Iranians were invited to visit and teach Indians how to do knotted rugs, which are now made in roughly equal numbers at the center and by individuals scattered throughout the highlands. The patterns are borrowed from huipiles. Such designs work well on items like my pillowcase, but not in significantly larger sizes on knotted rugs—indeed, this newly transplanted craft has not been very successful. However, there are centuries-old precedents for syntheses of Mexican Indian and foreign craft techniques. I am thinking especially of the Chinese influence on the lacquered plates of Uruapan and environs and on certain kinds of pottery, although in the broadest sense the entire world of Mexican crafts joins Spain and the New World.[28]

BOUTIQUES AND OTHER SOUVENIR STORES

These outlets, the most numerous kind, range from elegant to shabby, with quality and price of wares in proportion to proximity to the town square. They are run mostly by local Ladino businessmen whose main inspiration is profit, individuals not measurably more sympathetic to Indians than are local landowners. (A few owner-managers are American retirees with vaguely leftist politics who may be willing to accept lower profit margins than do the majority of rapacious local entrepreneurs.) In most of these stores, the Indian craftsperson faces the law of supply and demand, and, because overpopulation dictates that the supply is always high, remuneration is humiliatingly low. This keeps prices in the cooperatives and cottage industries well below value too, because all stores compete for tourists' dollars. In addition, the owners and managers of boutiques and souvenir stores have no particular commitment to *local* goods. These remain emphasized because tourists often prefer the local imprimatur on authenticity and because local items tend to be cheaper, because there are only modest transportation costs and no additional layers of middlemen. Nevertheless, a basic willingness to sell things from elsewhere, when combined with niche-carving, leads to many stores featuring local textiles plus, for instance, hand-blown glass from Guadalajara or carved animals from Oaxaca as well as stores selling only silver jewelry from Taxco or amber jewelry.

Although unalloyed authenticity is always a chimera, in these stores authenticity is present *much* more in rhetoric than in fact. A very few "authentic" huipiles, as sold in Sna Jolobil, hang beside endless arrays of cheaper ones decorated with varieties of flower patterns (some older local designs, but many spur-of-the-moment or proper to elsewhere in Mexico) and beside garments not in tradition, such as full-length, one-piece dresses decorated with traditional patterns crowded nearly beyond recognition, intensified to the point of caricature. Nevertheless, even the product seeming to be the least authentic at first glance can incorporate forms of the processes that shape items like my pillowcase. For instance, some overdecorated dresses have traditional roots in even their gaudiest features. The most typical decorations added as supplements to patterns like "ancestors" are of pictorial flowers and birds, which have places in tradition in some highland communities, even if not that of the source of the basic pattern on the dress. And decorations placed on "new" parts of a garment often are linked in trails of ornament with embroidery in traditional locations. Uses of color can be analyzed similarly. But at some point the chains of connections between tradition and innovation, however logically convincing, lose their emotive power and an article becomes as cheap in appearance as it is in price.

Of course, boutiques do have important functions beyond the enrichment of Ladino businessmen. Many tourists who fly to Chiapas cannot extend their trips to the rest of Mexico and are grateful to have crafts from throughout the nation available in San Cristóbal. By the same token, craftspersons from elsewhere are happy to make sales away from their own homes. And many of these crafts do express some sort of authenticity on the national rather than the local level. Finally, souvenir purchases of any kind can warm up the tourist's purchasing inclinations—preparing them psychologically to buy more authentic and pricey goods.

THE SANTO DOMINGO MARKET

Many inexpensive crafts are sold by women sitting in rows in what has coalesced into an enduring crafts market in the grounds around the Santo Domingo church and the old cloister (itself now occupied by the most prestigious cooperative, Sna Jolobil). The location is optimal because tourist traffic is heavy. The market's proximity to Sna Jolobil points up some remarkable contrasts. The huipiles sold in the cooperative look like those worn routinely a few generations ago, or in revival today, but the blouses taking up perhaps a fourth of the area outdoors are of a variety of types that can be made quickly and thus sold cheaply. But whereas some of the goods offered in the market are historically unauthentic, the open-air experience is much more traditional in routine hard-edged bargaining and in parts of the ambiance that intrigue some tourists and repulse others: crowds, noise, and dirt. Finally, whereas the women that run Sna Jolobil are from various hamlets (a very new development), the women and children working in the market are originally from one village, Chamula (although some of them now reside in poorer sections of San Cristóbal).

A few stands, such as those for leather belts, represent specialized niches, however, most offer the same products and catch a potential customer's eye due to the particulars of display or the serendipity of the psychological moment, that is, that the tourist has wandered among near-identical stands for just the right length of time. Nevertheless, the interplay between things authentic in letter or spirit and imagination is still in evidence, all taking place supported by minimal budgets and desperate hopes for high turnover.

Blouses sold here are generally of manufactured thread embroidered on cheap muslin. The type of materials is traditional not in Chamula itself, but rather in the lowlands where men in the village used to go for seasonal work. The minimal quality of the muslin and the thread is untraditional: These women would not spend even the relatively short amounts of time invested in these objects made of materials apt to wear out quickly were these clothes for their own families—the low prices of the materials would be a false economy. But this matters less when blouses are destined for foreign bargain hunters who may buy them more as souvenirs than as clothing.

A second main category of goods sold here are sewn toys, little animals and dolls made with scraps of handwoven cloth (Indian children actually spend more time playing with cheap plastic toys). Half the dolls are a new model, the Subcomandante Marcos doll, which has achieved incredible popularity because of its novelty to politically liberal tourists. This does not suggest that the Indians lack respect for the subcomandante, but rather manifests the same informal familiarity with deeply respected images that inspires placing little plastic crucifixes and Virgin Marys on the dashboards of taxis and buses along with Disney figures. The new doll is really as abstract as the "ancestors" design—a gun and mask are schematic additions on the same order as the three lines above the man and the corn arms of the woman. The doll is modeled after a female doll holding a baby (thus, a fertility symbol parallel to that in the corn) rather than a rifle; a male partner has now been created in the subcomandante image. I bought a Marcos baseball hat for a friend back home and enjoyed dining in one of several restaurants outfitted with Subcomandante Marcos napkin holders. Marcos wanted to become a symbolic figure, and he has succeeded.

The last classification of goods sold here are miniatures of dolls, of hats, of pottery, and so on. These and more than a few of the textiles sold by the Chamulan women were purchased from Guatemalans living in squalid refugee camps between San Cristóbal and the border.

HAWKERS

It may seem that this last category would constitute a minor footnote in this list of opportunities to buy crafts, but it does not. Young women, often carrying babies, and children working alone pursue tourists down the street, energetically marketing woven wristbands and belts for small fees, prices swiftly lowered when the tourist resists. Their persistence crowds the tourist into an unpleasant choice, either to be rude to the very people he or she has come to see or to yield, thus acting in accordance with the unpalatable truth that many of these Indians do not embody a comfortable traditional way of life, but rather are poor on a scale that wipes out most shreds of dignity. Moreover, making a purchase does not relieve the pressure except from the individual hawker thus served, instead inspiring immediate assembly of a crowd.[29]

The minimal weavings these Indians sell are traditional in that they are made on backstrap looms using local wool. Also, they feature the diamond pattern that represents the universe. This might be due to the fact that this pattern can be shrunk to the smallest size, but Indian street vendors in Oaxaca weave diamonds less often. It is bitterly ironic that while other craftspersons in Chiapas are making a living marketing symbols dear to them, signs of an ethnicity and tradition that they wish to maintain, these mothers and children must sell tiny items that symbolize a way of life that they would dearly love to escape.

Crafts and Maintaining (or Transforming) a Traditional Way of Life

The average "ethnic" or "cultural" tourist who comes to San Cristóbal and ventures briefly into the surrounding villages is looking for some part of an idealized past, for a simpler and more fulfilling life on the land. Of course, tourists arriving in Chiapas after the Zapatista uprising began in 1994 must modify that rosy picture. The fear of stumbling into danger did inhibit tourism briefly, although great care was taken not to harm tourists—after all, supportive international publicity is among the central and best-realized goals of the rebellion. Tourists I encountered in the summer of 1997 considered the Zapatistas a romantic eccentricity of the state rather than a threat to themselves. However, the disturbance unveiled an ironic truth, that the part of Mexico that best draws visitors seeking an "authentic," peaceful idyll is actually the state in the most turmoil. And crafts illustrate this contradiction well. They are especially complex in manufacture and appearance, especially resonant with religion and local identities, precisely because cultivating a vivid and inward-looking ethnicity has been a re-action to political and economic repression over many centuries. How craft objects such as my pillowcase are designed, made, and marketed in modern Chiapas illustrate—and, indeed, fuel—trends in power relationships between Indians and outsiders, the position and transformation of religion, continuity and change in gender relationships, and how the individual Indian tries to maintain family and village identity.

POWER

The defense that a vigorous ethnicity offered against Chiapas's Indians' ill treatment by the Ladino oligarchy remained primarily a psychological bulwark until recently—a cultural strategy that mattered only to the Indians. Now, with tourism the main business of San Cristóbal and environs, certain manifestations of ethnicity have become economically indispensable to the state. Because it is how Indians look, their public practice of religion, and their crafts that draw affluent visitors to Chiapas, the Ladino businessmen who run San Cristóbal need the Indians to continue to cultivate their ethnicity. On the one hand, this extends centuries of exploitation: Most of the tourist money goes to these Ladinos. On the other hand, the tourists who observe Indians and take home their crafts represent the world outside of Chiapas, a world capable of being shocked by how the Indians are treated and exerting pressure on the Mexican central government for reform. The Zapatistas know this well: Their strongest weapon is the press communique. Finally, the Indians can and do limit tourists' access to some of their attractive features and products and thus have slightly more economic leverage in the relationship with the local power structure than before.

Each adult Indian represents a commodity valuable to the government, a vote. Nearly every vote from nearly every Indian community ends up on the PRI section of the ballot, due to pressure combined with fraud. Municipio *caciques* (bilingual Indian intermediaries, with considerable power) assure that the receipt of even the least of government services means a village lined up behind the PRI, but some Indian towns are demanding more for their votes. For instance, I was told several times that an unnamed woman leading a cooperative in one municipio had successfully demanded money for thread and equipment in exchange for continued loyalty.

Most of the paternalistic help that textile cooperatives and cottage industries get is from Mexicans who came from outside Chiapas, including those in government agencies such as FONART and INI, and from foreigners. Even though any relationship between Indian and outsider still is weighted on the side of the outsider, these strands weaken the historical stranglehold of the local power structure. Through experience with altruistic middlemen, Indians learn business and administrative practices that qualify them to work in the urban world. And the best intermediaries, like Morris and Past, try to become dispensable and are happy to turn over well-constructed enterprises to the Indians. This directly affects only a few thousand craftspersons, but gives hope to many more. It is important to remember that extensive nonexploitative interaction between any outsiders and the Maya is only a few decades old and that many of the new supportive relationships concern tourism, especially the production of crafts. It will not be too long before there are more businesses controlled by Indians from bottom to top, from sheep-tending to profit distribution.

RELIGION

Various Protestant sects continue to make massive inroads throughout the Mayan world, as throughout Latin America. Pentecostals, Presbyterians, Methodists, Baptists, Mormons, Jehovah's Witnesses, and Seventh-Day Adventists all find converts in Chiapas, but it is hard to know how many

leave Mayan Catholicism because of conviction and how many for economic reasons. Two basic problems plague traditional Indian religion. First,
large amounts of hard liquor (posh) must be imbibed during festivals, and
many men continue that consumption socially. Alcoholism has been a
horrible problem in the highlands.[30] It is not as bad today as a few decades
ago, due partly to Protestant preaching against it and partly to a liberal
Catholic reaction to losing souls to the Protestants. In particular, an organization called Catholic Action advocates substituting soft drinks for posh in
festivals and as routine libations—I saw as much Pepsi as posh in the church
in Chamula.

The second vulnerability of Mayan Catholicism is at its core, the cargo
system. Even as incomes have fallen in recent times, the caciques who have
come to control the sales of central materials for festivals (fireworks, posh,
soft drinks, flowers, candles) have extorted more money for these and organized their own armed forces to keep the cargo system running smoothly.
In several communities, notably Chamula, thousands of Protestants who
felt that they no longer needed to partake in the cargo system have been
expelled by these bands of thugs. Perhaps 25,000 refugees have ended up in
slums around San Cristóbal. They seek wage labor, but making and selling
crafts is very important to them. Most of the women and children pressing
woven wristbands on tourists are Protestant refugees.

In some of the villages, and certainly in cooperatives such as Sna Jolobil and cottage industries such as Kun Kun, traditional Mayan Catholics,
members of Catholic Action, and assorted Protestants work side by side.
They are all Indians and share a past, even if their futures may diverge. And
many converts are "economic" Protestants. For them, dropping out of the
cargo system came first because their falling incomes could not keep up
with its rising expenses. The Protestants offered spiritual refuge and much-
needed hospitality in San Cristóbal. Women who are economic Protestants
attend their new churches, but also can continue to pay heed to older
religion by weaving patterns like "ancestors."

GENDER

A few generations ago, Indian men earned some outside income, while
Indian women stayed home grinding corn, making tortillas, fetching water
and firewood, and weaving their family's clothing. The men considered
themselves farmers, but Ladino landowners had kept Indians from ever
acquiring substantial tracts of arable land. For generations, the average
Mayan farmer cultivated a small plot of rocky soil in the highlands, also

worked a small plot he owned or rented in the lowlands, and might find seasonal work on lowland coffee plantations. Today, lowland plots are fewer, many coffee plantations have become ranches (needing fewer workers), and ill-paid Guatemalan refugees have taken on much of the work on the remaining plantations. The growing highland organic coffee industry offers some limited promise, but is itself a source of contention between villagers and Ladino landlords. Highland men may find other wage labor, particularly in construction, but, overall, their incomes are shrinking.

Tourists buy textiles, most of which are made by women. Weaving allows women to feel "capable and productive" by carrying on tradition-sanctioned work in a time-honored way.[31] Others can appreciate their skills, and they can help with family expenses. But this traditional women's work can come to occupy untraditionally large blocks of time. Sometimes their work pays enough that they cannot afford to spend time weaving for their husbands and children, instead buying cheap, used, town clothes—I saw this especially in Chamula and among refugees from there. Under-employed men do not like these changes. They resent the very thought of fetching water or firewood. Several wives who have taken on a sort of secular cargo by becoming leaders in cooperatives have thereby earned savage beatings. But selling textiles has given women the new option of remaining single. "Why should I marry a drunk?" is an occasionally heard reaction to a widespread problem that could not be avoided before.[32]

Formerly, men linked the family to the outside world, other villages, the cities where they might find work, and the spiritual world: thus, the three lines constituting the body of the male figure in "ancestors," his arms raised heavenward, while the female figure enfolds the corn at home. Through commercial weaving, particularly in the cooperatives formed to serve the tourist market, women who formerly would not have had the self-confidence or opportunity to talk to women from other communities are working and socializing together.[33] Just a few years ago, a woman who wove "ancestors" into a huipil that she would wear was wrapping herself in the traditional role described in that pattern. Now, a woman who makes such a huipil for sale or puts it on an object such as a pillowcase, something that only an outsider would use, can honor the "ancestors" while she works, but can conceive of not living as the pattern dictates. After all, this very act of weaving for cash takes her beyond the nurturing of corn.

How surprising is the shift in gender roles attendant on the growth of income from women's crafts? Change is painful, but what are the alternatives? The old roles could not be sustained in the economic present.

Another model for new gender roles might be how the sexes relate in the city, but that would constitute a much more radical shift than that caused so far by working in crafts. And pursuing the other visible alternative, that exemplified in the Zapatista forces, would be even more wrenching. Women make up perhaps a third of the army and lead some squads, causing problems even in that "revolutionary" force. The recasting of gender roles seen in craft villages in the highlands may be the minimum possible in these changing times.

VILLAGE AND FAMILY

Modern Maya individuals, families, and villages who wish to hold fast to tradition as the world changes bewilderingly swiftly around them do as their ancestors did: They armor themselves in ethnicity. They do so in many ways, some of which resemble how crafts are intensified. Intensification through virtuosity offers the easiest parallel, when individuals and groups self-consciously and energetically cultivate knowledge of tradition and expertise in crafts. The huipiles sold in Sna Jolobil that illustrate intensification through virtuosity are made by weavers who embody this process's behavioral form. Second, people can certainly "perform" intensification through addition, by wearing more ethnicity-specific garments than in generations past, by making a point of speaking Tzotzil or Tzeltal when using Spanish would be as easy, and so on. And the intensification through selection so important in shaping my pillowcase is "performed" by innumerable Maya every day, when, for instance, they spend more time doing ethnicity-specific tasks like weaving than did their mothers, but are happy to give up their mothers' daily routine of fetching water or walking to town.

Christine Eber and Brenda Rosenbaum, who studied cooperatives in Chiapas during the 1970s and 1980s, found that weavers did not "talk about personal empowerment through the symbols they weave nor the solidarity they create," but rather of "service to the families and communities, at once practical and sacred."[34] Payment for handmade textiles remains absurdly low, but nevertheless buttresses fragile family finances. And, although the booming population still requires outmigration to prevent famine, income from crafts keeps many families and villages largely intact. In short, engagement with traditional crafts has become critical in these Indians' having a chance to maintain the first ingredient of a traditional way of life, the traditional community.

The municipios where crafts are helping stabilize income and community, where hope for improving the standard of living has thereby been rekindled, the municipios with something to lose are precisely the ones least likely to support the Zapatistas. San Andrés Larrainzar, where my pillowcase was made, is such a community, with its long history of flourishing cooperatives, its firm hold on the aesthetic center of the revival of weaving—"ancestors" is just one of the lovely patterns associated with this municipio—and with many of the difficult changes in gender relationships and other adjustments of shifting from a subsistence to a market economy negotiated as well as anywhere in the highlands. Its neighbor, Chenalhó, represents the many municipios that aspire to the success of San Andrés. Indeed, as early as 1989, Eber and Rosenbaum found four weaving cooperatives in Chenalhó, two supported by political parties (the PRI and the CNC), one by a government agency (the INI), and one private (a branch of Sna Jolobil).[35] But traditional weavings from this municipio are not as appealing as those from San Andrés, both to my eye and in the cumulative opinion of tourists as expressed in how much space is allotted Chenalhó's weavings in Sna Jolobil (much less than for San Andrés) and in the Casa de Artesanias (none). Weavers from Chenalhó have not been able to garner nearly as much craft-based income as have the truly successful craft villages.[36] Nevertheless, hope endures, hope all the more precious for being tenuous.

The 1997 massacre in an outlying hamlet of Chenalhó resulted from the clashing of views concerning how Indians can improve their collective lot. The crafts movement offers modest incomes and the prospect of gradual improvement in general welfare. Although the money earned is seldom substantial, it has the advantage of originating outside of the country, independent of the whims of the Mexican government and the vicissitudes of the Mexican economy. Conversely, the Zapatistas insist on dramatic and immediate change. The national government responded to the rebellion with its own rhetoric and with an effective strategy of double containment. Mexican troops now surround the Zapatista army, and the villages just outside of the revolutionary forces' rural enclaves are receiving money for jobs, housing, social services, and infrastructure such as roads, government-run stores, and potable water systems.[37] This money is welcome, but considered overdue and apt to evaporate when the immediate crisis subsides.

The Zapatistas often rub the most conservative Indians the wrong way with, for instance, the elevation of women into positions of command; having village women take on responsibility in weaving collectives had been grating enough. Worst of all, the very flares in publicity that have inspired cynical government expenditures in certain areas have repeatedly driven away large numbers of tourists, thereby abruptly depressing the economy of the entire highlands. The men that attacked the hamlet of Acteal at the end of 1997 were not just following the orders of some cacique representing the local PRI, they were fighting against a community whose actions in sheltering Indians sympathetic to the Zapatistas could be seen as taking food out of their own families' mouths. It is more than likely that the attackers included husbands and sons of weavers working in Chenalhó's many cooperatives. In such incidents, Indians who want food, land, and the chance to retain some measure of traditional identity are pitted against other Indians with the same desires, but with differing ideas of how to attain those goals.

Pierre Van Den Berghe ends his book on tourism in San Cristóbal with a section entitled "What Went Right?" He cites factors including an optimal degree of outsider access to the area; the intrinsic attractiveness of the Indians, climate, and scenery; that "ethnic" tourists are not apt to pollute; and that local development has remained sensibly small in scale.[38] My argument has focussed on how the attractiveness of the Indians to tourists stems from long-term oppression and how, despite the great degree to which the new tourist industry continues historical exploitation, making and selling crafts can be and often is done in a way that does not injure tradition. Moreover, the modest income from crafts helps protect aspects of traditional life. The Zapatistas desire faster and more comprehensive improvements. Which combination of paths to sorely needed change will prove most valuable is impossible to predict. Some form of armed struggle will continue—after all, this too is part of local tradition. At the same time, tourism and sales of crafts will continue to offer the best support for gradual change in the highlands.

Notes

1. Fábregas Puig and García, 42.
2. Noble et al., 801.
3. In a more recent illustration, twenty-five Indians in one hamlet were killed between 1965 and 1985 because they tried to occupy land granted to them by presidential decree in 1965, but that ranchers with hired gunmen declined to leave (Russell, 11).
4. See Cancian, *Economics.*
5. This has been studied intensively in the hamlet of Zinacantan (see bibliography in Vogt).

6. *Guide,* 18–19.

7. Cancian, *The Decline,* 201.

8. Collier, 15, following Aguirre Beltran.

9. Vogt, 103.

10. See Franck and Lanks; Garner; Gilpatrick; Goolsby; and Jackson.

11. Greene, 153, 168.

12. Huxley, 12.

13. MacCannell, 13.

14. Graburn, 26.

15. Krippendorf, 23.

16. Cohen, 2.

17. McKean, 126.

18. Morris, *Living,* 116.

19. *Programa,* 2. "Los antepasados cuidan la sociedad y enseñan como vivir a través de los sueños. Son seres sobrenaturales como los santos." Morris (*Living,* 153) has best summarized the position of the Ancestors in Indian cosmology:

> The Totil Me'il, literally "Fathers-Mothers," also known as the Ancestors, reside in the mountains above each community and watch over the lives of their children. The Ancestors summon those with strong souls in their dreams to show them the proper and holy path of life and give them power over the jealous witches and demons that plague the night. People who ignore the Ancestors' teachings ignore the path that was laid down at the beginning of the world. Those with weak souls will grow ill.
>
> The Ancestors represent the first people who learned how to plant corn, praise their creator, and live as proper human beings. Like the saints, they are not anyone's direct ancestors but supernatural beings who guard the entire community. The Ancestors and the saints are members of a family who meet to discuss the state of the world. God has empowered them both to intercede on behalf of mankind. The saints are the more remote group, for they are the stars that wander across the distant sky. The Ancestors dwell in the nearly [*sic*] mountains and hear more clearly their children's pleas for health and knowledge.

20. Morris, personal communication, 1997.

21. Morris, *A Millennium,* 11.

22. FONART is the Fondo Nacional para el Fomento de las Artesanias (National Foundation for the Encouragement of Folk Arts). INI is the Instituto Nacional Indigenista (National Indian Institute).

23. Past, personal communication, 1997. See also Eber and Rosenbaum, 176 n. 6.

24. Past, personal communication, 1997.

25. McKean, 135.

26. Van Den Berghe, 64–65; on the history of cooperatives in Chiapas, see Eber and Rosenbaum.

27. Morris, personal communication, 1997.

28. See Oettinger.

29. Van Den Berghe, 68.

30. See Eber.

31. Eber and Rosenbaum, 165.

32. Morris, *Living,* 70.

33. Ibid., 46.

34. Eber and Rosenbaum, 175.

35. Ibid., 167. CNC is La Confederación Nacional Campesina (National Peasant Confederation).

36. Eber and Rosenbaum, 167, 173.

37. Russell, 84.

38. Van Den Berghe, 147–51.

Works Cited

Aguirre Beltran, Gonzalo. *Regions of Refuge.* 1967. Reprint, Washington, D.C.: Society for Applied Anthropology, 1979.

Cancian, Frank. *The Decline of Community in Zinacantan: Economy, Public Life, and Social Stratification, 1960–1987.* Stanford, Calif.: Stanford University Press, 1992.

——. *Economics and Prestige in a Maya Community: The Religious Cargo System in Zinacantan.* Stanford, Calif.: Stanford University Press, 1965.

Cohen, Erik. "Authenticity and Commoditization in Tourism." *Annals of Tourism Research* 15, no. 3 (1988): 371–86.

Collier, George A. *Fields of the Tzotzil: The Ecological Bases of Tradition in Highland Chiapas.* Austin: University of Texas Press, 1975.

Eber, Christine. *Women and Alcohol in a Highland Town: Water of Hope, Water of Sorrow.* Austin: University of Texas Press, 1995.

Eber, Christine, and Brenda Rosenbaum. "'That We May Serve Beneath Your Hands and Feet': Women Weavers in Highland Chiapas, Mexico." Pp. 155–79 in *Crafts in the World Market: The Impact of Global Exchange in Middle American Artisans,* ed. June Nash. Albany: State University of New York Press, 1993.

Fábregas Puig, Andrés, and Carlos Román García. *Al Fin del Milenio: El Rostro de la Frontera Sur.* Tuxtla Gutiérrez, Chiapas, Mexico: Gobierno del Estado de Chiapas y Instituto Chiapenéco de Cultura, 1994.

Franck, Harry A., and Herbert C. Lanks. *The Pan American Highway: From the Rio Grande to the Canal Zone.* New York: D. Appleton-Century Company, 1942.

Garner, Bess Adams. *Mexico: Notes in the Margin*. Boston: Houghton Mifflin, 1937.

Gilpatrick, Wallace. *The Man Who Likes Mexico*. New York: The Century Company, 1911.

Goolsby, William Berlin. *Guide to Mexico for the Motorist*. Mexico D.F.: privately published, 1936.

Graburn, Nelson H. H. "Tourism: The Sacred Journey." Pp. 21–36 in *Hosts and Guests,* ed. Valene Smith. Oxford, U.K.: Blackwell, 1989.

Greene, Graham. *Another Mexico*. New York: Viking Press, 1939.

Guide: San Juan Chamula, Chiapas. Tuxtla Gutiérrez, Chiapas, Mexico: Talleres Gráficos del Estado, 1995.

Huxley, Aldous. *Along the Road*. London: Chatto and Windus, 1925.

Jackson, John Henry. *Mexican Interlude*. New York: MacMillan, 1937.

Krippendorf, Jost. *The Holiday Makers: Understanding the Impact of Leisure and Travel*. Trans. Vera Andrassy. London: Heinemann, 1987.

MacCannell, Dean. *The Tourist: A New Theory of the Leisure Class*. New York: Schocken Books, 1975.

McKean, Philip F. "Towards a Theoretical Analysis of Tourism: Involution in Bali." Pp. 124–44 in *Hosts and Guests,* ed. Valene Smith. Oxford, U.K.: Blackwell, 1989.

Morris, Walter F., Jr. *Living Maya*. New York: Harry N. Abrams, 1987.

——. *A Millennium of Weaving in Chiapas: An Introduction to the Pellizzi Collection of Chiapas Textiles*. San Cristóbal, Chiapas, Mexico: Gobierno del Estado de Chiapas, 1984.

Noble, John, et al. *Mexico: A Lonely Planet Travel Survival Kit*. 5th ed. Hawthorn, Victoria, Australia: Lonely Planet Publications, 1995.

Oettinger, Marion, Jr. *El Alma del Pueblo: El Arte Popular de España y las Américas*. San Antonio, Tex.: San Antonio Museum of Art, 1997.

Past, Ambar. *Bon: Tintes Naturales*. Bilingual in Tzotzil and Spanish. San Cristóbal, Chiapas, Mexico: Taller Leñateros, 1980.

Past, Ambar, and Juan Bañuelos. *Conjuros y Ebriedades: Cantos de Mujeres Mayas*. San Cristóbal de las Casas, Mexico: Taller Leñateros, 1997.

Programa Antesanal del dif Regional Zona II Altos. n.d., 2-page photocopied typescript given out in Casa de Artesanias, San Cristóbal, Chiapas, Mexico.

Russell, Philip J. *The Chiapas Rebellion*. Austin, Tex.: Mexico Resource Center, 1995.

Van Den Berghe, Pierre L. *The Quest for the Other: Ethnic Tourism in San Cristóbal, Mexico*. Seattle: University of Washington Press, 1994.

Vogt, Evon Z. *Fieldwork among the Maya: Reflections on the Harvard Chiapas Project*. Albuquerque: University of New Mexico Press, 1994.

About the Contributors

S. ELIZABETH BIRD is professor of anthropology at the University of South Florida. She is the editor of *Dressing in Feathers: The Construction of the Indian in American Popular Culture* (Westview Press, 1996) and author of *For Enquiring Minds: A Cultural Study of Supermarket Tabloids* (University of Tennessee Press, 1992) as well as numerous articles and book chapters in the fields of folklore, popular culture, and media studies.

CHRIS GOERTZEN trained as an ethnomusicologist under Bruno Nettl. He has taught at Earlham College, Kenyon College, the University of Minnesota, the University of North Carolina, the University of Southern Mississippi, and the University of Trondheim (Norway). He has published work on American, Norwegian, and Austrian folk and popular music. He is currently writing a book exploring various aspects of the confluence of crafts, festivals, and tourism in contemporary Mexico.

SARAH H. HILL earned a Ph.D. in American studies from Emory University in 1991. She is an independent scholar living in Atlanta and is the author of a history of Southeastern Cherokee women entitled *Weaving New Worlds: Cherokee Women and Their Basketry* (University of North Carolina Press, 1997). As guest curator at the Atlanta History Center, she conceived and developed the exhibition "Native Lands: Indians and Georgia." She is an adjunct faculty member of Emory University, director of the Georgia chapter of the National Trail of Tears Commission, member of the Georgia Council on American Indian Concerns, and an editor of the *Journal of Cherokee Studies*.

KATIE N. JOHNSON is assistant professor of English at Miami University. Her work has appeared in *Theatre Journal, American Drama,* and *The Encyclopedia of American Cultural and Intellectual History.* Her current book project examines how representations of prostitutes on the New York stage intersect with antiprostitution reform in the early twentieth century.

CARTER JONES MEYER received her Ph.D. in American civilization from Brown University and is currently an associate professor of history and convener of the American Studies Program at Ramapo College of New Jersey. Her research and writings have focused on American Indians and the constructions of culture in the United States in the late nineteenth and early twentieth centuries.

NANCY J. PAREZO is curator of ethnology at the Arizona State Museum and professor of American Indian studies and anthropology at the University of Arizona. She is president of the Council for Museum Anthropology and cochair of the Council for the Preservation of Anthropological Records. Her publications include *Navajo Sandpaintings: From Religious Act to Commercial Art* (University of Arizona Press, 1983), *Hidden Scholars: Women Anthropologists and the Native American Southwest* (University of New Mexico Press, 1993), *Preserving the Anthropological Record* (Wenner-Gran Foundation for Anthropological Research, 1995), and numerous articles. She is currently working on a book on the anthropology exhibits at the 1904 World's Fair and a comparative study of the archaeology exhibits at international expositions between 1876 and 1915 (with Don. D. Fowler).

DIANA ROYER is associate professor of English at Miami University. She has published on Ambrose Bierce, Nathaniel Hawthorne, Edgar Allan Poe, Yusuf Idris, Virginia Woolf, and American Indian topics. She is the author of *Nawal El Saadawi: Works Toward a New Egypt* (The Edwin Mellen Press, forthcoming) and coeditor of *Breaking Boundaries: New Perspectives on Women's Regional Writing* (University of Iowa, 1997) with Sherrie A. Inness.

JOHN W. TROUTMAN is a Ph.D. candidate in the Department of History at the University of Texas at Austin. He completed his M.A. in American Indian studies at the University of Arizona in 1997, writing his thesis on Native American experiences at the St. Louis World's Fair.

ERIK TRUMP is assistant professor of political science at Saginaw Valley State University. He received his Ph.D. in American studies from Boston University. His publications include articles about the 1893 Columbian Exposition and the Indian fiction of Oliver La Farge.

PAULINE TUTTLE is a Ph.D. candidate in ethnomusicology at the University of Washington, Seattle. She has conducted extensive field research on Plains and Northwest Coast music, as well as intercontinental interchanges among indigenous Bahá'í musicians. As a CERLAC Fellow, she completed a collection and documentation project on Calypso, Pan, and Mas' in the context of Carnival in Canada for the National Museum of Civilization and conducted field research in Trinidad, Barbados, Toronto, and Montreal. She currently teaches courses on American Indian and world music at the University of Washington.

TAMARA UNDERINER is assistant professor of theatre history and literature at the University of Minnesota, where she specializes in theatre of the Americas. Her work has appeared in *Theatre Survey* and *Theatre Journal*. She is currently writing a book on contemporary Mayan theater in southern Mexico.

Index

Mesa Verde, 194
mestizo, 237, 255
Mooney, James, 26–27, 39n. 95, 220
Moore, Thomas (Tomas), 21, 22, 24
Mulberry Craft Center, 227
Museum of New Mexico, 190, 193, 194–96, 200, 204

Namias, June, 69, 80
National Congress of American Indians, xviii
Navajo Indians: at Louisiana Purchase Exposition, 14, 15, 34n. 42; romanticized image of, 160; at World's Columbian Exposition, 163
New Age, 64, 76–77, 110–12, 114, 119, 144n. 44; and Bahá'í Faith, 106, 141n. 15; conception of Indians, xiii, 88
New Mexico Archaeological Society, 94
Northern Exposure, 57, 83–84
Northrup, Jim, xiii

Olds, Fred, 219
Oneida Indians, 10
Oskenonton, 202
O'Sullivan, John Louis, xiii

Paiute Indians, 192
Palmer, Edward, 220
Parker, Quanah, 9, 35n. 48
Past, Ambar, 248–49, 255–56, 261
Pearsall, Mrs. Marion C., 165
Philbrook Art Center, 212
Pima Indians, 10, 14, 15
Pocahontas, 62, 78, 79, 82, 85, 86, 88
Pomo Indians: at Louisiana Purchase Exposition, 10, 14, 15; romanticized image of, 160
pottery: Hopi, 4; Pueblo, 10, 11, 198, 202; Rookwood, 163; of Southwestern Indians, 163; Zuni, 4

Pratt, Richard, 168
Ptehincala Ska Win. *See* White Buffalo Calf Maiden
Pueblo Indians, xvii, 3, 87, 182n. 15; at Louisiana Purchase Exposition, 3–5, 10, 11, 14, 23, 34n. 34; 1920s reformers and, 190–211; romanticized image of, 160. *See also* pottery, Pueblo
Pueblo Pottery Fund. *See* Indian Arts Fund

Radin, Paul, 63
Redfeather, Tsianina, 202
Reel, Estelle, 170, 218–19
Roe, Mr. and Mrs. Walter C., 169–70
Root, Deborah, 52, 56, 57
Rose, Wendy, xi
Rousseau, Jean-Jacques, xii-xiii, 140n. 4

Sandoz, Marie, 101
Santa Fe Fiesta, 195
Sargeant, Elizabeth Shepley, 196
Savage Spirit, 73
School of American Research, xvii, 190, 193–96, 200–202, 204
Seri Indians, 17–19, 36n. 55
shamanism, white, xi-xii, xiii
Sioux Indians, 3, 10, 14, 23, 25, 27
Sitting Bull, 103, 105, 109, 125, 132
Skiff, Frederick J.V., 6, 27
Slocum, William F., 5, 6
Smoke Signals, 87
Southern Highland Handicraft Guild, 221
Southwest Indian Fair, 200–202, 206
Sparhawk, Frances, 167, 169; and establishment of Indian Industries League, 161; writings of, 162
Speck, Frank, 220
Stamper, Lottie Queen, 225

TECHNOLOGY OF TRAVEL COLLAPSES GEOG, BORDERS &
     BOUNDARIES —
HOW MANY HOMES HAVE I HAD?
DISTINQUISH MEANING FROM PHYSICAL BOUNDARIES

SLIDES — ASTOUNDING
          STUNNING
          ATTENTION GRABBING

WHAT DO YOU SEE?
                 UGLIENESS
DOES BEAUTY HAVE BOUNDARIES?
     AUTHENTICITY — FAKE
       ORIGINALITY — COPYING

PAULINE TUTTLE FOR "MY" PERFORMANCE